TABLE OF CONTENTS

Visions of Loveliness

Ruffles and bows, hearts and lace ...
if you're a romantic at heart,
these beautifully tempting cover-ups
are for you! This section includes
light, airy afghans and luxuriously rich
wraps to delight the senses. They make
wonderful gifts for Mother's Day,
Baby's christening, or any occasion.

crochet
WITH ♥ RED HEART YARNS ™
Best-Loved
AFGHANS

*F*rom its very first issue in 1996, Crochet With Heart *magazine has been beloved for its exciting variety of afghans and other great-looking needlecraft projects. We've gathered 49 of our favorite cover-ups from its pages to fill this very special book, including several prize-winning afghans submitted by readers.*

Take a few minutes to browse through the pages … you're sure to spot several wraps you'd like to crochet right away for your own family or for gifts. And you'll be impressed with the easy-to-follow instructions and clear stitch diagrams. There is a wide variety of yarns from which you may choose to crochet your afghans; just remember to work a swatch to make sure you match the gauge given in the instructions.

Turn to the Visions of Loveliness collection for delicate, lacy beauties, or discover snuggly winter blankets in Warm & Cozy. Classic Elegance offers wraps with style, and Just for Fun will delight you with bright, whimsical afghans. Garden Gathering features a beautiful bouquet of color and texture.

No matter which afghan you choose to make first, this collection of crochet will capture your heart!

LEISURE ARTS, INC.
and
OXMOOR HOUSE, INC.

EDITORIAL STAFF

Editor-at-Large: Anne Van Wagner Childs
Vice President and Editor-in-Chief: Sandra Graham Case
Administrative Coordinator: Debra Nettles
Editorial Director: Susan Frantz Wiles
Publications Director: Susan White Sullivan
Creative Art Director: Gloria Bearden
Photography Director: Karen Hall
Art Operations Director: Jeff Curtis

PRODUCTION
Senior Technical Editor: Cathy Hardy
Instructional Editors: Susan Ackerman Carter and Sue Galucki

EDITORIAL
Managing Editor: Linda L. Trimble
Associate Editor: Suzie Puckett

ART
Art Director: Mark Hawkins
Senior Production Artist: Clint Hanson
Color Technician: Mark Potter
Staff Photographer: Russell Ganser
Photography Stylists: Tiffany Huffman and Janna Laughlin
Publishing Systems Administrator: Becky Riddle
Publishing Systems Assistants: Myra S. Means and
    Chris Wertenberger

PROMOTIONS
Managing Editor: Alan Caudle
Associate Editor: Steven M. Cooper
Designer: Dale T. Rowett
Graphic Artist: Deborah Kelly

BUSINESS STAFF

Publisher: Rick Barton
Vice President, Finance: Tom Siebenmorgen
Vice President, Retail Marketing: Bob Humphrey
Director of Corporate Planning and Development:
    Laticia Mull Cornett
Vice President, National Accounts: Pam Stebbins
Retail Marketing Director: Margaret Sweetin
General Merchandise Manager: Cathy Laird
Vice President, Operations: Jim Dittrich
Distribution Director: Rob Thieme
Retail Customer Service Manager: Wanda Price
Print Production Manager: Fred F. Pruss

Crochet With Heart: Best-Loved Afghans
from the *Crochet Treasury* Series
Published by Leisure Arts, Inc., and Oxmoor House, Inc.

Hardcover ISBN 1-57486-199-9
Softcover ISBN 1-57486-200-6

Stunning Shells

The subtle beauty of this wrap will make you
stop and take notice! Three puff stitches make up
each shell, and aran yarn lends classic appeal.

Finished Size: 42½" x 62½"

MATERIALS

Red Heart Worsted Weight Yarn
[8 ounces (452 yards) per skein]: 6 skeins
Crochet hook, size J (6.00 mm) **or** size needed for gauge

GAUGE: In pattern, 2 repeats and
12 rows = 6"

STITCH GUIDE

> **PUFF ST**
> ★ YO, insert hook in sc or sp indicated, YO and pull up a loop even with last st made; repeat from ★ 2 times **more**, YO and draw through all 7 loops on hook.
>
> **SHELL**
> Work Puff St in sc or sp indicated, (ch 2, work Puff St in same sc or sp) twice.
>
> **BACK POST DOUBLE CROCHET**
> *(abbreviated BPdc)*
> YO, insert hook from **back** to **front** around post of dc indicated *(Fig. 13, page 126)*, YO and pull up a loop even with last st made, (YO and draw through 2 loops on hook) twice. Skip dc in front of BPdc.
>
> **FRONT POST DOUBLE CROCHET**
> *(abbreviated FPdc)*
> YO, insert hook from **front** to **back** around post of dc indicated *(Fig. 13, page 126)*, YO and pull up a loop even with last st made, (YO and draw through 2 loops on hook) twice. Skip dc behind FPdc.

AFGHAN BODY

Ch 136 **loosely**.

Row 1: Sc in second ch from hook and in each ch across: 135 sc.

Row 2 (Right side): Ch 3 **(counts as first dc, now and throughout)**, turn; dc in next 4 sc, ★ skip next 2 sc, work Shell in next sc, ch 1, skip next 2 sc, dc in next 5 sc; repeat from ★ across: 13 Shells and 70 dc.

Row 3: Ch 3, turn; (work BPdc around next dc, dc in next dc) twice, ★ ch 1, skip next ch-1 sp, (sc in next ch-2 sp, ch 1) twice, dc in next dc, (work BPdc around next dc, dc in next dc) twice; repeat from ★ across: 96 sts and 39 ch-1 sps.

Row 4: Ch 3, turn; ★ (dc in next BPdc, work FPdc around next dc) twice, skip next ch-1 sp, work Shell in next ch-1 sp, ch 1, work FPdc around next dc; repeat from ★ across to last 4 sts, dc in next BPdc, work FPdc around next dc, dc in last 2 sts: 13 Shells and 70 sts.

Row 5: Ch 3, turn; (work BPdc around next dc, dc in next FPdc) twice, ★ ch 1, skip next ch-1 sp, (sc in next ch-2 sp, ch 1) twice, dc in next FPdc, (work BPdc around next dc, dc in next st) twice; repeat from ★ across: 96 sts and 39 ch-1 sps.

Rows 6-121: Repeat Rows 4 and 5, 58 times; do **not** finish off.

EDGING

Rnd 1: Ch 1, turn; sc in first dc, work 135 sc evenly spaced across to last dc, 3 sc in last dc; work 189 sc evenly spaced across end of rows; working in free loops of beginning ch *(Fig. 15b, page 127)*, 3 sc in ch at base of first sc, work 135 sc evenly spaced across to last ch, 3 sc in last ch; work 189 sc evenly spaced across end of rows, 2 sc in same st as first sc; join with slip st to first sc: 660 sc.

Rnd 2: Do **not** turn; slip st in next 2 sc, ch 1, sc in same st, ch 1, skip next 2 sc, work Shell in next sc, ch 1, skip next 2 sc, ★ sc in next sc, ch 1, skip next 2 sc, work Shell in next sc, ch 1, skip next 2 sts; repeat from ★ around; join with slip st to first sc, finish off.

Soft Hearts for Baby

Baby will know she's loved when you wrap her in this comfy cover-up! Soft fringe and heartwarming motifs make it an ideal gift for your smallest sweetheart.

Finished Size: 32" x 38"

MATERIALS
Red Heart Baby Sport Weight Yarn
[7 ounces (700 yards) per skein]:
White - 2 skeins
Pink - 2 skeins
Crochet hook, size G (4.00 mm) **or** size needed for gauge

GAUGE: Each Strip = 5¼" wide
In pattern, 17 sts = 4";
Rows 1-7 = 3"

STRIP (Make 6)
With White, ch 18 **loosely**.
Row 1: Sc in second ch from hook and in each ch across: 17 sc.
Row 2 (Right side): Ch 3 **(counts as first dc, now and throughout)**, turn; dc in next 5 sc, ch 2, skip next 2 sc, dc in next sc, ch 2, skip next 2 sc, dc in last 6 sc: 13 dc and 2 ch-2 sps.
Note: Mark last row as **right** side and bottom edge.
Row 3: Ch 3, turn; dc in next 4 dc, ch 2, skip next dc, 3 dc in next dc, ch 2, skip next dc, dc in last 5 dc.
Row 4: Ch 3, turn; dc in next 3 dc, ch 2, skip next dc, 2 dc in each of next 3 dc, ch 2, skip next dc, dc in last 4 dc: 14 dc and 2 ch-2 sps.
Row 5: Ch 3, turn; dc in next 2 dc, ch 2, skip next dc, 2 dc in next dc, dc in next 4 dc, 2 dc in next dc, ch 2, skip next dc, dc in last 3 dc.
Row 6: Ch 3, turn; dc in next 2 dc, ch 3, sc in next dc, hdc in next dc, 3 dc in next dc, ch 2, slip st in next 2 dc, ch 2, 3 dc in next dc, hdc in next dc, sc in next dc, ch 3, dc in last 3 dc: 18 sts and 4 sps.
Row 7: Ch 3, turn; dc in next 2 dc, skip next ch-3 sp and next 2 sts, tr in next dc, ch 2, skip next dc, dc in next dc, ch 3, skip next 2 slip sts, dc in next dc, ch 2, skip next dc, tr in next dc, skip next ch-3 sp, dc in last 3 dc: 10 sts and 3 sps.
Row 8: Ch 1, turn; sc in first 4 sts, 2 sc in next ch-2 sp, sc in next dc, 3 sc in next ch-3 sp, sc in next dc, 2 sc in next ch-2 sp, sc in last 4 sts: 17 sc.
Row 9: Ch 1, turn; sc in each sc across.
Row 10: Ch 3, turn; dc in next 5 sc, ch 2, skip next 2 sc, dc in next sc, ch 2, skip next 2 sc, dc in last 6 sc: 13 dc and 2 ch-2 sps.
Rows 11-88: Repeat Rows 3-10, 9 times; then repeat Rows 3-8 once **more**.
Finish off.

EDGING
Rnd 1: With **right** side facing, join Pink with sc in first sc *(see Joining With Sc, page 126)*; sc in same st and in each sc across to last sc, 3 sc in last sc; work 152 sc evenly spaced across end of rows; working in free loops of beginning ch *(Fig. 15b, page 127)*, 3 sc in ch at base of first sc, sc in each ch across to last ch, 3 sc in last ch; work 152 sc evenly spaced across end of rows, sc in same st as first sc; join with slip st to Back Loop Only of first sc *(Fig. 14, page 126)*: 346 sc.
Rnd 2: Ch 3, working in Back Loops Only, 2 dc in same st, dc in next sc and in each sc around working 3 dc in center sc of each corner 3-sc group; join with slip st to first dc, finish off: 354 dc.
Trim: With **right** side facing and working in free loops of sc on Rnd 1, join Pink with sc in any sc; sc in each sc around working 3 sc in center sc of each corner 3-sc group; join with slip st to first sc, finish off.

ASSEMBLY
Place two Strips with **wrong** sides together and bottom edges at same end. Matching stitches and working through **both** loops of each stitch on **both** pieces, join Pink with slip st in center dc of first corner 3-dc group; (ch 1, slip st in next dc) across ending in center dc of next corner 3-dc group; finish off.
Join remaining Strips in same manner, always working in same direction.

BORDER
Rnd 1: With **right** side facing, join Pink with sc in center dc of top right corner 3-dc group; sc in same st and in each dc and each joining around working 3 sc in center dc of each corner 3-dc group, sc in same st as first sc; join with slip st to first sc.
Rnd 2: Ch 1, sc in same st and in each sc across to center sc of next corner 3-sc group, (ch 1, slip st in next sc) across to center sc of next corner 3-sc group, sc in center sc and in each sc across to center sc of next corner 3-sc group, (ch 1, slip st in next sc) across; join with slip st to first sc, finish off.

Holding four 13" strands of Pink together for each fringe, add fringe across short edges of Afghan *(Figs. 20a & b, page 127)*.

Summer Lace

The light and lacy touch of this afghan makes it perfect for summer! Each curvy motif features a multitude of picots in a dreamy color that's reminiscent of a soft, grassy carpet.

Finished Size: 42½" x 62½"

MATERIALS

Red Heart Worsted Weight Yarn
[8 ounces (452 yards) per skein]: 4 skeins
Crochet hook, size G (4.00 mm) **or** size needed for gauge

GAUGE: Each Motif = 10"
Rnds 1-3 = 5¾"

STITCH GUIDE

PICOT
Ch 3, sc in top of dc just made.

FIRST MOTIF

Ch 6; join with slip st to form a ring.
Rnd 1 (Right side): Ch 8 **(counts as first dc plus ch 5, now and throughout)**, dc in ring, (ch 5, dc in ring) 6 times, ch 2, dc in first dc to form last ch-5 sp: 8 ch-5 sps.
Note: Mark last round as **right** side.
Rnd 2: Ch 1, sc in same sp, 8 dc in next ch-5 sp, (sc in next ch-5 sp, 8 dc in next ch-5 sp) around; join with slip st to first sc: 36 sts.
Rnd 3: Slip st in next dc, ch 6, sc in fourth ch from hook **(first Picot made)**, dc in next dc, (work Picot, dc in next dc) 6 times, ★ ch 5, skip next sc, dc in next dc, (work Picot, dc in next dc) 7 times; repeat from ★ 2 times **more**, ch 2, skip last st, dc in third ch of beginning ch-6 to form last ch-5 sp: 28 Picots and 4 ch-5 sps.
Rnd 4: Ch 8, skip next Picot, (sc in next Picot, ch 5, skip next Picot) 3 times, ★ (dc, ch 5) twice in next ch-5 sp, skip next Picot, (sc in next Picot, ch 5, skip next Picot) 3 times; repeat from ★ 2 times **more**, dc in same sp as first dc, ch 2, dc in first dc to form last ch-5 sp: 20 ch-5 sps.
Rnd 5: Ch 1, sc in same sp, 8 dc in next ch-5 sp, sc in next ch-5 sp, ch 5, sc in next ch-5 sp, ★ (8 dc in next ch-5 sp, sc in next ch-5 sp) twice, ch 5, sc in next ch-5 sp; repeat from ★ 2 times **more**, 8 dc in last ch-5 sp; join with slip st to first sc: 64 dc.
Rnd 6: Slip st in next dc, ch 6, sc in fourth ch from hook **(first Picot made)**, dc in next dc, (work Picot, dc in next dc) 6 times, sc in next ch-5 sp, ★ † skip next sc, dc in next dc, (work Picot, dc in next dc) 7 times †, ch 5, skip next sc, dc in next dc, (work Picot, dc in next dc) 7 times, sc in next ch-5 sp; repeat from ★ 2 times **more**, then repeat from † to † once, ch 2, skip last st, dc in third ch of beginning ch-6 to form last ch-5 sp: 56 Picots.

Rnd 7: Ch 8, ★ † (skip next Picot, sc in next Picot, ch 5) 3 times, skip next 2 Picots, (sc in next Picot, ch 5, skip next Picot) 3 times †, (dc, ch 5) twice in next corner ch-5 sp; repeat from ★ 2 times **more**, then repeat from † to † once, dc in same sp as first dc, ch 5; join with slip st to first dc, finish off: 32 ch-5 sps.

ADDITIONAL 23 MOTIFS

Work same as First Motif through Rnd 6: 56 Picots.
When joining to a Motif that has already been joined, slip st into same ch.
Rnd 7 (Joining rnd): Work One Side or Two Side Joining, arranging Motifs into 4 vertical rows of 6 Motifs each.

ONE SIDE JOINING

Rnd 7 (Joining rnd): Ch 8, ★ † (skip next Picot, sc in next Picot, ch 5) 3 times, skip next 2 Picots, (sc in next Picot, ch 5, skip next Picot) 3 times †, (dc, ch 5) twice in next corner ch-5 sp; repeat from ★ once **more**, then repeat from † to † once, dc in next corner ch-5 sp, ch 2; holding Motifs with **wrong** sides together, slip st in center ch of corresponding corner ch-5 on **adjacent Motif** *(Fig. 17, page 127)*, ch 2, dc in same sp on **new Motif**, ch 2, slip st in center ch of next ch-5 on **adjacent Motif**, ch 2, (skip next Picot on **new Motif**, sc in next Picot, ch 2, slip st in center ch of next ch-5 on **adjacent Motif**, ch 2) 3 times, skip next 2 Picots on **new Motif**, (sc in next Picot, ch 2, slip st in center ch of next ch-5 on **adjacent Motif**, ch 2, skip next Picot on **new Motif**) 3 times, dc in same sp as first dc, ch 2, slip st in center ch of next corner ch-5 on **adjacent Motif**, ch 2; join with slip st to first dc, finish off.

TWO SIDE JOINING

Rnd 7 (Joining rnd): Ch 8, † (skip next Picot, sc in next Picot, ch 5) 3 times, skip next 2 Picots, (sc in next Picot, ch 5, skip next Picot) 3 times †, (dc, ch 5) twice in next corner ch-5 sp, repeat from † to † once, dc in next corner ch-5 sp, ch 2; holding Motifs with **wrong** sides together, slip st in center ch of corresponding corner ch-5 on **adjacent Motif**, ♥ ch 2, dc in same sp on **new Motif**, ch 2, slip st in center ch of next ch-5 on **adjacent Motif**, ch 2, (skip next Picot on **new Motif**, sc in next Picot, ch 2, slip st in center ch of next ch-5 on **adjacent Motif**, ch 2) 3 times, skip next 2 Picots on **new Motif**, (sc in next Picot, ch 2, slip st in center ch of next ch-5 on **adjacent Motif**, ch 2, skip next Picot on **new Motif**) 3 times ♥, dc in next corner ch-5 sp, ch 2, slip st in center ch of next corner ch-5 on **adjacent Motif**, repeat from

♥ to ♥ once, dc in same sp as first dc, ch 2, slip st in center ch of next corner ch-5 on **adjacent Motif**, ch 2; join with slip st to first dc, finish off.

BORDER

Rnd 1: With **right** side facing, join yarn with sc in any corner ch-5 sp *(see Joining With Sc, page 126)*; ★ ♥ 8 dc in next ch-5 sp, (sc in next ch-5 sp, ch 5, sc in next ch-5 sp, 8 dc in next ch-5 sp) twice, † sc around next joining, 8 dc in next ch-5 sp, (sc in next ch-5 sp, ch 5, sc in next ch-5 sp, 8 dc in next ch-5 sp) twice †, repeat from † to † across to next corner ch-5 sp ♥, sc in corner ch-5 sp; repeat from ★ 2 times **more**, then repeat from ♥ to ♥ once; join with slip st to first sc: 480 dc and 40 ch-5 sps.

Rnd 2: Slip st in next dc, ch 6, sc in fourth ch from hook, ★ ♥ † dc in next dc, (work Picot, dc in next dc) 6 times, sc in next ch-5 sp, skip next sc, dc in next dc, (work Picot, dc in next dc) 7 times, sc in next ch-5 sp, skip next sc, dc in next dc, (work Picot, dc in next dc) 6 times, skip next 3 sts †; repeat from † to † across to last Motif on same side, dc in next dc, (work Picot, dc in next dc) 6 times, [sc in next ch-5 sp, skip next sc, dc in next dc, (work Picot, dc in next dc) 7 times] twice, ch 5 ♥, skip next corner sc, dc in next dc, work Picot; repeat from ★ 2 times **more**, then repeat from ♥ to ♥ once, skip last st; join with slip st to third ch of beginning ch-6, finish off.

Lacy Valentine

An incurable romantic will love this charming valentine wrap! The four pastel hearts of each block are joined as you go and then bordered with a decorative pattern to form a square. A scalloped edging completes the feminine look.

Finished Size: 46" x 67"

MATERIALS
Red Heart Worsted Weight Yarn
[3 ounces (170 yards) per skein]:
Ecru - 12 skeins
Blue - 2 skeins
Yellow - 2 skeins
Spruce - 2 skeins
Pink - 2 skeins
Crochet hook, size H (5.00 mm) **or** size needed for gauge

GAUGE: Each Heart = 3½"w x 3" h
Each Square = 10½"

STITCH GUIDE

> **DECREASE**
> Pull up a loop in next 3 sts, YO and draw through all 4 loops on hook **(counts as one sc).**

FIRST SQUARE
FIRST HEART
With Blue, ch 12 **loosely.**
Rnd 1 (Right side): 2 Sc in second ch from hook, sc in next 3 chs, decrease, sc in next 3 chs, 3 sc in last ch; working in free loops of beginning ch **(Fig. 15b, page 127),** sc in next 4 chs, 3 sc in next ch, sc in next 5 chs; join with slip st to first sc: 24 sc.
Note: Mark last round as **right** side.
Rnd 2: Ch 1, 2 sc in same st and in next sc, sc in next 2 sc, decrease, sc in next 2 sc, 2 sc in each of next 3 sc, sc in next 5 sc, 3 sc in next sc, sc in next 5 sc, 2 sc in last sc; join with slip st to first sc: 30 sc.
Rnd 3: Ch 1, 2 sc in same st and in each of next 2 sc, sc in next 2 sc, decrease, sc in next 2 sc, place marker around last sc made for st placement, 2 sc in each of next 5 sc, sc in next 6 sc, 3 sc in next sc, sc in next 6 sc, 2 sc in each of last 2 sc; join with slip st to first sc, finish off: 40 sc.
Rnd 4: With **right** side facing, join Ecru with sc in marked sc **(see Joining With Sc, page 126);** ch 3, skip next sc, (sc in next sc, ch 3, skip next sc) 8 times, (sc, ch 3) twice in next sc, skip next sc, sc in next sc, (ch 3, skip next sc, sc in next sc) 3 times, place marker around last ch-3 made for st placement, (ch 3, skip next sc, sc in next sc) 5 times, skip last 3 sc; join with slip st to first sc, finish off: 19 ch-3 sps.

SECOND HEART
With Yellow, work same as First Heart through Rnd 3: 40 sc.
Rnd 4 (Joining rnd): With **right** side facing, join Ecru with sc in marked sc; (ch 3, skip next sc, sc in next sc) 5 times, ch 1, holding Hearts with **wrong** sides together, sc in marked ch-3 sp on **First Heart (Fig. 17, page 127),** ch 1, ★ skip next sc on **Second Heart,** sc in next sc, ch 1, sc in next ch-3 sp on **First Heart,** ch 1; repeat from ★ 3 times **more,** sc in same st on **Second Heart,** (ch 3, skip next sc, sc in next sc) 4 times, place marker around last ch-3 made for st placement, (ch 3, skip next sc, sc in next sc) 5 times, skip last 3 sc; join with slip st to first sc, finish off: 19 sps.

THIRD HEART
With Spruce, work same as First Heart through Rnd 3: 40 sc.
Rnd 4 (Joining rnd): With **right** side facing, join Ecru with sc in marked sc; (ch 3, skip next sc, sc in next sc) 5 times, ch 1, holding Hearts with **wrong** sides together, sc in marked ch-3 sp on **Second Heart,** ch 1, skip next sc on **Third Heart,** sc in next sc, ch 1, ★ sc in next ch-3 sp on **Second Heart,** ch 1, skip next sc on **Third Heart,** sc in next sc, ch 1; repeat from ★ 2 times **more,** sc in side of sc joining corner sps of first two Hearts, ch 1, sc in same st on **Third Heart,** (ch 3, skip next sc, sc in next sc) 4 times, place marker around last ch-3 made for st placement, (ch 3, skip next sc, sc in next sc) 5 times, skip last 3 sc; join with slip st to first sc, finish off: 19 sps.

FOURTH HEART
With Pink, work same as First Heart through Rnd 3: 40 sc.
Rnd 4 (Joining rnd): With **right** side facing, join Ecru with sc in marked sc; (ch 3, skip next sc, sc in next sc) 5 times, ch 1, holding Hearts with **wrong** sides together, sc in marked ch-3 sp on **Third Heart,** ch 1, skip next sc on **Fourth Heart,** sc in next sc, ch 1, ★ sc in next ch-3 sp on **Third Heart,** ch 1, skip next sc on **Fourth Heart,** sc in next sc, ch 1; repeat from ★ 2 times **more,** sc in side of sc joining corner sps of first two Hearts (in same st as Third Heart joining), ch 1, sc in same st on **Fourth Heart,** † ch 1, sc in next ch-3 sp on **First Heart,** ch 1, skip next sc on **Fourth Heart,** sc in next sc †; repeat from † to † 3 times **more,** (ch 3, skip next sc, sc in next sc) 5 times, skip last 3 sc; join with slip st to first sc, finish off: 19 sps.

BORDER

When adding Rnd 1 to each Square, be sure to join yarn to the Heart marked with a dot on diagram.

Rnd 1: With **right** side facing, join Ecru with sc in first ch-3 sp to left of notch at center top of marked Heart; ch 2, (sc in next ch-3 sp, ch 2) twice, dc in next ch-3 sp, ch 2, tr in next ch-3 sp, ch 1, skip joining, tr in next ch-3 sp, ch 2, dc in next ch-3 sp, ch 2, ★ (sc in next ch-3 sp, ch 2) 6 times, dc in next ch-3 sp, ch 2, tr in next ch-3 sp, ch 1, skip joining, tr in next ch-3 sp, ch 2, dc in next ch-3 sp, ch 2; repeat from ★ 2 times **more**, (sc in next ch-3 sp, ch 2) 3 times; join with slip st to first sc: 40 sps.

Rnd 2: Slip st in first ch-2 sp, ch 2, slip st in next ch-2 sp, ch 2, dc in next ch-2 sp, ch 1, skip next ch-2 sp, in next ch-1 sp work [(dtr, ch 1) twice, tr tr, ch 2, tr tr, ch 1, (dtr, ch 1) twice], skip next ch-2 sp, dc in next ch-2 sp, ch 2, ★ (slip st in next ch-2 sp, ch 2) 5 times, dc in next ch-2 sp, ch 1, skip next ch-2 sp, in next ch-1 sp work [(dtr, ch 1) twice, tr tr, ch 2, tr tr, ch 1, (dtr, ch 1) twice], skip next ch-2 sp, dc in next ch-2 sp, ch 2; repeat from ★ 2 times **more**, (slip st in next ch-2 sp, ch 2) 3 times; join with slip st to first slip st: 52 sps.

Continued on page 14.

Rnd 3: Ch 1, sc in same st and in each sp and each st around working 3 sc in each corner ch-2 sp; join with slip st to first sc: 112 sc.

Rnd 4: Ch 1, sc in same st and in each sc around working 3 sc in center sc of each corner 3-sc group; join with slip st to first sc: 120 sc.

Rnd 5: Slip st in next sc, ch 1, sc in same st, ch 3, ★ skip next sc, (sc in next sc, ch 3, skip next sc) across to center sc of next corner 3-sc group, (sc, ch 3) twice in center sc; repeat from ★ 3 times **more**, skip next sc, (sc in next sc, ch 3, skip next st) across; join with slip st to first sc, finish off: 64 ch-3 sps.

ADDITIONAL SQUARES

Using Placement Diagram as a guide, work and join Squares in vertical rows from top to bottom.

Work same as First Square through Rnd 4 of Border: 120 sc.

Rnd 5 (Joining rnd): Work One or Two Side Joining.

ONE SIDE JOINING

Rnd 5 (Joining rnd): Slip st in next sc, ch 1, sc in same st, ch 3, skip next sc, (sc in next sc, ch 3, skip next sc) across to center sc of next corner 3-sc group, ★ (sc, ch 3) twice in center sc, skip next sc, (sc in next sc, ch 3, skip next sc) across to center sc of next corner 3-sc group; repeat from ★ once **more**, sc in center sc, ch 1, holding Squares with **wrong** sides together, sc in corresponding corner ch-3 sp on **adjacent Square**, ch 1, sc in same st on **new Square**, ch 1, sc in next ch-3 sp on **adjacent Square**, ch 1, (skip next sc on **new Square**, sc in next sc, ch 1, sc in next ch-3 sp on **adjacent Square**, ch 1) 15 times, sc in same st on **new Square**, ch 3, skip next sc, (sc in next sc, ch 3, skip next st) across; join with slip st to first sc, finish off: 64 sps.

TWO SIDE JOINING

Rnd 5 (Joining rnd): Slip st in next sc, ch 1, sc in same st, ch 3, skip next sc, (sc in next sc, ch 3, skip next sc) across to center sc of next corner 3-sc group, (sc, ch 3) twice in center sc, skip next sc, (sc in next sc, ch 3, skip next sc) across to center sc of next corner 3-sc group, sc in center sc, ch 1, holding Squares with **wrong** sides together, sc in corresponding corner ch-3 sp on **adjacent Square**, ch 1, sc in same st on **new Square**, ch 1, (sc in next ch-3 sp on **adjacent Square**, ch 1, skip next sc on **new Square**, sc in next sc, ch 1) 15 times, sc in next 3 corner sps on **adjacent Squares**, ch 1, sc in same st on **new Square**, ch 1, sc in next ch-3 sp on **adjacent Square**, ch 1, (skip next sc on **new Square**, sc in next sc, ch 1, sc in next ch-3 sp on **adjacent Square**, ch 1) 15 times, sc in same st on **new Square**, ch 3, skip next sc, (sc in next sc, ch 3, skip next st) across; join with slip st to first sc, finish off: 64 sps.

EDGING

Rnd 1: With **right** side of one short edge facing, join Ecru with sc in first ch-3 sp to left of top right corner ch-3 sp; † ch 1, (sc, ch 5, sc) in next ch-3 sp, ch 1, [(sc in next sp, ch 1) twice, (sc, ch 5, sc) in next sp, ch 1] across to within one ch-3 sp of next corner ch-3 sp, sc in next ch-3 sp, ch 1, in corner ch-3 sp work (sc, ch 1, sc, ch 5, sc), ch 1, [(sc in next sp, ch 1) twice, (sc, ch 5, sc) in next sp, ch 1] across to within one ch-3 sp of next corner ch-3 sp, sc in next ch-3 sp, ch 1, in corner ch-3 sp work [sc, ch 1, sc, ch 5, (sc, ch 1) twice] †, sc in next ch-3 sp, repeat from † to † once; join with slip st to first sc: 342 ch-1 sps and 114 ch-5 sps.

Rnd 2: Slip st in next 2 sts and in next ch-5 sp, ch 4, dc in same sp, (ch 1, dc in same sp) 4 times, skip next ch-1 sp, sc in next ch-1 sp, skip next ch-1 sp, ★ [dc in next ch-5 sp, (ch 1, dc in same sp) 5 times, skip next ch-1 sp, sc in next ch-1 sp, skip next ch-1 sp] across to next corner ch-5 sp, dc in corner ch-5 sp, (ch 1, dc in same sp) 7 times, skip next ch-1 sp, sc in next ch-1 sp, skip next ch-1 sp; repeat from ★ around; join with slip st to third ch of beginning ch-4: 578 ch-1 sps.

Rnd 3: Slip st in first ch-1 sp, ch 1, sc in same sp and in next ch-1 sp, ch 3, (sc, ch 5, sc) in next ch-1 sp, ch 3, ★ † [sc in next 4 ch-1 sps, ch 3, (sc, ch 5, sc) in next ch-1 sp, ch 3] across to within 5 ch-1 sps of next corner ch-1 sp, sc in next 3 ch-1 sps, ch 3, (sc in next ch-1 sp, ch 3) twice, (sc, ch 5, sc) in corner ch-1 sp, ch 3, (sc in next ch-1 sp, ch 3) twice †, sc in next 3 ch-1 sps, ch 3, (sc, ch 5, sc) in next ch-1 sp, ch 3; repeat from ★ 2 times **more**, then repeat from † to † once, sc in last ch-1 sp; join with slip st to first sc, finish off.

PLACEMENT DIAGRAM

First Square

KEY

♡ Yellow
♥ Pink
♥ Spruce
♥ Blue

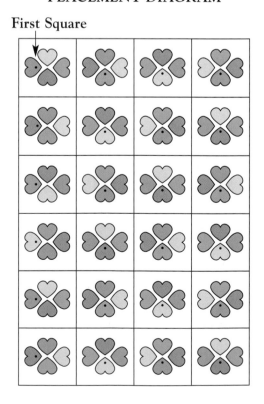

14

Lap of Luxury

Clusters worked in a sideways manner give this luxurious afghan a uniquely textured look! Fashioned in off-white and edged with generous fringe, the soft throw will be a leisure-time favorite.

Finished Size: 44" x 60½"

MATERIALS

Red Heart Worsted Weight Yarn
[8 ounces (452 yards) per skein]: 7 skeins
Crochet hook, size G (4.00 mm) **or** size
needed for gauge

GAUGE: In pattern, 2 repeats = 4¼";
            10 rows = 6"

STITCH GUIDE

> **FRONT POST CLUSTER**
> *(abbreviated FP Cluster)*
> ★ YO, insert hook from **front** to **back** around posts of last 3-dc group made *(Fig. 13, page 126)*, YO and pull up a loop, YO and draw through 2 loops on hook; repeat from ★ 2 times **more**, YO and draw through all 4 loops on hook.

AFGHAN

Ch 189 **loosely**.

Row 1: (2 Dc, ch 2, 2 dc) in sixth ch from hook, ★ skip next 2 chs, dc in next 3 chs, work FP Cluster, skip next 3 chs, (2 dc, ch 2, 2 dc) in next ch; repeat from ★ across to last 3 chs, skip next 2 chs, dc in last ch: 20 FP Clusters.

Row 2 (Right side): Ch 3 **(counts as first dc, now and throughout)**, turn; (2 dc, ch 2, 2 dc) in next ch-2 sp, ★ skip next 2 dc, dc in side of next FP Cluster and in next 3 dc, (2 dc, ch 2, 2 dc) in next ch-2 sp; repeat from ★ across to last 2 dc, skip last 2 dc, dc in next ch: 166 dc.
Note: Mark last row as **right** side.

Row 3: Ch 3, turn; (2 dc, ch 2, 2 dc) in next ch-2 sp, ★ skip next 2 dc, dc in next 3 dc, work FP Cluster, (2 dc, ch 2, 2 dc) in next ch-2 sp; repeat from ★ across to last 3 dc, skip next 2 dc, dc in last dc: 20 FP Clusters.

Row 4: Ch 3, turn; (2 dc, ch 2, 2 dc) in next ch-2 sp, ★ skip next 2 dc, dc in side of next FP Cluster and in next 3 dc, (2 dc, ch 2, 2 dc) in next ch-2 sp; repeat from ★ across to last 3 dc, skip next 2 dc, dc in last dc: 166 dc.

Rows 5-101: Repeat Rows 3 and 4, 48 times; then repeat Row 3 once **more**.
Finish off.

Holding ten 18" strands of yarn together for each fringe, add fringe across short edges of Afghan *(Figs. 20a & b, page 127)*.

Victorian Fans

*Create an atmosphere of nostalgia and grace in any room
with this "fan-ciful" afghan! The tasteful throw is patterned
after the traditional Grandmother's Fan quilt.*

Finished Size: 55" x 78"

MATERIALS

Red Heart Worsted Weight Yarn
[3 ounces (170 yards) per skein]:
Ecru - 15 skeins
Spruce - 4 skeins
Blue - 4 skeins
Pink - 4 skeins
Yellow - 4 skeins
Crochet hook, size H (5.00 mm) **or** size needed for gauge

GAUGE: Each Square = 12"

STITCH GUIDE

> **FRONT POST DOUBLE CROCHET**
> *(abbreviated FPdc)*
> YO, insert hook from **front** to **back** around post of st indicated (***Fig. 13, page 126***), YO and pull up a loop even with last dc made, (YO and draw through 2 loops on hook) twice. Skip st behind FPdc.
>
> **BACK POST DOUBLE CROCHET**
> *(abbreviated BPdc)*
> YO, insert hook from **back** to **front** around post of st indicated (***Fig. 13, page 126***), YO and pull up a loop even with last dc made, (YO and draw through 2 loops on hook) twice. Skip st in front of BPdc.

SQUARE (Make 24)

Row 1: With Ecru, ch 4, 6 dc in fourth ch from hook: 7 sts.

Row 2 (Right side): Ch 3 (**counts as first dc, now and throughout**), turn; 2 dc in next dc, (dc in next dc, 2 dc in next dc) twice, dc in top of beginning ch: 10 dc.

Note: Mark last row as **right** side.

Row 3: Ch 3, turn; 2 dc in next dc, (dc in next dc, 2 dc in next dc) 3 times, dc in last 2 dc: 14 dc.

Row 4: Ch 3, turn; dc in next dc and in each dc across; finish off.

Using the following colors for Rows 5-18, make 6 fans each of Spruce, Blue, Pink, and Yellow.

Row 5: With **wrong** side facing, join color indicated with slip st in first dc; ch 3, 2 dc in next dc, (dc in next dc, 2 dc in next dc) across to last 2 dc, dc in last 2 dc: 20 dc.

Row 6: Ch 3, turn; dc in next dc, ★ work FPdc around next dc, dc in next 2 dc; repeat from ★ across.

Row 7: Ch 3, turn; 2 dc in next dc, ★ work BPdc around next FPdc, dc in next dc, 2 dc in next dc; repeat from ★ across: 27 sts.

Row 8: Ch 3, turn; dc in next 2 dc, (work FPdc around next BPdc, dc in next 3 dc) across.

Row 9: Ch 3, turn; dc in next 2 dc, (work FPdc around next BPdc, dc in next 3 dc) across.

Row 10: Ch 3, turn; 2 dc in next dc, dc in next dc, ★ work FPdc around next BPdc, dc in next dc, 2 dc in next dc, dc in next dc; repeat from ★ across: 34 sts.

Row 11: Ch 3, turn; dc in next 3 dc, (work BPdc around next FPdc, dc in next 4 dc) across.

Row 12: Ch 3, turn; dc in next dc, 2 dc in next dc, dc in next dc, ★ work FPdc around next BPdc, dc in next 2 dc, 2 dc in next dc, dc in next dc; repeat from ★ across: 41 sts.

Row 13: Ch 3, turn; dc in next 4 dc, (work BPdc around next FPdc, dc in next 5 dc) across.

Row 14: Ch 3, turn; dc in next dc, 2 dc in next dc, dc in next 2 dc, ★ work FPdc around next BPdc, dc in next 2 dc, 2 dc in next dc, dc in next 2 dc; repeat from ★ across: 48 sts.

Row 15: Ch 3, turn; dc in next 5 dc, (work BPdc around next FPdc, dc in next 6 dc) across.

Row 16: Ch 3, turn; dc in next 2 dc, 2 dc in next dc, dc in next 2 dc, ★ work FPdc around next BPdc, dc in next 3 dc, 2 dc in next dc, dc in next 2 dc; repeat from ★ across: 55 sts.

Row 17: Ch 1, turn; sc in first 2 dc, dc in next 4 dc, sc in next dc, work BPdc around next FPdc, sc in next dc, ★ dc in next 5 dc, sc in next dc, work BPdc around next FPdc, sc in next dc; repeat from ★ across to last 6 dc, dc in next 4 dc, sc in last 2 dc.

Row 18: Ch 1, turn; sc in first sc, hdc in next sc, dc in next dc, (dc, ch 1, dc) in next dc, dc in next dc, hdc in next dc, sc in next sc, ★ skip next BPdc, sc in next sc, hdc in next dc, dc in next dc, (dc, ch 1, dc) in next dc, dc in next dc, hdc in next st, sc in next sc; repeat from ★ across; finish off.

Row 19: With **wrong** side facing, join Ecru with slip st in first sc; ch 5 (**counts as first dc plus ch 2**), sc in next ch-1 sp, ch 2, † skip next 3 sts, 3 dc in next sc, ch 3, sc in next ch-1 sp, ch 3 †; repeat from † to † once **more**, skip next 3 sts, 3 tr in next sc, ch 4, (3 tr, ch 4) twice in next ch-1 sp, skip next 3 sts, 3 tr in next sc, ch 3, sc in next ch-1 sp, ch 3, repeat from † to † once, skip next 3 sts, 3 dc in next sc, ch 2, sc in next ch-1 sp, ch 2, skip next 3 sts, dc in last sc: 15 sps.

Row 20: Ch 2 **(counts as first hdc)**, turn; (3 hdc in next ch-2 sp, ch 1) twice, (3 dc in next ch-3 sp, ch 1) twice, (3 tr in next sp, ch 1) 3 times, (3 tr, ch 3, 3 tr) in next ch-4 sp, (ch 1, 3 tr in next sp) 3 times, (ch 1, 3 dc in next ch-3 sp) twice, (ch 1, 3 hdc in next ch-2 sp) twice, hdc in last dc.

Row 21: Ch 1, turn; sc in first 4 hdc, ch 1, skip next hdc, sc in next hdc, (3 hdc in next ch-1 sp, skip next dc, hdc in next dc) twice, (3 dc in next ch-1 sp, skip next tr, dc in next tr) twice, (3 tr in next ch-1 sp, skip next tr, tr in next tr) twice, (3 tr, ch 3, 3 tr) in next ch-3 sp, (skip next tr, tr in next tr, 3 tr in next ch-1 sp) twice, (skip next tr, dc in next tr, 3 dc in next ch-1 sp) twice, (skip next dc, hdc in next dc, 3 hdc in next ch-1 sp) twice, skip next hdc, sc in next hdc, ch 1, skip next hdc, sc in last 4 hdc: 64 sts and 3 sps.

Begin working in rounds.

Rnd 1: Ch 1, turn; sc in first 5 sts, hdc in next 5 sts, dc in next 7 sts, tr in next 16 sts, (3 tr, ch 2, 3 tr) in next ch-2 sp, tr in next 16 sts, dc in next 7 sts, hdc in next 5 sts, sc in next 4 sts, (sc, ch 2, sc) in next sc; working in end of rows, skip first row, sc in next 3 rows, skip next row, 2 sc in each of next 3 rows, sc in next row, 2 sc in each of next 7 rows, sc in next row, 2 sc in each of last 4 rows; (2 dc, ch 2, 2 dc) in free loop of beginning ch; working in end of rows, 2 sc in each of first 4 rows, sc in next row, 2 sc in each of next 7 rows, sc in next row, 2 sc in each of next 3 rows, skip next row, sc in next 3 rows, skip last row, sc in same st as first sc, ch 2; join with slip st to first sc: 144 sts and 4 ch-2 sps.

Rnd 2: Ch 3, do **not** turn; ★ dc in next st and in each st across to next ch-2 sp, (dc, ch 3, dc) in ch-2 sp; repeat from ★ around; join with slip st to first dc, finish off: 152 dc.

Continued on page 18.

ASSEMBLY

Use diagram as a guide for placement and always work in the same direction. Join Squares forming 4 vertical strips of 6 Squares each as follows: Holding two Squares with **wrong** sides together and working through **inside** loops of each st on **both** pieces, join Ecru with slip st in center ch of first corner ch-3; slip st in each ch and in each dc across ending in center ch of next corner ch-3; finish off.

Join strips together in same manner, working in slip sts between Squares.

PLACEMENT DIAGRAM

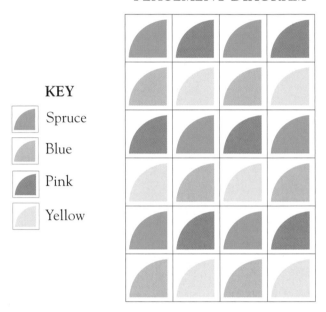

KEY

- Spruce
- Blue
- Pink
- Yellow

EDGING

Rnd 1: With **right** side facing, join Ecru with slip st in top right corner ch-3 sp; ch 3, 2 dc in same sp, ★ dc in each dc and in each ch and each joining across to next corner ch-3 sp, (3 dc, ch 3, 3 dc) in corner ch-3 sp; repeat from ★ 2 times **more**, dc in each dc and in each ch and each joining across, 3 dc in same sp as first dc, ch 1, hdc in first dc to form last ch-3 sp: 832 dc and 4 ch-3 sps.

Rnd 2: Ch 4 **(counts as first dc plus ch 1)**, dc in same sp, ch 1, ★ skip next dc, (dc in next dc, ch 1, skip next dc) across to next corner ch-3 sp, (dc, ch 1, dc, ch 3, dc, ch 1, dc) in corner ch-3 sp, ch 1; repeat from ★ 2 times **more**, skip next dc, (dc in next dc, ch 1, skip next dc) across, (dc, ch 1, dc) in same sp as first dc, ch 1, hdc in first dc to form last ch-3 sp: 430 dc, 426 ch-1 sps, and 4 ch-3 sps.

Rnd 3: Ch 3, dc in same sp, † dc in each dc and in each ch-1 sp across to next corner ch-3 sp, (2 dc, ch 2, 2 dc) in corner ch-3 sp, 2 dc in next dc, dc in each ch-1 sp and in each dc across to within one dc of next corner ch-3 sp, 2 dc in next dc †, (2 dc, ch 2, 2 dc) in corner ch-3 sp, repeat from † to † once, 2 dc in same sp as first dc, ch 1, sc in first dc to form last ch-2 sp: 876 dc and 4 ch-2 sps.

Rnd 4: Ch 1, sc in same sp, ★ ♥ skip next dc, 5 dc in next dc, † skip next 2 dc, sc in next dc, skip next 2 dc, 5 dc in next dc †; repeat from † to † across to within one dc of next corner ch-2 sp, skip next dc ♥, sc in corner ch-2 sp; repeat from ★ 2 times **more**, then repeat from ♥ to ♥ once; join with slip st to first sc, finish off.

Blue Breeze

Shades of periwinkle contrasted with off-white give definition to the pretty shell stitches in this mile-a-minute afghan. The wrap is a breeze to make because it's assembled using the popular and quick "join-as-you-go" method.

Finished Size: 45" x 61"

MATERIALS

Red Heart Worsted Weight Yarn
[8 ounces (452 yards) per skein]:
Light Blue - 2 skeins
Blue - 2 skeins
Off-White - 3 skeins
Crochet hook, size H (5.00 mm) **or** size needed for gauge

GAUGE: In pattern, 2 repeats = 3¼"
Each Strip = 5" wide

STITCH GUIDE

SHELL (3 Dc, ch 2, 3 dc) in st or sp indicated. **PICOT** Ch 4, slip st in top of dc just made.

FIRST STRIP

With Light Blue, ch 208 **loosely**.

Rnd 1 (Right side): (2 Dc, ch 2, 3 dc) in fourth ch from hook, (skip next 2 chs, sc in next ch, skip next 2 chs, work Shell in next ch) across, ch 2; working in free loops of beginning ch *(Fig. 15b, page 127)*, work Shell in same st as last Shell made, (skip next 2 chs, sc in next ch, skip next 2 chs, work Shell in next ch) 34 times, ch 2; join with slip st to top of beginning ch, finish off: 70 Shells.

Note: Mark last round as **right** side.

Rnd 2: With **right** side facing, join Blue with slip st in ch-2 sp at either end; ch 3 **(counts as first dc, now and throughout)**, (2 dc, ch 2, 3 dc) in same sp, † ch 1, work Shell in next Shell (ch-2 sp), (dc in next sc, work Shell in next Shell) across to ch-2 sp at opposite end, ch 1 †, work Shell in end ch-2 sp, repeat from † to † once; join with slip st to first dc, finish off: 76 sps.

Rnd 3: With **right** side facing, join Off-White with slip st in ch-2 sp at either end; ch 3, (2 dc, ch 2, 3 dc) in same sp, † ch 1, 3 dc in next ch-1 sp, ch 1, work Shell in next Shell, (skip next 3 dc, dc in next dc, work Shell in next Shell) across to next ch-1 sp, ch 1, 3 dc in next ch-1 sp, ch 1 †, work Shell in end ch-2 sp, repeat from † to † once; join with slip st to first dc, do **not** finish off: 80 sps.

Rnd 4: Slip st in next 2 dc and in next ch-2 sp, ch 1, (sc in same sp, ch 4) twice, † (sc, ch 4) twice in each of next 2 ch-1 sps, (sc, ch 4, sc) in next Shell, ★ ch 2, skip next 3 dc, dc in next dc, work Picot, ch 2, (sc, ch 4, sc) in next Shell; repeat from ★ across to next ch-1 sp, ch 4, (sc, ch 4) twice in each of next 2 ch-1 sps †, (sc, ch 4) twice in next Shell, repeat from † to † once; join with slip st to first sc, finish off: 228 sps and 68 Picots.

Continued on page 20.

19

REMAINING 8 STRIPS

Work same as First Strip through Rnd 3: 80 sps.

Rnd 4 (Joining rnd)**:** Slip st in next 2 dc and in next ch-1 sp, ch 1, (sc, ch 4) twice in same sp and in each of next 2 ch-1 sps, (sc, ch 4, sc) in next Shell, ★ ch 2, skip next 3 dc, dc in next dc, work Picot, ch 2, (sc, ch 4, sc) in next Shell; repeat from ★ across to next ch-1 sp, ch 4, (sc, ch 4) twice in each of next 2 ch-1 sps, (sc, ch 4) twice in next Shell and in each of next 2 ch-1 sps, sc in next Shell, ch 2, holding Strips with **wrong** sides together, slip st in corresponding ch-4 sp on **previous Strip** (*Fig. 17, page 127*), ch 2, sc in same Shell on **new Strip**, † ch 2, skip next 3 dc, dc in next dc, ch 2, slip st in next Picot on **previous Strip**, ch 2, slip st in dc just made on **new Strip**, ch 2, sc in next Shell, ch 2, slip st in next ch-4 sp on **previous Strip**, ch 2, sc in same Shell on **new Strip** †; repeat from † to † across to next ch-1 sp, ch 4, (sc, ch 4) twice in each of last 2 ch-1 sps; join with slip st to first sc, finish off.

Light & Airy

The simplicity of this airy afghan makes it an ideal project for beginners. Featuring shades of off-white and spruce, the wrap will be a welcome companion for a restful evening at home.

Finished Size: 47" x 65"

MATERIALS

Red Heart Worsted Weight Yarn
[3½ ounces (198 yards) per skein]:
Spruce - 8 skeins
Off-White - 4 skeins
Crochet hook, size I (5.50 mm) **or** size needed for gauge

GAUGE: In pattern, 2 repeats = 4¼";
               8 rows = 4½ "

STITCH GUIDE

> **PICOT**
> Ch 6, slip st in top of last dc made.

AFGHAN BODY

With Spruce, ch 159 **loosely**.

Row 1 (Right side)**:** Dc in fourth ch from hook **(3 skipped chs count as first dc)** and in next 2 chs, ch 2, skip next 2 chs, dc in next ch, work Picot, ch 2, ★ skip next 2 chs, dc in next 3 chs, ch 2, skip next 2 chs, dc in next ch, work Picot, ch 2; repeat from ★ across to last 6 chs, skip next 2 chs, dc in last 4 chs: 19 Picots.

Note: Mark last row as **right** side.

Row 2: Ch 3 **(counts as first dc, now and throughout)**, turn; ★ dc in next 3 dc, ch 2, sc in next Picot, ch 2; repeat from ★ across to last 4 dc, dc in last 4 dc.

Row 3: Ch 3, turn; ★ dc in next 3 dc, ch 2, dc in next sc, ch 2; repeat from ★ across to last 4 dc, dc in last 4 dc; finish off.

Row 4: With **wrong** side facing and working in Front Loops Only (*Fig. 14, page 126*), join Off-White with slip st in first dc; ch 3, dc in next dc and in each st across; finish off: 157 dc.

Row 5: With **right** side facing and working in **both** loops, join Spruce with slip st in first dc; ch 3, dc in next 3 dc, ch 2, skip next 2 dc, dc in next dc, work Picot, ch 2, ★ skip next 2 dc, dc in next 3 dc, ch 2, skip next 2 dc, dc in next dc, work Picot, ch 2; repeat from ★ across to last 6 dc, skip next 2 dc, dc in last 4 dc; do **not** finish off.

Rows 6-107: Repeat Rows 2-5, 25 times; then repeat Rows 2 and 3 once **more**.

EDGING

Rnd 1: With **wrong** side facing and working in Front Loops Only, join Off-White with slip st in first dc on last row; ch 3, 2 dc in same st, dc in each st across to last dc, 5 dc in last dc; work 215 dc evenly spaced across end of rows; working in free loops of beginning ch (*Fig. 15b, page 127*), 5 dc in ch at base of first dc, dc in each ch across to last ch, 5 dc in last ch; work 215 dc evenly spaced across end of rows, 2 dc in same st as first dc; join with slip st to first dc, finish off: 760 dc.

Rnd 2: With **right** side facing and working in **both** loops, join Spruce with slip st in same st as joining; ch 3, 2 dc in same st, dc in each dc around working 5 dc in center dc of each corner 5-dc group, 2 dc in same st as first dc; join with slip st to first dc: 776 dc.

Rnd 3: Ch 4, do **not** turn; (dc, work Picot, ch 1, dc) in same st, ch 1, skip next dc, dc in next dc, work Picot, ch 1, skip next dc, † dc in next dc, ch 1, skip next dc, dc in next dc, work Picot, ch 1, skip next dc †; repeat from † to † across to center dc of next corner 5-dc group, ★ (dc, ch 1, dc, work Picot, ch 1, dc) in center dc, ch 1, skip next dc, dc in next dc, work Picot, ch 1, skip next dc, repeat from † to † across to center dc of next corner 5-dc group; repeat from ★ around; join with slip st to third ch of beginning ch-4, finish off.

Warm & Cozy

When the nights turn cool and Jack Frost starts nipping at your nose, it's time to snuggle up by the fire with a cozy afghan! In this collection, we've included thick, rustic wraps as well as handsome, tailored styles for formal settings. Go all out with rich texture and vivid hues to warm both heart and home.

Handsome Chevron

*Warmly contrasting ripples give this eye-catching afghan a masculine feel,
but it will look handsome in any decor. The grand cover-up is worked in strips,
which are bordered by a single crochet trim and then whipstitched together.*

Finished Size: 49$\frac{1}{2}$" x 66"

MATERIALS
Red Heart Worsted Weight Yarn
[3$\frac{1}{2}$ ounces (198 yards) per skein]:
Teal - 8 skeins
Tan - 6 skeins
Crochet hook, size H (5.00 mm) **or** size needed for gauge
Yarn needle

GAUGE: Each Strip = 5$\frac{1}{2}$" wide;
One repeat (4 rows) = 3"

STITCH GUIDE

> **DECREASE** (uses next 2 sts)
> ★ YO, insert hook in **next** st, YO and pull up a loop, YO and draw through 2 loops on hook; repeat from ★ once **more**, YO and draw through all 3 loops on hook (**counts as one dc**).

Note: Strips are worked in Back Loops Only throughout (**Fig. 14, page 126**).

STRIP A (Make 5)
With Teal, ch 18 **loosely**.
Row 1 (Right side): Working in back ridge of each ch (**Fig. 2b, page 125**), tr in fifth ch from hook (**4 skipped chs count as first tr, now and throughout**), dc in next 5 chs, 5 dc in next ch, dc in next 5 chs, tr in last 2 chs: 19 sts.
Note: Mark last row as **right** side and bottom edge.
Row 2: Ch 3 (**counts as first dc, now and throughout**), turn; decrease twice, dc in next 4 dc, 5 dc in next dc, dc in next 4 dc, decrease twice, dc in last tr changing to Tan (**Fig. 16, page 127**).
Row 3: Ch 3, turn; decrease twice, dc in next 4 dc, 5 dc in next dc, dc in next 4 dc, decrease twice, dc in last dc.
Row 4: Ch 3, turn; decrease twice, dc in next 4 dc, 5 dc in next dc, dc in next 4 dc, decrease twice, dc in last dc changing to Teal.
Row 5: Ch 3, turn; decrease twice, dc in next 4 dc, 5 dc in next dc, dc in next 4 dc, decrease twice, dc in last dc.
Row 6: Ch 3, turn; decrease twice, dc in next 4 dc, 5 dc in next dc, dc in next 4 dc, decrease twice, dc in last dc changing to Tan.
Rows 7-87: Repeat Rows 3-6, 20 times; then repeat Row 3 once **more**.
Row 88: Ch 3, turn; decrease twice, dc in next 4 dc, 5 dc in next dc, dc in next 4 dc, decrease twice, dc in last dc; finish off.

STRIP B (Make 4)
With Tan, ch 18 **loosely**.
Row 1 (Right side): Working in back ridge of each ch, tr in fifth ch from hook, dc in next 5 chs, 5 dc in next ch, dc in next 5 chs, tr in last 2 chs: 19 sts.
Note: Mark last row as **right** side and bottom edge.
Row 2: Ch 3, turn; decrease twice, dc in next 4 dc, 5 dc in next dc, dc in next 4 dc, decrease twice, dc in last tr changing to Teal.
Row 3: Ch 3, turn; decrease twice, dc in next 4 dc, 5 dc in next dc, dc in next 4 dc, decrease twice, dc in last dc.
Row 4: Ch 3, turn; decrease twice, dc in next 4 dc, 5 dc in next dc, dc in next 4 dc, decrease twice, dc in last dc changing to Tan.
Row 5: Ch 3, turn; decrease twice, dc in next 4 dc, 5 dc in next dc, dc in next 4 dc, decrease twice, dc in last dc.
Row 6: Ch 3, turn; decrease twice, dc in next 4 dc, 5 dc in next dc, dc in next 4 dc, decrease twice, dc in last dc changing to Teal.
Rows 7-87: Repeat Rows 3-6, 20 times; then repeat Row 3 once **more**.
Row 88: Ch 3, turn; decrease twice, dc in next 4 dc, 5 dc in next dc, dc in next 4 dc, decrease twice, dc in last dc; finish off.

EDGING
FIRST SIDE
With **right** side facing and working in end of rows, join Teal with sc in Row 1 (**see Joining With Sc, page 126**); work 197 sc evenly spaced across; finish off: 198 sc.

SECOND SIDE
With **right** side facing and working in end of rows, join Teal with sc in Row 88; work 197 sc evenly spaced across; finish off: 198 sc.
Repeat for remaining Strips.

ASSEMBLY
Alternating Strips and beginning and ending with Strip A, lay out Strips with **right** sides facing and marked edges at bottom. To join Strips, place two Strips with **wrong** sides together and bottom edges at same end. With Teal and working through **inside** loops of each sc on **both** Strips, whipstitch Strips together (**Fig. 19a, page 127**).

Repeat to join remaining Strips.

Kingly Cover-up

*Crocheted in colors fit for a king, this regal afghan will make
Dad feel like the lord of the manor on Father's Day — or any day!
The wrap, with its contrasting stripes and lively gold fringe, is
sure to command attention wherever it's displayed.*

Finished Size: 46" x 65"

MATERIALS
Red Heart Worsted Weight Yarn
[3½ ounces (198 yards) per skein]:
Black - 6 skeins
Red - 5 skeins
Ecru - 3 skeins
Gold - 2 skeins
Crochet hook, size H (5.00 mm) **or** size needed for
gauge

GAUGE: 14 dc = 4"; 8 dc rows = 4 ½"

Note: Each row is worked across length of Afghan.

PANEL A (Make 3)
CENTER
With Red, ch 217 **loosely**.
Row 1 (Right side)**:** Dc in back ridge of fourth ch from
hook **(3 skipped chs count as first dc)** and each ch across
(Fig. 2b, page 125): 215 dc.
Note: Mark first dc on last row as **right** side and bottom
edge.
Rows 2-10: Ch 3 **(counts as first dc, now and
throughout)**, turn; dc in next dc and in each dc across.
Finish off.

BORDER
FIRST SIDE
Row 1: With **right** side facing, join Gold with sc in first
dc *(see Joining With Sc, page 126)*; sc in next dc and in
each dc across; finish off: 215 sc.
Row 2: With **wrong** side facing and working in Front
Loops Only *(Fig. 14, page 126)*, join Ecru with sc in first
sc; sc in next sc and in each sc across.
Rows 3-6: Ch 1, turn; sc in Front Loop Only of each sc
across.
Finish off.

Trim: With **right** side facing, Row 1 toward you, and
working in free loops of sc on Row 3 *(Fig. 15a,
page 127)*, join Ecru with slip st in first sc; ch 3, ★ skip
next sc, sc in next sc, ch 3; repeat from ★ across to last
2 sc, skip next sc, slip st in last sc; finish off.
Repeat Trim on Row 5.

SECOND SIDE
Row 1: With **right** side facing and working in free loops
of beginning ch *(Fig. 15b, page 127)*, join Gold with sc
in first ch; sc in next 214 chs; finish off: 215 sc.

Complete same as First Side.

PANEL B (Make 2)
With Black, ch 216 **loosely**.
Row 1: Sc in back ridge of second ch from hook and each
ch across: 215 sc.
Row 2 (Right side)**:** Ch 3, turn; dc in Front Loop Only of
next sc and each sc across.
Note: Mark first dc on last row as **right** side and bottom
edge.
Row 3: Ch 1, turn; sc in Front Loop Only of each dc
across.
Rows 4-22: Repeat Rows 2 and 3, 9 times; then repeat
Row 2 once **more**.
Finish off.

ASSEMBLY
Alternating Panels and beginning and ending with
Panel A, lay out Panels with **right** sides facing and marked
edges at bottom. To join Panels, place first two Panels
with **wrong** sides together and bottom edges to your right.
Working through **both** loops of each stitch on **both** pieces,
join Black with sc in first st; sc in next st and in each st
across; finish off.

Repeat to join remaining Panels.

EDGING
SIDE
Row 1: With **right** side of one long edge facing, join
Black with sc in first sc; sc in next sc and in each sc
across: 215 sc.
Row 2: Ch 1, do **not** turn; working from **left** to **right**,
work reverse sc in each sc across *(Figs. 11a-d, page 126)*;
finish off.

Repeat for opposite edge of Afghan.

TOP AND BOTTOM
Row 1: With **wrong** side of one short edge facing and
working in end of rows, join Black with sc in first row;
work 169 sc evenly spaced across: 170 sc.
Row 2: Ch 1, turn; sc in each sc across; finish off.

Row 3: With **wrong** side facing, join Red with sc in first sc; sc in next sc, ★ ch 1, skip next sc, sc in next 2 sc; repeat from ★ across: 56 ch-1 sps.

Row 4: Ch 1, turn; sc in first sc, ch 1, (2 sc in next ch-1 sp, ch 1) across to last 2 sc, skip next sc, sc in last sc; finish off: 57 ch-1 sps.

Row 5: With **wrong** side facing, join Black with sc in first sc; 2 sc in next ch-1 sp, 3-sc in each ch-1 sp across to last ch-1 sp, 2 sc in last ch-1 sp, sc in last sc; finish off: 171 sc.

Row 6: With **right** side facing, join Gold with sc in first sc; sc in next sc and in each sc across; finish off.

Repeat for opposite edge of Afghan.

Holding four 12" strands of Gold for each fringe, add fringe across short edges of Afghan *(Figs. 20a & b, page 127)*.

Blacklight Beauty

Distinguished by the majestic hues of midnight, this afghan is striking in any setting. Textured stitches accentuate the bold color scheme and lend a reversible quality to the unique wrap.

Finished Size: 50" x 63½"

MATERIALS
Red Heart Worsted Weight Yarn
[8 ounces (452 yards) per skein]:
Black - 5 skeins
Purple - 2 skeins
Teal - 2 skeins
Blue - 1 skein
Crochet hook, size G (4.00 mm) **or** size needed for gauge

GAUGE: 13 dc and 8 dc rows = 4"

STITCH GUIDE

FRONT POST CLUSTER *(abbreviated FP Cluster)*
YO twice, insert hook from **front** to **back** around post of dc one row **below** next dc *(Fig. 13, page 126)*, YO and pull up a loop, (YO and draw through 2 loops on hook) twice, YO twice, insert hook from **back** to **front** around post of **same** dc (**below** prior loops made), YO and pull up a loop, (YO and draw through 2 loops on hook) twice, YO and draw through all 3 loops on hook.

FRONT POPCORN
4 Dc in dc indicated, drop loop from hook, insert hook from the **front** in first dc of 4-dc group, hook dropped loop and draw through st.

BACK POPCORN
4 Dc in dc indicated, drop loop from hook, insert hook from the **back** in first dc of 4-dc group, hook dropped loop and draw through st.

CROSS ST
Skip next dc, dc in next dc, working **around** dc just made *(Fig. 18, page 127)*, dc in skipped dc.

Note: Each row is worked across length of Afghan.

FIRST SIDE
With Black, ch 205 **loosely**.
Row 1 (Right side): Dc in back ridge of fourth ch from hook (**3 skipped chs count as first dc**) and each ch across *(Fig. 2b, page 125)*: 203 dc.
Note: Mark last row as **right** side.
Row 2: Ch 3 (**counts as first dc, now and throughout**), turn; dc in next dc and in each dc across changing to Purple in last dc *(Fig. 16, page 127)*.
Row 3: Ch 3, turn; dc in next 4 dc, (work FP Cluster, dc in next 5 dc) across changing to Teal in last dc.

Row 4: Ch 3, turn; ★ dc in next 3 dc, work FP Cluster, dc in next FP Cluster, work FP Cluster; repeat from ★ across to last 4 dc, dc in last 4 dc changing to Blue in last dc.
Row 5: Ch 3, turn; dc in next 2 dc, work FP Cluster, dc in next 3 sts, work FP Cluster, ★ dc in next dc, work FP Cluster, dc in next 3 sts, work FP Cluster; repeat from ★ across to last 3 dc, dc in last 3 dc changing to Purple in last dc.
Row 6: Ch 3, turn; dc in next dc, work FP Cluster, (dc in next 5 sts, work FP Cluster) across to last 2 dc, dc in last 2 dc changing to Black in last dc.
Rows 7 and 8: Ch 3, turn; dc in next dc and in each st across.
Row 9: Ch 3, turn; work Front Popcorn in next dc, dc in next dc, ★ work Back Popcorn in next dc, dc in next dc, work Front Popcorn in next dc, dc in next dc; repeat from ★ across.
Row 10: Ch 1, turn; sc in each st across changing to Blue in last sc.
Row 11: Ch 1, turn; sc in each sc across changing to Purple in last sc.
Row 12: Ch 1, turn; sc in each sc across changing to Black in last sc.
Row 13: Ch 3, turn; dc in next sc and in each sc across changing to Teal in last dc.
Row 14: Ch 1, turn; sc in each dc across changing to Black in last sc.
Rows 15 and 16: Ch 3, turn; dc in next st and in each st across.
Row 17: Ch 3, turn; dc in next dc and in each dc across changing to Purple in last dc.
Row 18: Ch 3, turn; dc in next dc and in each dc across changing to Blue in last dc.
Row 19: Ch 1, turn; sc in each dc across.
Row 20: Ch 1, turn; sc in each sc across changing to Purple in last sc.
Row 21: Ch 3, turn; dc in next sc and in each sc across changing to Black in last dc.
Rows 22 and 23: Ch 3, turn; dc in next dc and in each dc across.
Row 24: Ch 3, turn; dc in next dc and in each dc across changing to Teal in last dc.
Row 25: Ch 1, turn; sc in each dc across changing to Black in last sc.
Row 26: Ch 3, turn; dc in next sc and in each sc across changing to Purple in last dc.
Row 27: Ch 1, turn; sc in each dc across changing to Blue in last sc.
Row 28: Ch 1, turn; sc in each sc across changing to Black in last sc.
Row 29: Ch 3, turn; dc in next sc and in each sc across.

Row 30: Ch 3, turn; work Cross Sts across to last 2 dc, dc in last 2 dc.

Row 31: Ch 3, turn; dc in next dc, work Cross Sts across to last dc, dc in last dc.

Row 32: Ch 3, turn; dc in next dc and in each dc across.

Row 33: Ch 3, turn; dc in next dc and in each dc across changing to Purple in last dc.

Rows 34-37: Repeat Rows 3-6.

Rows 38-42: Ch 3, turn; dc in next dc and in each st across.

Row 43: Ch 3, turn; work Front Popcorn in next dc, dc in next dc, ★ work Back Popcorn in next dc, dc in next dc, work Front Popcorn in next dc, dc in next dc; repeat from ★ across.

Rows 44-47: Ch 3, turn; dc in next st and in each st across.

Row 48: Ch 3, turn; dc in next dc and in each dc across changing to Purple in last dc.

Rows 49-52: Repeat Rows 3-6.

Row 53: Ch 3, turn; dc in next dc and in each st across; finish off.

SECOND SIDE

Row 1: With **right** side facing and working in free loops of beginning ch *(Fig. 15b, page 127)*, join Black with slip st in first ch; ch 3, dc in next 202 chs: 203 dc.

Rows 2-53: Work same as First Side.

EDGING

Rnd 1: With **right** side facing, join Black with sc in any st *(see Joining With Sc, page 126)*; sc evenly around entire Afghan working 3 sc in each corner; join with slip st to first sc.

Rnd 2: Ch 1, sc in same st and in each sc around working 3 sc in center sc of each corner 3-sc group; join with slip st to first sc, finish off.

29

Harvest Wrap

*This earthy afghan resembles a neatly cultivated field
ready for the harvest. Rows of popcorn and post stitches
in natural colors yield a pattern that's comforting,
whether you live on the farm or in the city.*

Finished Size: 44" x 74"

MATERIALS
Red Heart Worsted Weight Yarn
[3 ounces (170 yards) per skein]:
Yellow - 5 skeins
Brown - 2 skeins
Rose - 2 skeins
Crochet hook, size G (4.00 mm) **or** size needed for
gauge

GAUGE: In pattern, (2 dc, Popcorn) 4 times and
one repeat (9 rows) = 3$\frac{1}{2}$ "

STITCH GUIDE

FRONT POST TREBLE CROCHET
(abbreviated FPtr)
YO twice, working in **front** of last 2 dc made, insert hook
from **front** to **back** around post of dc indicated **(Fig. 13,
page 126)**, YO and pull up a loop, (YO and draw
through 2 loops on hook) 3 times.

BACK POST TREBLE CROCHET
(abbreviated BPtr)
YO twice, working **behind** last 2 dc made, insert hook
from **back** to **front** around post of FPtr indicated
(Fig. 13, page 126), YO and pull up a loop, (YO and
draw through 2 loops on hook) 3 times.

POPCORN
4 Dc in next sc changing to Brown in last dc made, drop
loop from hook, insert hook in first dc of 4-dc group,
hook dropped loop and draw through.

PICOT
Ch 4, dc in fourth ch from hook.

Note: Each row is worked across length of Wrap.

WRAP BODY
With Brown, ch 251 **loosely**.
Row 1: Sc in second ch from hook and in each ch across:
250 sc.
When changing colors, work over unused color, holding it
with normal tension and keeping yarn to **wrong** side.

Row 2 (Right side): Ch 3 **(counts as first dc)**, turn; ★ dc
in next 2 sc changing to Rose in last dc made, work
Popcorn; repeat from ★ across to last 3 sc, cut Rose, dc in
last 3 sc: 82 Popcorns.
Note: Mark last row as **right** side.
Row 3: Ch 1, turn; sc in each dc and in each Popcorn
across; finish off: 250 sc.
Row 4: With **right** side facing and working in Back Loops
Only **(Fig. 14, page 126)**, join Yellow with sc in first sc
(see Joining With Sc, page 126); sc in next sc and in
each sc across.
Row 5: Ch 2 **(counts as first hdc, now and throughout)**,
turn; working in **both** loops, dc in next sc and in each sc
across to last sc, hdc in last sc.
Row 6: Ch 3 **(counts as first hdc plus ch 1)**, turn; ★ skip
next dc, dc in next 2 dc, work FPtr around skipped dc,
ch 1; repeat from ★ across to last 3 sts, skip next dc, dc in
next dc, hdc in last hdc.
Row 7: Ch 2, turn; dc in next dc, ch 1, ★ skip next ch
and next FPtr, dc in next 2 dc, work BPtr around skipped
FPtr, ch 1; repeat from ★ across to last 2 sts, skip next ch,
hdc in last hdc.
Row 8: Ch 1, turn; sc in first hdc, (skip next ch-1 sp, sc
in next 3 sts) across to last ch-1 sp, sc in last ch-1 sp and
in last 2 sts; finish off: 250 sc.
Row 9: With **right** side facing and working in Front
Loops Only, join Brown with sc in first sc; sc in each sc
across.
Row 10: Ch 1, turn; sc in both loops of each sc across.
Rows 11-110: Repeat Rows 2-10, 11 times; then repeat
Row 2 once **more**.
Row 111: Ch 1, turn; sc in each dc and in each Popcorn
across; do **not** finish off: 250 sc.

EDGING
Ch 1, turn; sc in first sc, work Picot, (skip next 2 sc, sc in
next sc, work Picot) across; working in end of rows, skip
first row, (sc in next row, work Picot, skip next row)
across; working in free loops of beginning ch **(Fig. 15b,
page 127)**, sc in ch at base of first sc, work Picot, (skip
next 2 chs, sc in next ch, work Picot) across; working in
end of rows, skip first row, (sc in next row, work Picot,
skip next row) across; join with slip st to first sc, finish off.

Clam Shell Sensation

This Aran afghan is as unique as the textured clam shells that wash up on the beach! Rows of stitch combinations resembling seashells are flanked by cables formed using post stitches. The result is a cozy blanket that you'll love to wrap around yourself.

Finished Size: 52¹/₂ " x 72"

MATERIALS

Red Heart Worsted Weight Yarn
[8 ounces (452 yards) per skein]: 9 skeins
Crochet hook, size J (6.00 mm) **or** size needed for gauge

GAUGE: In pattern, one repeat = 6¹/₂ ";
　　　　　6 rows = 3"

STITCH GUIDE

BACK POST DOUBLE CROCHET
(abbreviated BPdc)
YO, insert hook from **back** to **front** around post of st indicated *(Fig. 13, page 126)*, YO and pull up a loop even with last st made, (YO and draw through 2 loops on hook) twice.

FRONT POST DOUBLE CROCHET
(abbreviated FPdc)
YO, insert hook from **front** to **back** around post of st indicated *(Fig. 13, page 126)*, YO and pull up a loop even with last st made, (YO and draw through 2 loops on hook) twice.

FRONT POST TREBLE CROCHET
(abbreviated FPtr)
YO twice, working front of last 2 FPdc made, insert hook from **front** to **back** around post of BPdc indicated *(Fig. 13, page 126)*, YO and pull up a loop even with last st made, (YO and draw through 2 loops on hook) 3 times.

3-DC POPCORN
3 Dc in st or sp indicated, drop loop from hook, insert hook in first dc of 3-dc group, hook dropped loop and draw through.

4-DC POPCORN
4 Dc in dc indicated, drop loop from hook, insert hook in first dc of 4-dc group, hook dropped loop and draw through.

AFGHAN BODY

Ch 139 **loosely**.
Row 1: Dc in fourth ch from hook **(3 skipped chs count as first dc)** and in each ch across: 137 dc.

Row 2 (Right side)**:** Ch 3 **(counts as first dc, now and throughout)**, turn; (work FPdc around next dc, dc in next dc) 4 times, ★ † work 4-dc Popcorn in next dc, dc in next dc, work FPdc around next dc, dc in next dc, work FPdc around each of next 3 dc, dc in next dc, work FPdc around next dc, dc in next dc, work 4-dc Popcorn in next dc, dc in next dc †, skip next 2 dc, work 3-dc Popcorn in next dc, (ch 2, work 3-dc Popcorn in same st) twice, skip next 2 dc, dc in next dc; repeat from ★ 5 times **more**, then repeat from † to † once, (work FPdc around next dc, dc in next dc) 4 times.

Row 3: Ch 3, turn; (work BPdc around next FPdc, dc in next dc) 4 times, ★ † dc in next 4-dc Popcorn and in next dc, work BPdc around next FPdc, dc in next dc, work BPdc around each of next 3 FPdc, dc in next dc, work BPdc around next FPdc, dc in next dc and in next 4-dc Popcorn, dc in next dc †, ch 2, (sc in next ch-2 sp, ch 2) twice, skip next 3-dc Popcorn, dc in next dc; repeat from ★ 5 times **more**, then repeat from † to † once, (work BPdc around next FPdc, dc in next dc) 4 times.

Row 4: Ch 3, turn; (work FPdc around next BPdc, dc in next dc) 4 times, ★ † work 4-dc Popcorn in next dc, dc in next dc, work FPdc around next BPdc, dc in next dc, skip next BPdc, work FPdc around each of next 2 BPdc, work FPtr around skipped BPdc, dc in next dc, work FPdc around next BPdc, dc in next dc, work 4-dc Popcorn in next dc, dc in next dc †, ch 2, (sc in next sc, ch 2) twice, dc in next dc; repeat from ★ 5 times **more**, then repeat from † to † once, (work FPdc around next BPdc, dc in next dc) 4 times.

Row 5: Ch 3, turn; (work BPdc around next FPdc, dc in next dc) 4 times, ★ † dc in next 4-dc Popcorn and in next dc, work BPdc around next FPdc, dc in next dc, work BPdc around each of next 3 sts, dc in next dc, work BPdc around next FPdc, dc in next dc and in next 4-dc Popcorn, dc in next dc †, ch 2, (sc in next sc, ch 2) twice, dc in next dc; repeat from ★ 5 times **more**, then repeat from † to † once, (work BPdc around next FPdc, dc in next dc) 4 times.

Row 6: Ch 3, turn; (work FPdc around next BPdc, dc in next dc) 4 times, ★ † work 4-dc Popcorn in next dc, dc in next dc, work FPdc around next BPdc, dc in next dc, work FPdc around each of next 3 BPdc, dc in next dc, work FPdc around next BPdc, dc in next dc, work 4-dc Popcorn in next dc, dc in next dc †, skip next ch-2 sp, work 3-dc Popcorn in next ch-2 sp, (ch 2, work 3-dc Popcorn in same sp) twice, dc in next dc; repeat from ★ 5 times **more**, then repeat from † to † once, (work FPdc around next BPdc, dc in next dc) 4 times.

Rows 7-138: Repeat Rows 3-6, 33 times.

Row 139: Ch 3, turn; (work BPdc around next FPdc, dc in next dc) 4 times, ★ † dc in next 4-dc Popcorn and in next dc, work BPdc around next FPdc, dc in next dc, work BPdc around each of next 3 FPdc, dc in next dc, work BPdc around next FPdc, dc in next dc and in next 4-dc Popcorn †, dc in next dc, 2 dc in next ch-2 sp, dc in next 3-dc Popcorn, 2 dc in next ch-2 sp, skip next 3-dc Popcorn, dc in next dc; repeat from ★ 5 times **more**, then repeat from † to † once, skip next dc, (work BPdc around next FPdc, dc in next dc) 4 times; do **not** finish off: 136 sts.

EDGING

Rnd 1: Ch 1, turn; (sc, ch 2) twice in first dc, (skip next 2 sts, sc in next st, ch 2) across to last 3 sts, skip next 2 sts, (sc, ch 2) twice in last dc; working in end of rows, skip first row, sc in next row, ch 2, (skip next row, sc in next row, ch 2) across to last row, sc in last row, ch 2; working in free loops of beginning ch *(Fig. 15b, page 127)*, (sc, ch 2) twice in ch at base of first dc, skip next 3 chs, sc in next ch, ch 2, (skip next 2 chs, sc in next ch, ch 2) across to last 3 chs, skip next 2 chs, (sc, ch 2) twice in last ch; working in end of rows, sc in first row, ch 2, (sc in next row, ch 2, skip next row) across; join with slip st to first sc: 236 ch-2 sps.

Rnd 2: Slip st in first ch-2 sp, ch 3, 2 dc in same sp, drop loop from hook, insert hook in first dc of 3-dc group, hook dropped loop and draw through **(beginning 3-dc Popcorn made)**, (ch 2, work 3-dc Popcorn in same sp) twice, skip next ch-2 sp, ★ work 3-dc Popcorn in next ch-2 sp, (ch 2, work 3-dc Popcorn in same sp) twice, skip next ch-2 sp; repeat from ★ around; join with slip st to top of beginning 3-dc Popcorn.

Rnd 3: Slip st in first ch-2 sp, ch 1, sc in same sp, ch 3, sc in third ch from hook, ch 1, ★ sc in next ch-2 sp, ch 3, sc in third ch from hook, ch 1; repeat from ★ around; join with slip st to first sc, finish off.

Terrific Texture

Wrap yourself in waves of textured comfort with this terrific throw! The cover-up's vivid color blend enhances its pattern and attracts the eye. What an irresistible invitation to relax!

Finished Size: 46" x 61"

MATERIALS
Red Heart Worsted Weight Yarn
[3½ ounces (198 yards) per skein]:
Grey - 6 skeins
Dark Rose - 6 skeins
Crochet hook, size H (5.00 mm) **or** size needed for gauge

GAUGE: In pattern, (2 dc, ch 1) 4 times = 3½ ";
8 rows = 3¼ "

STITCH GUIDE

> **LONG DOUBLE CROCHET** (*abbreviated LDC*)
> YO, working **around** previous row (*Fig. 18, page 127*), insert hook in st indicated, YO and pull up a loop even with last st made, (YO and draw through 2 loops on hook) twice (*Fig. 10, page 126*).
> **PICOT**
> Ch 6, slip st in sixth ch from hook.

Note: Each row is worked across length of Afghan.

AFGHAN BODY
With Grey, ch 200 **loosely**.
Row 1 (Wrong side): Sc in back ridge of second ch from hook (*Fig. 2b, page 125*) and each ch across; finish off: 199 sc.
Note: Mark **back** of any sc on last row as **right** side.
Row 2: With **right** side facing, join Dark Rose with slip st in first sc; ch 3 (**counts as first dc, now and throughout**), 2 dc in same st, ★ ch 1, skip next 2 sc, 2 dc in next sc; repeat from ★ across; finish off: 135 dc and 66 ch-1 sps.
Row 3: With **wrong** side facing, join Grey with sc in first dc (*see Joining With Sc, page 126*); ch 1, skip next dc, work LDC in second sc of skipped 2-sc group one row **below** next ch-1, ★ sc in next dc, ch 1, skip next dc, work LDC in second sc of skipped 2-sc group one row **below** next ch-1; repeat from ★ across to last 3 dc, skip next 2 dc, sc in last dc; finish off: 133 sts and 66 ch-1 sps.

Row 4: With **right** side facing, join Dark Rose with slip st in first sc; ch 3, 2 dc in same st, (ch 1, 2 dc in next sc) across; finish off: 135 dc and 66 ch-1 sps.
Row 5: With **wrong** side facing, join Grey with sc in first dc; ch 1, skip next dc, work LDC in LDC one row **below** next ch-1, ★ skip next dc, sc in next dc, ch 1, work LDC in LDC one row **below** next ch-1; repeat from ★ across to last 3 dc, skip next 2 dc, sc in last dc; finish off: 133 sts and 66 ch-1 sps.
Row 6: With **right** side facing, join Dark Rose with slip st in first sc; ch 3, 2 dc in same st, (ch 1, 2 dc in next sc) across; finish off: 135 dc and 66 ch-1 sps.
Row 7: With **wrong** side facing, join Grey with sc in first dc; ch 1, skip next dc, work LDC in LDC one row **below** next ch-1, ★ sc in next dc, ch 1, skip next dc, work LDC in LDC one row **below** next ch-1; repeat from ★ across to last 3 dc, skip next 2 dc, sc in last dc; finish off: 133 sts and 66 ch-1 sps.
Rows 8-108: Repeat Rows 4-7, 25 times; then repeat Row 4 once **more**.
Row 109: With **wrong** side facing, join Grey with sc in first dc; ch 1, skip next dc, work LDC in LDC one row **below** next ch-1, ★ skip next dc, sc in next dc, ch 1, work LDC in LDC one row **below** next ch-1; repeat from ★ across to last 3 dc, skip next 2 dc, sc in last dc; do **not** finish off: 133 sts and 66 ch-1 sps.

EDGING
Rnd 1: Ch 1, turn; 3 sc in first sc, sc in each st and in each ch-1 sp across to last sc, 3 sc in last sc; working in end of rows, sc in first row, (2 sc in next row, sc in next row) across; working in free loops of beginning ch (*Fig. 15b, page 127*), 3 sc in ch at base of first sc, sc in each ch across to last ch, 3 sc in last ch; working in end of rows, sc in first row, (2 sc in next row, sc in next row) across; join with slip st to first sc: 732 sc.
Rnd 2: Do **not** turn; work Picot, (slip st in next sc, work Picot) twice, ★ (skip next sc, slip st in next sc, work Picot) across to center sc of next corner 3-sc group, (slip st in next sc, work Picot) twice; repeat from ★ 2 times **more**, skip next sc, (slip st in next sc, work Picot, skip next sc) across; join with slip st to joining slip st, finish off.

Rich Reflection

The rich hues of autumn are reflected in this warm, wonderful afghan. Featuring an interwoven pattern of diamond-shaped stripes, the cover-up will be a treasure in any season.

Finished Size: 50" x 68"

MATERIALS

Red Heart Worsted Weight Yarn
[8 ounces (452 yards) per skein]:
Brown - 4 skeins
Ecru - 3 skeins
Yellow - 3 skeins
Black - 2 skeins
Crochet hook, size H (5.00 mm) **or** size needed for gauge

GAUGE: In pattern, 14 sts = 4"; 8 rows = 2¼"

Note: Each row is worked across length of Afghan. When joining yarn and finishing off, leave a 9" end to be worked into fringe.

AFGHAN BODY

With Brown, ch 240 **loosely**.

Row 1: Sc in second ch from hook and in each ch across: 239 sc.

Row 2 (Right side): Ch 1, turn; sc in first sc, ★ ch 1, skip next sc, sc in next sc; repeat from ★ across: 120 sc and 119 ch-1 sps.

Note: Mark last row as **right** side.

Row 3: Ch 1, turn; sc in first sc, working **behind** next ch-1 (*Fig. 18, page 127*), dc in skipped sc one row **below** ch-1, sc in next sc, ch 1, skip next ch-1 sp, sc in next sc, ★ (working **behind** next ch-1, dc in skipped sc one row **below** ch-1, sc in next sc) 3 times, ch 1, skip next ch-1 sp, sc in next sc; repeat from ★ across to last 2 sts, working **behind** next ch-1, dc in skipped sc one row **below** ch-1, sc in last sc; finish off: 239 sts.

Row 4: With **right** side facing, join Ecru with sc in first sc (*see Joining With Sc, page 126*); ch 2, skip next 2 sts, working in **front** of next ch-1, tr in skipped sc 2 rows **below** ch-1, ch 2, skip next 2 sts, sc in next sc, ★ ch 1, skip next dc, sc in next sc, ch 2, skip next 2 sts, working in **front** of next ch-1, tr in skipped sc 2 rows **below** ch-1, ch 2, skip next 2 sts, sc in next sc; repeat from ★ across; finish off.

Row 5: With **wrong** side facing, join Brown with sc in first sc; working **behind** next ch-2, dc in first skipped st one row **below** ch-2, ch 1, sc in next tr, ch 1, working **behind** next ch-2, dc in second skipped st one row **below** ch-2, sc in next sc, ★ working **behind** next ch-1, dc in skipped dc one row **below** ch-1, sc in next sc, working **behind** next ch-2, dc in first skipped st one row **below** ch-2, ch 1, sc in next tr, ch 1, working **behind** next ch-2, dc in second skipped st one row **below** ch-2, sc in next sc; repeat from ★ across; finish off.

Row 6: With **right** side facing, join Yellow with sc in first sc; ch 1, skip next dc, working in **front** of next ch-1, tr in skipped sc 2 rows **below** ch-1, ch 1, skip next sc, working in **front** of next ch-1, tr in skipped sc 2 rows **below** ch-1, ★ ch 2, skip next 2 sts, sc in next dc, ch 2, skip next 2 sts, working in **front** of next ch-1, tr in skipped sc 2 rows **below** ch-1, ch 1, skip next sc, working in **front** of next ch-1, tr in skipped sc 2 rows **below** ch-1; repeat from ★ across to last 2 sts, ch 1, skip next dc, sc in last sc; finish off.

Row 7: With **wrong** side facing, join Black with sc in first sc; (ch 1, skip next ch-1 sp, sc in next tr) twice, ch 1, ★ working **behind** next ch-2, dc in second skipped st one row **below** ch-2, sc in next sc, working **behind** next ch-2, dc in first skipped st one row **below** ch-2, ch 1, sc in next tr, ch 1, skip next ch-1 sp, sc in next tr, ch 1; repeat from ★ across to last 2 sts, skip next ch-1 sp, sc in last sc; finish off.

Row 8: With **right** side facing, join Ecru with sc in first sc; working in **front** of next ch-1, tr in skipped dc 2 rows **below** ch-1, (ch 1, skip next sc, working in **front** of next ch-1, tr in skipped st 2 rows **below** ch-1) twice, ★ ch 1, skip next dc, sc in next sc, ch 1, skip next dc, working in **front** of next ch-1, tr in skipped dc 2 rows **below** ch-1, (ch 1, skip next sc, working in **front** of next ch-1, tr in skipped st 2 rows **below** ch-1) twice; repeat from ★ across to last sc, sc in last sc; finish off.

Row 9: With **wrong** side facing, join Black with sc in first sc; sc in next tr, (ch 1, skip next ch-1 sp, sc in next tr) twice, ★ (working **behind** next ch-1, dc in skipped dc one row **below** ch-1, sc in next st) twice, (ch 1, skip next ch-1 sp, sc in next tr) twice; repeat from ★ across to last sc, sc in last sc; finish off.

Row 10: With **right** side facing, join Yellow with sc in first sc; ch 1, (skip next sc, working in **front** of next ch-1, tr in skipped sc 2 rows **below** ch-1, ch 1) twice, ★ (skip next sc, sc in next dc, ch 1) twice, (skip next sc, working in **front** of next ch-1, tr in skipped sc 2 rows **below** ch-1, ch 1) twice; repeat from ★ across to last 2 sc, skip next sc, sc in last sc; finish off.

Row 11: With **wrong** side facing, join Brown with sc in first sc; working **behind** next ch-1, dc in skipped sc one row **below** ch-1, sc in next tr, ch 1, skip next ch-1 sp, sc in next tr, ★ (working **behind** next ch-1, dc in skipped sc one row **below** ch-1, sc in next st) 3 times, ch 1, skip next ch-1 sp, sc in next tr; repeat from ★ across to last 2 sts, working **behind** next ch-1, dc in skipped sc one row **below** ch-1, sc in last sc; finish off.

Continued on page 38.

Rows 12-172: Repeat Rows 4-11, 20 times; then repeat Row 4 once **more**.

Row 173: With **wrong** side facing, join Brown with sc in first sc; (working **behind** next ch-2, dc in each of 2 skipped sts one row **below** ch-2, sc in next st) twice, ★ working **behind** next ch-1, dc in skipped dc one row **below** ch-1, sc in next sc, (working **behind** next ch-2, dc in each of 2 skipped sts one row **below** ch-2, sc in next st) twice; repeat from ★ across; do **not** finish off.

Row 174: Ch 1, turn; sc in each st across; do **not** finish off.

EDGING
FIRST SIDE

Row 1: Ch 1, turn; sc in first 2 sc, ch 1, ★ skip next sc, sc in next sc, ch 1; repeat from ★ across to last 3 sc, skip next sc, sc in last 2 sc.

Row 2: Ch 1, turn; slip st in first sc, ch 1, ★ skip next sc, slip st in next ch-1 sp, ch 1; repeat from ★ across to last 2 sc, skip next sc, slip st in last sc; finish off.

SECOND SIDE

Row 1: With **wrong** side facing and working in free loops of beginning ch (*Fig. 15b, page 127*), join Brown with sc in first ch; sc in next ch, ch 1, ★ skip next ch, sc in next ch, ch 1; repeat from ★ 116 times **more**, skip next ch, sc in next 2 chs.

Row 2: Ch 1, turn; slip st in first sc, ch 1, ★ skip next sc, slip st in next ch-1 sp, ch 1; repeat from ★ across to last 2 sc, skip next sc, slip st in last sc; finish off.

Holding three 16" strands of corresponding color yarn together for each fringe, add additional fringe across short edges of Afghan (*Figs. 20a & b, page 127*).

Big on Ripples

This thick and cozy wrap is big on ripples! Made with variegated yarn, the afghan works up quickly because you hold four strands of yarn together as you crochet with a size Q hook.

Finished Size: 54" x 68"

MATERIALS
Red Heart Worsted Weight Yarn
[6 ounces (348 yards) per skein]: 20 skeins
Crochet hook, size Q (15.00 mm) **or** size needed for gauge

GAUGE: One repeat (from point to point) = 9";
Rows 1-4 = 4"

STITCH GUIDE

DECREASE (uses next 4 sc)
YO, insert hook in next sc, YO and pull up a loop, YO and draw through 2 loops on hook, YO, skip next 2 sc, insert hook in next sc, YO and pull up a loop, YO and draw through 2 loops on hook, YO and draw through all 3 loops on hook (**counts as one dc**).

ENDING DECREASE (uses last 2 sc)
★ YO, insert hook in next sc, YO and pull up a loop, YO and draw through 2 loops on hook; repeat from ★ once **more**, YO and draw through all 3 loops on hook (**counts as one dc**).

Note: Entire Afghan is worked holding four strands of yarn together.

AFGHAN
Ch 113 **loosely**.

Row 1 (Right side): Working in back ridge of each ch (*Fig. 2b, page 125*), sc in second ch from hook and in next 7 chs, 3 sc in next ch, sc in next 8 chs, ★ skip next 2 chs, sc in next 8 chs, 3 sc in next ch, sc in next 8 chs; repeat from ★ across: 114 sc.

Row 2: Ch 1, turn; sc in first sc, skip next sc, sc in next 7 sc, 3 sc in next sc, ★ sc in next 8 sc, skip next 2 sc, sc in next 8 sc, 3 sc in next sc; repeat from ★ 4 times **more**, sc in next 7 sc, skip next sc, sc in last sc.

Row 3: Ch 2, turn; dc in next sc, ★ † skip next sc, (dc, ch 1, dc) in next sc, skip next 2 sc, (dc, ch 1, dc) in next sc, skip next sc, dc in next sc, ch 1, (dc, ch 1) twice in next sc, dc in next sc, skip next sc, (dc, ch 1, dc) in next sc, skip next 2 sc, (dc, ch 1, dc) in next sc, skip next sc †, decrease; repeat from ★ 4 times **more**, then repeat from † to † once, work ending decrease: 79 dc and 42 ch-1 sps.

Row 4: Ch 1, turn; sc in first dc, skip next dc, ★ † (sc in next ch-1 sp and in next 2 dc) twice, skip next ch-1 sp, sc in next dc, 3 sc in next ch-1 sp, sc in next dc, skip next ch-1 sp, (sc in next 2 dc and in next ch-1 sp) twice †, sc in next dc, skip next dc, sc in next dc; repeat from ★ 4 times **more**, then repeat from † to † once, skip next dc, sc in last dc, leave remaining ch-2 unworked: 114 sc.

Repeat Rows 2-4 until Afghan measures approximately 68" from beginning ch, ending by working Row 2; finish off.

Reindeer Forest

*Playful reindeer frolic through an evergreen forest on
this merry afghan! Front post and long double crochets form
the wintry motifs as well as the crisscross pattern above them.*

Finished Size: 43" x 64"

MATERIALS

Red Heart Worsted Weight Yarn
[8 ounces (452 yards) per skein]: 7 skeins
Crochet hook, size I (5.50 mm) **or** size needed for gauge

GAUGE: 14 sts and 13 rows = 4"

STITCH GUIDE

LONG DOUBLE CROCHET (abbreviated LDC)
YO, insert hook from **bottom** to **top** in free loop of st
indicated (*Fig. 15a, page 127*), YO and pull up a loop
even with last st made, (YO and draw through 2 loops on
hook) twice (*Fig. 10, page 126*). Skip sc behind LDC.

FRONT POST DOUBLE CROCHET
(*abbreviated FPdc*)
YO, insert hook from **front** to **back** around post of st
indicated (*Fig. 13, page 126*), YO and pull up a loop
even with last st made, (YO and draw through 2 loops on
hook) twice. Skip st behind FPdc.

Note: Each row is worked across the length of Afghan.
When joining yarn and finishing off, always leave a 7"
end to be worked into fringe.

AFGHAN

Ch 226 **loosely**.
Row 1 (Right side)**:** Sc in back ridge of second ch from
hook and each ch across (*Fig. 2b, page 125*); finish off:
225 sc.
Note: Mark last row as **right** side.
Work in Back Loops Only unless otherwise specified
(*Fig. 14, page 126*).
Rows 2-5: With **right** side facing, join yarn with sc in
first sc; sc in each sc across; finish off.
Row 6: With **right** side facing, join yarn with sc in first sc;
sc in next 19 sc, † work LDC in sc one row **below** next sc,
sc in next 4 sc, work LDC in sc one row **below** each of
next 7 sc, sc in next 19 sc, work LDC in sc one row **below**
next sc †, sc in next 22 sc, repeat from † to † once, sc in
next 4 sc, work LDC in sc one row **below** each of next
7 sc, sc in next 4 sc, ♥ work LDC in sc one row **below**
next sc, sc in next 19 sc, work LDC in sc one row **below**
each of next 7 sc, sc in next 4 sc, work LDC in sc one row
below next sc ♥, sc in next 22 sc, repeat from ♥ to ♥ once,
sc in last 18 sc; finish off: 43 LDC and 182 sc.

Row 7: With **right** side facing, join yarn with sc in first sc;
sc in next st and in each st across; finish off: 225 sc.
Row 8: With **right** side facing, join yarn with sc in first sc;
sc in next 8 sc, work LDC in sc one row **below** next sc, sc
in next 9 sc, work LDC in sc one row **below** next sc, † sc
in next 8 sc, work FPdc around LDC one row **below** next
sc, sc in next 11 sc, work LDC in sc one row **below** next
sc, sc in next 9 sc, work LDC in sc one row **below** next
sc †, sc in next 12 sc, work LDC in sc one row **below** next
sc, sc in next 9 sc, work LDC in sc one row **below** next sc,
repeat from † to † once, sc in next 8 sc, work FPdc around
LDC one row **below** next sc, sc in next 8 sc, ♥ work LDC
in sc one row **below** next sc, sc in next 9 sc, work LDC in
sc one row **below** next sc, sc in next 11 sc, work FPdc
around LDC one row **below** next sc, sc in next 8 sc, work
LDC in sc one row **below** next sc, sc in next 9 sc, work
LDC in sc one row **below** next sc ♥, sc in next 12 sc,
repeat from ♥ to ♥ once, sc in last 7 sc; finish off: 16 LDC,
5 FPdc, and 204 sc.
Row 9: With **right** side facing, join yarn with sc in first sc;
sc in next st and in each st across; finish off: 225 sc.
Row 10: With **right** side facing, join yarn with sc in first
sc; sc in next 7 sc, † work LDC in sc one row **below** next
sc, sc in next 10 sc, work FPdc around LDC one row
below next sc, sc in next 8 sc, work FPdc around FPdc one
row **below** next sc, sc in next 10 sc, work LDC in sc one
row **below** next sc, sc in next 10 sc, work FPdc around
LDC one row **below** next sc †, sc in next 11 sc, repeat
from † to † once, sc in next 8 sc, work FPdc around FPdc
one row **below** next sc, sc in next 8 sc, ♥ work FPdc
around LDC one row **below** next sc, sc in next 10 sc, work
LDC in sc one row **below** next sc, sc in next 10 sc, work
FPdc around FPdc one row **below** next sc, sc in next 8 sc,
work FPdc around LDC one row **below** next sc, sc in next
10 sc, work LDC in sc one row **below** next sc ♥, sc in next
11 sc, repeat from ♥ to ♥ once, sc in last 6 sc; finish off:
8 LDC, 13 FPdc, and 204 sc.
Row 11: With **right** side facing, join yarn with sc in first
sc; sc in next st and in each st across; finish off: 225 sc.
Row 12: With **right** side facing, join yarn with sc in first
sc; sc in next 7 sc, † work FPdc around LDC one row
below next sc, sc in next 8 sc, work LDC in sc one row
below each of next 2 sc, work FPdc around FPdc one row
below next sc, sc in next 8 sc, work FPdc around FPdc one
row **below** next sc, sc in next 10 sc, work FPdc around
LDC one row **below** next sc, sc in next 8 sc, work LDC in
sc one row **below** each of next 2 sc, work FPdc around
FPdc one row **below** next sc †, sc in next 11 sc, repeat
from † to † once, (sc in next 8 sc, work FPdc around FPdc

Continued on page 42.

one row **below** next sc) twice, ♥ work LDC in sc one row **below** each of next 2 sc, sc in next 8 sc, work FPdc around LDC one row **below** next sc, sc in next 10 sc, work FPdc around FPdc one row **below** next sc, sc in next 8 sc, work FPdc around FPdc one row **below** next sc, work LDC in sc one row **below** each of next 2 sc, sc in next 8 sc, work FPdc around LDC one row **below** next sc ♥, sc in next 11 sc, work FPdc around FPdc one row **below** next sc, repeat from ♥ to ♥ once, sc in last 6 sc; finish off: 16 LDC, 21 FPdc, and 188 sc.

Row 13: With **right** side facing, join yarn with sc in first sc; sc in next st and in each st across; finish off: 225 sc.

Row 14: With **right** side facing, join yarn with sc in first sc; sc in next 7 sc, work FPdc around FPdc one row **below** next sc, sc in next 8 sc, work FPdc around LDC one row **below** next sc, † sc in next 5 sc, work LDC in sc one row **below** each of next 5 sc, work FPdc around FPdc one row **below** next sc, work LDC in sc one row **below** each of next 5 sc, sc in next 5 sc, work FPdc around st one row **below** next sc, sc in next 8 sc, work FPdc around st one row **below** next sc †, sc in next 13 sc, work FPdc around FPdc one row **below** next sc, sc in next 8 sc, work FPdc around LDC one row **below** next sc, repeat from † to † 3 times, sc in next 13 sc, work FPdc around LDC one row **below** next sc, sc in next 8 sc, work FPdc around FPdc one row **below** next sc, repeat from † to † once, sc in last 6 sc; finish off: 50 LDC, 21 FPdc, and 154 sc.

Row 15: With **right** side facing, join yarn with sc in first sc; sc in next st and in each st across; finish off: 225 sc.

Row 16: With **right** side facing, join yarn with sc in first sc; sc in next 7 sc, ♥ † work FPdc around FPdc one row **below** next sc, work LDC in sc one row **below** each of next 8 sc, work FPdc around FPdc one row **below** next sc, sc in next 6 sc, work FPdc around st one row **below** each of next 9 sc, sc in next 6 sc, work FPdc around FPdc one row **below** next sc, work LDC in sc one row **below** each of next 8 sc, work FPdc around FPdc one row **below** next sc †, sc in next 13 sc, repeat from † to † once, sc in next 6 sc ♥, work FPdc around st one row **below** each of next 9 sc, sc in next 6 sc, repeat from ♥ to ♥ once; finish off: 64 LDC, 61 FPdc, and 100 sc.

Row 17: With **right** side facing, join yarn with sc in first sc; sc in next st and in each st across; finish off: 225 sc.

Row 18: With **right** side facing, join yarn with sc in first sc; sc in next 9 sc, † work FPdc around st one row **below** each of next 8 sc, sc in next 7 sc, work FPdc around FPdc one row **below** each of next 7 sc, sc in next 9 sc, work FPdc around st one row **below** each of next 8 sc †, sc in next 15 sc, repeat from † to † once, sc in next 7 sc, work FPdc around FPdc one row **below** each of next 7 sc, sc in next 7 sc, ♥ work FPdc around st one row **below** each of next 8 sc, sc in next 9 sc, work FPdc around FPdc one row **below** each of next 7 sc, sc in next 7 sc, work FPdc around st one row **below** each of next 8 sc ♥, sc in next 15 sc, repeat from ♥ to ♥ once, sc in last 8 sc; finish off: 99 FPdc and 126 sc.

Row 19: With **right** side facing, join yarn with sc in first sc; sc in next st and in each st across; finish off: 225 sc.

Row 20: With **right** side facing, join yarn with sc in first sc; sc in next 9 sc, † work FPdc around FPdc one row **below** each of next 8 sc, work LDC in sc one row **below** next sc, sc in next 7 sc, work FPdc around FPdc one row **below** each of next 5 sc, sc in next 10 sc, work FPdc around FPdc one row **below** each of next 8 sc, work LDC in sc one row **below** next sc †, sc in next 14 sc, repeat from † to † once, sc in next 7 sc, work FPdc around FPdc one row **below** each of next 5 sc, sc in next 7 sc, ♥ work LDC in sc one row **below** next sc, work FPdc around FPdc one row **below** each of next 8 sc, sc in next 10 sc, work FPdc around FPdc one row **below** each of next 5 sc, sc in next 7 sc, work LDC in sc one row **below** next sc, work FPdc around FPdc one row **below** each of next 8 sc ♥, in next 14 sc, repeat from ♥ to ♥ once, sc in last 8 sc; finish off: 8 LDC, 89 FPdc, and 128 sc.

Row 21: With **right** side facing, join yarn with sc in first sc; sc in next st and in each st across; finish off: 225 sc.

Row 22: With **right** side facing, join yarn with sc in first sc; sc in next 8 sc, † work LDC in sc one row **below** next sc, work FPdc around FPdc one row **below** each of next 2 sc, sc in next 6 sc, work FPdc around LDC one row **below** next sc, sc in next 8 sc, work FPdc around FPdc one row **below** each of next 3 sc, sc in next 10 sc, work LDC in sc one row **below** next sc, work FPdc around FPdc one row **below** each of next 2 sc, sc in next 6 sc, work FPdc around LDC one row **below** next sc †, sc in next 13 sc, repeat from † to † once, sc in next 8 sc, work FPdc around FPdc one row **below** each of next 3 sc, sc in next 8 sc, ♥ work FPdc around LDC one row **below** next sc, sc in next 6 sc, work FPdc around FPdc one row **below** each of next 2 sc, work LDC in sc one row **below** next sc, sc in next 10 sc, work FPdc around FPdc one row **below** each of next 3 sc, sc in next 8 sc, work FPdc around LDC one row **below** next sc, sc in next 6 sc, work FPdc around FPdc one row **below** each of next 2 sc, work LDC in sc one row **below** next sc ♥, sc in next 13 sc, repeat from ♥ to ♥ once, sc in last 7 sc; finish off: 8 LDC, 39 FPdc, and 178 sc.

Row 23: With **right** side facing, join yarn with sc in first sc; sc in next st and in each st across; finish off: 225 sc.

Row 24: With **right** side facing, join yarn with sc in first sc; sc in next 8 sc, † work FPdc around st one row **below** each of next 2 sc, sc in next 17 sc, work FPdc around FPdc one row **below** next sc, sc in next 11 sc, work FPdc around st one row **below** each of next 2 sc †, sc in next 21 sc, repeat from † to † once, sc in next 17 sc, work FPdc around FPdc one row **below** next sc, sc in next 17 sc, ♥ work FPdc around st one row **below** each of next 2 sc, sc in next 11 sc, work FPdc around FPdc one row **below** next sc, sc in next 17 sc, work FPdc around st one row **below** each of next 2 sc ♥, sc in next 21 sc, repeat from ♥ to ♥ once, sc in last 7 sc; finish off: 21 FPdc and 204 sc.

Row 25: With **right** side facing, join yarn with sc in first sc; sc in next st and in each st across; finish off: 225 sc.

Row 26: With **right** side facing, join yarn with sc in first sc; sc in next 7 sc, † work LDC in sc one row **below** next sc, work FPdc around FPdc one row **below** each of next 2 sc, sc in next 13 sc, work LDC in sc one row **below** each of next 4 sc, work FPdc around FPdc one row **below** next sc, work LDC in sc one row **below** each of next 4 sc, sc in next 6 sc, work LDC in sc one row **below** next sc, work FPdc around FPdc one row **below** each of next 2 sc †, sc in next 20 sc, repeat from † to † once, sc in next 13 sc, work LDC in sc one row **below** each of next 4 sc, work FPdc around FPdc one row **below** next sc, work LDC in sc one row **below** each of next 4 sc, sc in next 13 sc, ♥ work FPdc around FPdc one row **below** each of next 2 sc, work LDC in sc one row **below** next sc, sc in next 6 sc, work LDC in sc one row **below** each of next 4 sc, work FPdc around FPdc one row **below** next sc, work LDC in sc one row **below** each of next 4 sc, sc in next 13 sc, work FPdc around FPdc one row **below** each of next 2 sc, work LDC in sc one row **below** next sc ♥, sc in next 20 sc, repeat from ♥ to ♥ once, sc in last 6 sc; finish off: 48 LDC, 21 FPdc, and 156 sc.

Row 27: With **right** side facing, join yarn with sc in first sc; sc in next st and in each st across; finish off: 225 sc.

Row 28: With **right** side facing, join yarn with sc in first sc; sc in next 6 sc, † work LDC in sc one row **below** next sc, work FPdc around st one row **below** each of next 3 sc, work LDC in sc one row **below** each of next 3 sc, sc in next 11 sc, work FPdc around st one row **below** each of next 7 sc, sc in next 6 sc, work LDC in sc one row **below** next sc, work FPdc around st one row **below** each of next 3 sc, work LDC in sc one row **below** each of next 3 sc †, sc in next 16 sc, repeat from † to † once, sc in next 11 sc, work FPdc around st one row **below** each of next 7 sc, sc in next 11 sc, ♥ work LDC in sc one row **below** each of next 3 sc, work FPdc around st one row **below** each of next 3 sc, work LDC in sc one row **below** next sc, sc in next 6 sc, work FPdc around st one row **below** each of next 7 sc, sc in next 11 sc, work LDC in sc one row **below** each of next 3 sc, work FPdc around st one row **below** each of next 3 sc, work LDC in sc one row **below** next sc ♥, sc in next 16 sc, repeat from ♥ to ♥ once, sc in last 5 sc; finish off: 32 LDC, 59 FPdc, and 134 sc.

Row 29: With **right** side facing, join yarn with sc in first sc; sc in next st and in each st across; finish off: 225 sc.

Row 30: With **right** side facing, join yarn with sc in first sc; sc in next 9 sc, † work FPdc around FPdc one row **below** next sc, sc in next 3 sc, work LDC in sc one row **below** next sc, sc in next 11 sc, work FPdc around FPdc one row **below** each of next 5 sc, sc in next 10 sc, work FPdc around FPdc one row **below** next sc, sc in next 3 sc, work LDC in sc one row **below** next sc †, sc in next 18 sc, repeat from † to † once, sc in next 11 sc, work FPdc around FPdc one row **below** each of next 5 sc, sc in next 11 sc, ♥ work LDC in sc one row **below** next sc, sc in next 3 sc, work FPdc around FPdc one row **below** next sc, sc in next 10 sc, work FPdc around FPdc one row **below** each of next 5 sc, sc in next 11 sc, work LDC in sc one row **below** next sc, sc in next 3 sc, work FPdc around FPdc one row **below** next sc ♥, sc in next 18 sc, repeat from ♥ to ♥ once, sc in last 8 sc; finish off: 8 LDC, 33 FPdc, and 184 sc.

Row 31: With **right** side facing, join yarn with sc in first sc; sc in next st and in each st across; finish off: 225 sc.

Row 32: With **right** side facing, join yarn with sc in first sc; sc in next 9 sc, † work FPdc around FPdc one row

below next sc, sc in next 3 sc, work FPdc around LDC one row **below** next sc, sc in next 12 sc, work FPdc around FPdc one row **below** each of next 3 sc, sc in next 11 sc, work FPdc around FPdc one row **below** next sc, sc in next 3 sc, work FPdc around LDC one row **below** next sc †, sc in next 18 sc, repeat from † to † once, sc in next 12 sc, work FPdc around FPdc one row **below** each of next 3 sc, sc in next 12 sc, ♥ work FPdc around LDC one row **below** next sc, sc in next 3 sc, work FPdc around FPdc one row **below** next sc, sc in next 11 sc, work FPdc around FPdc one row **below** each of next 3 sc, sc in next 12 sc, work FPdc around LDC one row **below** next sc, sc in next 3 sc, work FPdc around FPdc one row **below** next sc ♥, sc in next 18 sc, repeat from ♥ to ♥ once, sc in last 8 sc; finish off: 31 FPdc and 194 sc.

Row 33: With **right** side facing, join yarn with sc in first sc; sc in next st and in each st across; finish off: 225 sc.

Row 34: With **right** side facing, join yarn with sc in first sc; sc in next 10 sc, † work LDC in sc one row **below** next sc, sc in next 16 sc, work FPdc around FPdc one row **below** next sc, sc in next 13 sc, work LDC in sc one row **below** next sc †, sc in next 22 sc, repeat from † to † once, sc in next 16 sc, work FPdc around FPdc one row **below** next sc, sc in next 14 sc, ♥ work LDC in sc one row **below** next sc, sc in next 15 sc, work FPdc around FPdc one row **below** next sc, sc in next 14 sc, work LDC in sc one row **below** next sc ♥, sc in next 22 sc, repeat from ♥ to ♥ once, sc in last 11 sc; finish off: 8 LDC, 5 FPdc, and 212 sc.

Row 35: With **right** side facing, join yarn with sc in first sc; sc in next st and in each st across; finish off: 225 sc.

Row 36: With **right** side facing, join yarn with sc in first sc; ♥ sc in next 24 sc, † work LDC in sc one row **below** each of next 3 sc, work FPdc around FPdc one row **below** next sc, work LDC in sc one row **below** each of next 3 sc † ♥, sc in next 47 sc, repeat from † to † once, then repeat from ♥ to ♥ twice, sc in next 47 sc, repeat from † to † once, sc in last 23 sc; finish off: 30 LDC, 5 FPdc, and 190 sc.

Row 37: With **right** side facing, join yarn with sc in first sc; sc in next st and in each st across; finish off: 225 sc.

Row 38: With **right** side facing, join yarn with sc in first sc; sc in next 25 sc, work FPdc around st one row **below** each of next 5 sc, sc in next 49 sc, work FPdc around st one row **below** each of next 5 sc, ★ sc in next 26 sc, work FPdc around st one row **below** each of next 5 sc; repeat from ★ once **more**, sc in next 49 sc, work FPdc around st one row **below** each of next 5 sc, sc in last 24 sc; finish off: 25 FPdc and 200 sc.

Row 39: With **right** side facing, join yarn with sc in first sc; sc in next st and in each st across; finish off: 225 sc.

Row 40: With **right** side facing, join yarn with sc in first sc; sc in next 26 sc, work FPdc around FPdc one row **below** each of next 3 sc, sc in next 51 sc, work FPdc around FPdc one row **below** each of next 3 sc, ★ sc in next 28 sc, work FPdc around FPdc one row **below** each of next 3 sc; repeat from ★ once **more**, sc in next 51 sc, work FPdc around FPdc one row **below** each of next 3 sc, sc in last 25 sc; finish off: 15 FPdc and 210 sc.

Continued on page 44.

Row 41: With **right** side facing, join yarn with sc in first sc; sc in next st and in each st across; finish off: 225 sc.

Row 42: With **right** side facing, join yarn with sc in first sc; sc in next 27 sc, work FPdc around FPdc one row **below** next sc, sc in next 53 sc, work FPdc around FPdc one row **below** next sc, ★ sc in next 30 sc, work FPdc around FPdc one row **below** next sc; repeat from ★ once **more**, sc in next 53 sc, work FPdc around FPdc one row **below** next sc, sc in last 26 sc; finish off: 5 FPdc and 220 sc.

Rows 43 and 44: With **right** side facing, join yarn with sc in first sc; sc in next st and in each st across; finish off: 225 sc.

Row 45: With **right** side facing, join yarn with sc in first sc; sc in next sc, work LDC in sc one row **below** next sc, ★ sc in next 9 sc, work LDC in sc one row **below** next sc; repeat from ★ across to last 2 sc, sc in last 2 sc; finish off: 23 LDC and 202 sc.

Row 46: With **right** side facing, join yarn with sc in first sc; sc in next 2 sts, work LDC in st one row **below** next sc, sc in next 7 sc, work LDC in st one row **below** next sc, ★ sc in next LDC, work LDC in st one row **below** next sc, sc in next 7 sc, work LDC in st one row **below** next sc; repeat from ★ across to last 3 sts, sc in last 3 sts; finish off: 44 LDC and 181 sc.

Row 47: With **right** side facing, join yarn with sc in first sc; sc in next 3 sts, work LDC in sc one row **below** next sc, sc in next 5 sc, work LDC in sc one row **below** next sc, ★ sc in next 3 sts, work LDC in sc one row **below** next sc, sc in next 5 sc, work LDC in sc one row **below** next sc; repeat from ★ across to last 4 sts, sc in last 4 sts; finish off.

Row 48: With **right** side facing, join yarn with sc in first sc; sc in next 4 sts, work LDC in sc one row **below** next sc, sc in next 3 sc, work LDC in sc one row **below** next sc, ★ sc in next 5 sts, work LDC in sc one row **below** next sc, sc in next 3 sc, work LDC in sc one row **below** next sc; repeat from ★ across to last 5 sts, sc in last 5 sts; finish off.

Row 49: With **right** side facing, join yarn with sc in first sc; sc in next 5 sts, work LDC in sc one row **below** next sc, sc in next sc, work LDC in sc one row **below** next sc, ★ in next 7 sts, work LDC in sc one row **below** next sc, sc in next sc, work LDC in sc one row **below** next sc; repeat from ★ across to last 6 sts, sc in last 6 sts; finish off.

Row 50: With **right** side facing, join yarn with sc in first sc; sc in next 6 sts, work LDC in sc one row **below** next sc, ★ sc in next 9 sts, work LDC in sc one row **below** next sc; repeat from ★ across to last 7 sts, sc in last 7 sts; finish off: 22 LDC and 203 sc.

Row 51: With **right** side facing, join yarn with sc in first sc; sc in next 5 sc, work LDC in LDC one row **below** next sc, sc in next LDC, work LDC in LDC one row **below** next sc, ★ sc in next 7 sc, work LDC in LDC one row **below** next sc, sc in next LDC, work LDC in LDC one row **below** next sc; repeat from ★ across to last 6 sc, sc in last 6 sc; finish off: 44 LDC and 181 sc.

Continued on page 46.

Quick & Toasty

This throw will keep you toasty all winter! Worked with a size Q hook, three strands of jewel-tone yarn create the warming bulk of this quick project.

Finished Size: 45" x 61"

MATERIALS
Red Heart Worsted Weight Yarn
[5 ounces (290 yards) per skein (Variegated) or 6 ounces (325 yards) per skein (Red)]:
Variegated - 9 skeins
Red - 6 skeins
Crochet hook, size Q (15.00 mm)

GAUGE: In pattern, 8 sts = 5³/4 ";
4 rows = 3³/4 "

STITCH GUIDE

> **LONG DOUBLE CROCHET (abbreviated LDC)**
> YO, working **around** next ch-1 **(Fig. 18, page 127)**, insert hook in st one row **below** ch-1, YO and pull up a loop even with last st made, (YO and draw through 2 loops on hook) twice **(Fig. 10, page 126)**.

Note: Entire Afghan is worked holding three strands of yarn together and each row is worked across length of Afghan.

AFGHAN
With Red, ch 86 **loosely**.

Row 1: Sc in second ch from hook and in each ch across: 85 sc.

Row 2 (Right side): Ch 4 **(counts as first dc plus ch 1, now and throughout)**, turn; skip next sc, dc in next sc, ★ ch 1, skip next sc, dc in next sc; repeat from ★ across; finish off: 43 dc and 42 ch-1 sps.

Note: Mark last row as **right** side.

Row 3: With **right** side facing, join Variegated with sc in first dc **(see Joining With Sc, page 126)**; (work LDC, sc in next dc) across; finish off: 85 sts.

Row 4: With **right** side facing, join Red with slip st in first sc; ch 4, skip next LDC, dc in next sc, ★ ch 1, skip next LDC, dc in next sc; repeat from ★ across; finish off: 43 dc and 42 ch-1 sps.

Repeat Rows 3 and 4 until Afghan measures approximately 44" from beginning ch, ending by working Row 3.

Last Row: With **right** side facing, join Red with slip st in first sc; ch 3, dc in next LDC and in each st across; finish off.

Holding five 16" strands of Variegated and four 16" strands of Red together for each fringe, add fringe across short edges of Afghan *(Figs. 20a & b, page 127)*.

REINDEER *continued from page 44*
Row 52: With **right** side facing, join yarn with sc in first sc; sc in next 4 sc, work LDC in sc one row **below** next sc, sc in next 3 sts, work LDC in sc one row **below** next sc, ★ sc in next 5 sc, work LDC in sc one row **below** next sc, sc in next 3 sts, work LDC in sc one row **below** next sc; repeat from ★ across to last 5 sc, sc in last 5 sc; finish off.
Row 53: With **right** side facing, join yarn with sc in first sc; sc in next 3 sc, work LDC in sc one row **below** next sc, sc in next 5 sts, work LDC in sc one row **below** next sc, ★ sc in next 3 sc, work LDC in sc one row **below** next sc, sc in next 5 sts, work LDC in sc one row **below** next sc; repeat from ★ across to last 4 sc, sc in last 4 sc; finish off.
Row 54: With **right** side facing, join yarn with sc in first sc; sc in next 2 sc, work LDC in sc one row **below** next sc, sc in next 7 sts, work LDC in sc one row **below** next sc,
★ sc in next sc, work LDC in sc one row **below** next sc, sc in next 7 sts, work LDC in sc one row **below** next sc; repeat from ★ across to last 3 sc, sc in last 3 sc; finish off.
Row 55: With **right** side facing, join yarn with sc in first sc; sc in next sc, work LDC in sc one row **below** next sc, ★ sc in next 9 sts, work LDC in sc one row **below** next sc; repeat from ★ across to last 2 sc, sc in last 2 sc; finish off: 23 LDC and 202 sc.
Rows 56-135: Repeat Rows 46-55, 8 times.
Rows 136-139: With **right** side facing, join yarn with sc in first sc; sc in each st across; finish off.

Holding five 15" strands of yarn together for each fringe, add additional fringe across short edges of Afghan **(Figs. 20a & b, page 127)**.

Splendid Stripes

Rows of double crochets in variegated colors alternate with turquoise stripes of single crochet stitches on our plush afghan. Made with lustrous jewel-tone yarns, this exquisite wrap is crocheted holding two strands of yarn together.

Finished Size: 46" x 61"

MATERIALS
Red Heart Worsted Weight Yarn
[6 ounces (325 yards) per skein (Turquoise) or 5 ounces (290 yards) per skein (Variegated)]:
Turquoise - 8 skeins
Variegated - 5 skeins
Crochet hook, size N (9.00 mm) **or** size needed for gauge

Note: Entire Afghan is worked holding two strands of yarn together, and each row is worked across length of Afghan.

GAUGE: In pattern, 7 sts and 4 rows = 3"

AFGHAN BODY
With two strands of Turquoise, ch 143 **loosely**.
Row 1 (Right side)**:** Sc in back ridge of second ch from hook **(Fig. 2b, page 125)** and each ch across: 142 sc.
Note: Mark last row as **right** side.
Row 2: Ch 1, turn; sc in each sc across; finish off.
Row 3: With **right** side facing and holding one strand of Turquoise and one strand of Variegated together, join yarn with slip st in first sc; ch 3 **(counts as first dc, now and throughout)**, ★ skip next sc, dc in next 3 sc, working **around** last 3 dc made **(Fig. 18, page 127)**, dc in skipped sc; repeat from ★ across to last sc, dc in last sc.
Row 4: Ch 3, turn; ★ skip next dc, dc in next 3 dc, working **around** last 3 dc made, dc in skipped dc; repeat from ★ across to last dc, dc in last dc; finish off.
Row 5: With **right** side facing and holding two strands of Turquoise together, join yarn with sc in first dc **(see Joining With Sc, page 126)**; sc in next dc and in each dc across.
Row 6: Ch 1, turn; sc in each sc across; finish off.
Rows 7-58: Repeat Rows 3-6, 13 times.

EDGING
FIRST SIDE
Row 1: With **right** side facing and holding one strand of Turquoise and one strand of Variegated together, join yarn with sc in first sc on last row; sc in same st and in each sc across: 143 sc.
Row 2: Ch 1, turn; sc in first sc, ★ ch 3, skip next sc, sc in next sc; repeat from ★ across; finish off.

SECOND SIDE
Row 1: With **right** side facing, working in free loops of beginning ch, and holding one strand of Turquoise and one strand of Variegated together, join yarn with sc in first ch; sc in same st and in next 141 chs: 143 sc.
Row 2: Ch 1, turn; sc in first sc, ★ ch 3, skip next sc, sc in next sc; repeat from ★ across; finish off.

Holding three 18" strands of Turquoise and three 18" strands of Variegated together for each fringe, add fringe across short edges of Afghan **(Figs. 20a & b, page 127)**.

Classic Elegance

These timeless wraps will never
go out of style! They're perfect
for formal settings. Filet hearts,
floral motifs, and pineapples
are just a few of the classic
patterns from which to choose,
as well as wraps with rich
texture and color.
Get set to show your style!

Double-Cozy Cover-up

*Quickly worked holding two strands of yarn together,
our extra-cozy afghan is created with rows of open
V-stitches and a sprinkling of bobbles.*

Finished Size: 48" x 70"

MATERIALS
Red Heart Worsted Weight Yarn
[8 ounces (452 yards) per skein]: 11 skeins
Crochet hook, size K (6.50 mm) **or** size needed for
gauge

GAUGE: In pattern, 2 repeats and 5 rows = 4½ "

STITCH GUIDE

DECREASE (uses next 2 sts)
★ YO, insert hook in **next** st, YO and pull up a loop, YO
and draw through 2 loops on hook; repeat from ★ once
more, YO and draw through all 3 loops on hook (**counts
as one dc**).

DOUBLE DECREASE
YO, † insert hook in **next** dc or ch-2 sp, YO and pull up
a loop, YO and draw through 2 loops on hook †, YO,
skip next st, repeat from † to † once, YO and draw
through all 3 loops on hook (**counts as one dc**).

V-ST
(Dc, ch 2, dc) in dc indicated.

CLUSTER
★ YO, insert hook in sp indicated, YO and pull up a
loop, YO and draw through 2 loops on hook; repeat from
★ once **more**, YO and draw through all 3 loops on hook
(**counts as one dc**).

BOBBLE
★ YO, insert hook in dc indicated, YO and pull up a
loop, YO and draw through 2 loops on hook; repeat from
★ 3 times **more**, YO and draw through all 5 loops on
hook. Push Bobble to **right** side.

Note: Entire Afghan is worked holding two strands of yarn
together.

AFGHAN
Ch 151 **loosely**.
Row 1 (Right side): YO, insert hook in fourth ch from
hook (**3 skipped chs count as first dc**), YO and pull up a
loop, YO and draw through 2 loops on hook, YO, insert
hook in next ch, YO and pull up a loop, YO and draw
through 2 loops on hook, YO and draw through all 3 loops
on hook, dc in next ch, 3 dc in next ch, dc in next ch,
★ YO, † insert hook in **next** ch, YO and pull up a loop,

YO and draw through 2 loops on hook †, YO, skip next
2 chs, repeat from † to † once, YO and draw through all
3 loops on hook, dc in next ch, 3 dc in next ch, dc in next
ch; repeat from ★ across to last 3 chs, decrease, dc in last
ch: 129 sts.
Row 2: Ch 3 (**counts as first dc, now and throughout**),
turn; working in Front Loops Only (*Fig. 14, page 126*),
decrease, dc in next dc, 3 dc in next dc, dc in next dc,
★ double decrease, dc in next dc, 3 dc in next dc, dc in
next dc; repeat from ★ across to last 3 sts, decrease, dc in
last dc.
Row 3: Ch 3, turn; skip next dc, working in Back Loops
Only, dc in next dc, ★ ch 2, skip next dc, work V-St in
next dc, ch 2, skip next dc, double decrease; repeat from ★
across: 63 ch-2 sps.
Row 4: Ch 3, turn; work Cluster in next ch-2 sp, working
in both loops, dc in next dc, 3 dc in next ch-2 sp, dc in
next dc, ★ double decrease, dc in next dc, 3 dc in next
ch-2 sp, dc in next dc; repeat from ★ across to last ch-2 sp,
work Cluster in last ch-2 sp, dc in next dc, leave
remaining dc unworked: 129 dc.
Row 5: Ch 3, turn; working in Back Loops Only,
decrease, dc in next dc, 3 dc in next dc, dc in next dc,
★ double decrease, dc in next dc, 3 dc in next dc,
dc in next dc; repeat from ★ across to last 3 dc, decrease,
dc in last dc.
Row 6: Ch 3, turn; working in Front Loops Only,
decrease, dc in next dc, ch 1, work Bobble in next dc,
ch 1, dc in next dc, ★ double decrease, dc in next dc,
ch 1, work Bobble in next dc, ch 1, dc in next dc; repeat
from ★ across to last 3 dc, decrease, dc in last dc.
Row 7: Ch 3, turn; working in Back Loops Only of dc and
in **both** loops of Bobbles, decrease, dc in next ch, 3 dc in
next Bobble, dc in next ch, ★ double decrease, dc in next
ch, 3 dc in next Bobble, dc in next ch; repeat from ★
across to last 3 dc, decrease, dc in last dc.
Row 8: Ch 3, turn; working in Front Loops Only,
decrease, dc in next dc, 3 dc in next dc, dc in next dc,
★ double decrease, dc in next dc, 3 dc in next dc,
dc in next dc; repeat from ★ across to last 3 dc, decrease,
dc in last dc.
Rows 9-77: Repeat Rows 3-8, 11 times; then repeat
Rows 3-5 once **more**.
Finish off.

Holding ten 18" strands of yarn together for each fringe,
add fringe at points across short edges of Afghan
(*Figs. 20a & b, page 127*).

Pretty Petals

With its delightfully textured stitches and subtle floral pattern, this afghan appeals to your senses of touch and sight. Each square features a four-petal motif formed by back post stitches in shades of spruce and cream.

Finished Size: 43½" x 64"

MATERIALS
Red Heart Worsted Weight Yarn
[8 ounces (452 yards) per skein]:
Dark Spruce - 3 skeins
Spruce - 2 skeins
Cream - 2 skeins
Crochet hook, size H (5.00 mm) **or** size needed for gauge
Yarn needle

GAUGE: Each Square = 6¾"

STITCH GUIDE

BACK POST SINGLE CROCHET
(abbreviated BPsc)
Insert hook from **back** to **front** around post of sc indicated *(Fig. 13, page 126)*, YO and pull up a loop, YO and draw through both loops on hook.

BACK POST HALF DOUBLE CROCHET
(abbreviated BPhdc)
YO, insert hook from **back** to **front** around post of sc indicated *(Fig. 13, page 126)*, YO and pull up a loop, YO and draw through all 3 loops on hook.

BACK POST DOUBLE CROCHET
(abbreviated BPdc)
YO, insert hook from **back** to **front** around post of st indicated *(Fig. 13, page 126)*, YO and pull up a loop, (YO and draw through 2 loops on hook) twice.

DECREASE
Pull up a loop in next 2 dc, YO and draw through all 3 loops on hook **(counts as one sc)**.

SQUARE (Make 54)
Rnd 1 (Right side): With Cream, ch 3, 11 hdc in third ch from hook; join with slip st to top of beginning ch-3: 12 sts.
Note: Mark last round as **right** side.
Rnd 2: Ch 3 **(counts as first dc, now and throughout)**, dc in same st, 2 dc in next hdc, ch 2, skip next hdc, ★ 2 dc in each of next 2 hdc, ch 2, skip next hdc; repeat from ★ 2 times **more**; join with slip st to first dc, finish off: 16 dc and 4 ch-2 sps.

Rnd 3: With **right** side facing, join Spruce with slip st in same st as joining; ★ † ch 7 **loosely**, working in back ridge of each ch *(Fig. 2b, page 125)*, hdc in third ch from hook, dc in next 3 chs, tr in last ch, skip next 2 dc on Rnd 2, slip st in Back Loop Only of next dc *(Fig. 14, page 126)*, ch 3 †, slip st in Back Loop Only of next dc; repeat from ★ 2 times **more**, then repeat from † to † once; join with slip st to **both** loops of joining slip st, finish off: 4 Points.
Rnd 4: With **right** side facing and working in **front** of Rnd 3 ch-3, join Dark Spruce with slip st in any ch-2 sp on Rnd 2; ch 3, dc in same sp, ★ † skip next slip st on Rnd 3; working in free loops of ch-7 *(Fig. 15a, page 127)*, sc in next 5 chs, (sc, ch 2, sc) in ch-2 sp at end of Point; working in **both** loops of each st across opposite side of Point, sc in next 5 sts †, working in **front** of Rnd 3 ch-3, 2 dc in next ch-2 sp on Rnd 2; repeat from ★ 2 times **more**, then repeat from † to † once; join with slip st to first dc, do **not** finish off: 56 sts and 4 ch-2 sps.
Rnd 5: Ch 1, pull up a loop in same st and in next dc, YO and draw through all 3 loops on hook **(counts as first sc)**, ★ † slip st in next sc, sc in next 5 sc, (sc, ch 3, sc) in next ch-2 sp, sc in next 5 sc, slip st in next sc †, decrease; repeat from ★ 2 times **more**, then repeat from † to † once; join with slip st to first sc, finish off: 60 sts and 4 ch-3 sps.
Rnd 6: With **right** side facing, join Spruce with slip st in same st as joining; ch 3, 2 dc in same st, ★ † ch 1, skip next 2 sts, hdc in next sc, sc in next 4 sc, (2 sc, ch 2, 2 sc) in next ch-3 sp, sc in next 4 sc, hdc in next sc, ch 1, skip next 2 sts †, 3 dc in next sc; repeat from ★ 2 times **more**, then repeat from † to † once; join with slip st to first dc, finish off: 68 sts and 12 sps.
Rnd 7: With **right** side facing, join Cream with slip st in same st as joining; ch 3, dc in next 2 dc, ★ † ch 1, work BPdc around next hdc, work BPhdc around each of next 4 sc, work BPsc around each of next 2 sc, ch 3, work BPsc around each of next 2 sc, work BPhdc around each of next 4 sc, work BPdc around next hdc, ch 1 †, dc in next 3 dc; repeat from ★ 2 times **more**, then repeat from † to † once; join with slip st to first dc, finish off.
Rnd 8: With **right** side facing, join Dark Spruce with sc in any corner ch-3 sp *(see Joining With Sc, page 126)*; (sc, ch 2, 2 sc) in same sp, ★ sc in each st and in each ch-1 sp across to next corner ch-3 sp, (2 sc, ch 2, 2 sc) in corner ch-3 sp; repeat from ★ 2 times **more**, sc in each st and in each ch-1 sp across; join with slip st to first sc, finish off: 92 sc and 4 ch-2 sps.

ASSEMBLY

With Dark Spruce and working through **both** loops of each stitch on **both** pieces, whipstitch Squares together forming 6 vertical strips of 9 Squares each (*Fig. 19b, page 127*), beginning in second ch of first corner ch-2 and ending in first ch of next corner ch-2; then whipstitch strips together in same manner.

EDGING

Rnd 1: With **right** side facing, join Cream with slip st in any sc; ch 3, dc evenly around entire Afghan working 3 dc in each corner ch-2 sp; join with slip st to first dc, finish off.

Rnd 2: With **right** side facing, join Spruce with sc in any dc; sc in each dc around working 3 sc in center dc of each corner 3-dc group; join with slip st to first sc, finish off.

Rnd 3: With **right** side facing, join Dark Spruce with slip st from **back** to **front** around post of any sc; ch 3, work BPdc around each sc around working 3 BPdc around center sc of each corner 3-sc group; join with slip st to first dc, finish off.

Serenity

Hexagons crocheted in soft white and spruce create a serene wrap for summer lounging. The motifs are worked separately and then whipstitched together later, so this project is great to take along when you know you'll have little bits of time on your hands.

Finished Size: 46" x 62"

MATERIALS
Red Heart Worsted Weight Yarn
[8 ounces (452 yards) per skein]:
White - 4 skeins
Spruce - 3 skeins
Crochet hook, size I (5.50 mm) **or** size needed for gauge
Yarn needle

GAUGE: Each Motif = 7¹/₂"
(from straight edge to straight edge)

STITCH GUIDE

BEGINNING CLUSTER
Ch 3, ★ YO twice, insert hook in sp indicated, YO and pull up a loop, (YO and draw through 2 loops on hook) twice; repeat from ★ once **more**, YO and draw through all 3 loops on hook.

CLUSTER
★ YO twice, insert hook in sp indicated, YO and pull up a loop, (YO and draw through 2 loops on hook) twice; repeat from ★ 2 times **more**, YO and draw through all 4 loops on hook.

MOTIF A (Make 25)
With Spruce, ch 8; join with slip st to form a ring.
Rnd 1 (Right side): Ch 1, 18 sc in ring; join with slip st to first sc.
Note: Mark last round as **right** side.
Rnd 2: Ch 1, sc in same st, ch 5, skip next 2 sc, ★ sc in next sc, ch 5, skip next 2 sc; repeat from ★ around; join with slip st to first sc: 6 ch-5 sps.
Rnd 3: Slip st in first ch-5 sp, ch 4 **(counts as first tr, now and throughout)**, 7 tr in same sp, 8 tr in each ch-5 sp around; join with slip st to first tr: 48 tr.
Rnd 4: Ch 1, sc in same st and in next 3 tr, ch 3, (sc in next 4 tr, ch 3) around; join with slip st to first sc, finish off: 12 ch-3 sps.
Rnd 5: With **right** side facing, join White with slip st in last ch-3 sp (before joining); work (beginning Cluster, ch 4, Cluster) in same sp, ch 3, work (Cluster, ch 5, Cluster) in next ch-3 sp, ch 3, ★ work (Cluster, ch 4, Cluster) in next ch-3 sp, ch 3, work (Cluster, ch 5, Cluster) in next ch-3 sp, ch 3; repeat from ★ around; join with slip st to top of beginning Cluster, finish off: 24 sps.

Rnd 6: With **right** side facing, join Spruce with sc in any corner ch-5 sp *(see Joining With Sc, page 126)*; (2 sc, ch 3, 3 sc) in same sp, 3 sc in each of next 3 sps, ★ (3 sc, ch 3, 3 sc) in next ch-5 sp, 3 sc in each of next 3 sps; repeat from ★ around; join with slip st to first sc: 90 sc and 6 ch-3 sps.
Rnd 7: Ch 1, sc in same st and in each sc around working 3 sc in each ch-3 sp; join with slip st to first sc, finish off: 108 sc.

MOTIF B (Make 24)
With White, ch 8; join with slip st to form a ring.
Rnd 1 (Right side): Ch 1, 18 sc in ring; join with slip st to first sc.
Note: Mark last round as **right** side.
Rnd 2: Ch 1, sc in same st, ch 5, skip next 2 sc, ★ sc in next sc, ch 5, skip next 2 sc; repeat from ★ around; join with slip st to first sc: 6 ch-5 sps.
Rnd 3: Slip st in first ch-5 sp, ch 4, 7 tr in same sp, 8 tr in each ch-5 sp around; join with slip st to first tr: 48 tr.
Rnd 4: Ch 1, sc in same st and in next 3 tr, ch 3, (sc in next 4 tr, ch 3) around; join with slip st to first sc, finish off: 12 ch-3 sps.
Rnd 5: With **right** side facing, join Spruce with slip st in last ch-3 sp (before joining); work (beginning Cluster, ch 4, Cluster) in same sp, ch 3, work (Cluster, ch 5, Cluster) in next ch-3 sp, ch 3, ★ work (Cluster, ch 4, Cluster) in next ch-3 sp, ch 3, work (Cluster, ch 5, Cluster) in next ch-3 sp, ch 3; repeat from ★ around; join with slip st to top of beginning Cluster, finish off: 24 sps.
Rnd 6: With **right** side facing, join White with sc in any corner ch-5 sp; (2 sc, ch 3, 3 sc) in same sp, 3 sc in each of next 3 sps, ★ (3 sc, ch 3, 3 sc) in next ch-5 sp, 3 sc in each of next 3 sps; repeat from ★ around; join with slip st to first sc: 90 sc and 6 ch-3 sps.
Rnd 7: Ch 1, sc in same st and in each sc around working 3 sc in each ch-3 sp; join with slip st to first sc, finish off: 108 sc.

ASSEMBLY
With corresponding color, using Placement Diagram as a guide, page 55, and working through **inside** loops only, whipstitch Motifs together *(Fig. 19a, page 127)*, forming 5 horizontal strips of 5 Motifs each **and** 4 horizontal strips of 6 Motifs each, beginning in center sc of first corner 3-sc group and ending in center sc of next corner 3-sc group; then whipstitch strips together in same manner.

PLACEMENT DIAGRAM

KEY

◯ Motif A

⬡ Motif B

EDGING

Rnd 1: With **right** side facing, join White with sc in any st; sc evenly around entire Afghan working an even number of sc; join with slip st to first sc.

Rnd 2: Ch 2, hdc in same st, skip next sc, ★ slip st in next sc, ch 2, hdc in same st, skip next sc; repeat from ★ around; join with slip st to first slip st, finish off.

TASSELS

Cut a piece of cardboard 3" wide and as long as you want your finished tassel to be. Wind a double strand of White around the cardboard approximately 12 times. Cut an 18" length of yarn and insert it under all of the strands at the top of the cardboard; pull up **tightly** and tie securely. Leave the yarn ends long enough to attach the tassel. Cut the yarn at the opposite end of the cardboard and then remove it **(Fig. 1a)**. Cut a 6" length of yarn and wrap it **tightly** around the tassel twice, 1" below the top **(Fig. 1b)**; tie securely. Trim the ends. Add tassels at points across short edges of Afghan.

Fig. 1a

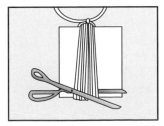

Fig. 1b

Hearts Aplenty

Airy rows of filet hearts make this afghan perfect for someone you love.
Crocheted with cotton yarn, it offers warmth for body and soul!

Finished Size: 46" x 61"

MATERIALS
Red Heart Cotton Worsted Weight Yarn
[2½ ounces (127 yards) per skein]: 16 skeins
Crochet hook, size F (3.75 mm) **or** size needed for gauge

GAUGE: 16 dc and 8 rows = 4"

STITCH GUIDE

ADD ON DC
YO, insert hook into base of last dc made **(Fig. 1)**, YO and pull up a loop, YO and draw through one loop on hook, (YO and draw through 2 loops on hook) twice. Repeat as many times as instructed.

Fig. 1

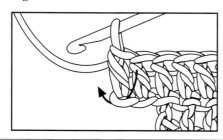

Note: Each row is worked across length of Afghan.

AFGHAN
Ch 213.
Row 1 (Right side): Dc in back ridge of fourth ch from hook **(3 skipped chs count as first dc, now and throughout)** and each ch across **(Fig. 2b, page 125):** 211 dc.
Row 2: Ch 5, turn; dc in fourth ch from hook and in next ch, dc in next dc, ★ ch 2, skip next 2 dc, dc in next dc; repeat from ★ across, add on 3 dc: 217 sts.
Row 3: Ch 5, turn; dc in fourth ch from hook and in next ch, dc in next dc, ch 2, skip next 2 dc, dc in next dc, ch 2, dc in next dc, 2 dc in next ch-2 sp, ★ dc in next dc, (ch 2, dc in next dc) 5 times, 2 dc in next ch-2 sp; repeat from ★ 10 times **more**, (dc in next dc, ch 2) 3 times, skip next 2 dc, dc in last dc, add on 3 dc: 223 sts.
Row 4: Ch 5, turn; dc in fourth ch from hook and in next ch, dc in next dc, ch 2, skip next 2 dc, dc in next dc, (ch 2, dc in next dc) twice, 2 dc in next ch-2 sp, dc in

next 4 dc, 2 dc in next ch-2 sp, ★ dc in next dc, (ch 2, dc in next dc) 3 times, 2 dc in next ch-2 sp, dc in next 4 dc, 2 dc in next ch-2 sp; repeat from ★ 10 times **more**, (dc in next dc, ch 2) twice, skip next 2 dc, dc in last dc, add on 3 dc: 229 sts.
Row 5: Ch 5, turn; dc in fourth ch from hook and in next ch, dc in next dc, ch 2, skip next 2 dc, ★ (dc in next dc, ch 2) twice, dc in next 10 dc, 2 dc in next ch-2 sp; repeat from ★ 11 times **more**, (dc in next dc, ch 2) 3 times, skip next 2 dc, dc in last dc, add on 3 dc: 235 sts.
Row 6: Ch 5, turn; dc in fourth ch from hook and in next ch, dc in next dc, ch 2, skip next 2 dc, dc in next dc, (ch 2, dc in next dc) twice, 2 dc in next ch-2 sp, dc in next 10 dc, ch 2, ★ skip next 2 dc, dc in next dc, ch 2, dc in next dc, 2 dc in next ch-2 sp, dc in next 10 dc, ch 2; repeat from ★ 10 times **more**, skip next 2 dc, (dc in next dc, ch 2) 4 times, skip next 2 dc, dc in last dc, add on 3 dc: 241 sts.
Row 7: Turn; slip st in first 4 dc, ch 3 **(counts as first dc, now and throughout)**, 2 dc in next ch-2 sp, dc in next dc, (ch 2, dc in next dc) 3 times, 2 dc in next ch-2 sp, dc in next 10 dc, ch 2, skip next 2 dc, dc in next dc, ★ ch 2, dc in next dc, 2 dc in next ch-2 sp, dc in next 10 dc, ch 2, skip next 2 dc, dc in next dc; repeat from ★ 10 times **more**, (ch 2, dc in next dc) twice, 2 dc in next ch-2 sp, dc in next dc, leave remaining 3 dc unworked: 235 sts.
Row 8: Turn; slip st in first 4 dc, ch 3, 2 dc in next ch-2 sp, dc in next dc, (ch 2, dc in next dc) twice, ★ ch 2, skip next 2 dc, dc in next 10 dc, (ch 2, dc in next dc) twice; repeat from ★ 11 times **more**, 2 dc in next ch-2 sp, dc in next dc, leave remaining 3 dc unworked: 229 sts.
Row 9: Turn; slip st in first 4 dc, ch 3, 2 dc in next ch-2 sp, (dc in next dc, ch 2) twice, skip next 2 dc, dc in next 4 dc, ch 2, skip next 2 dc, dc in next dc, ★ ch 2, (dc in next dc, ch 2) 3 times, skip next 2 dc, dc in next 4 dc, ch 2, skip next 2 dc, dc in next dc; repeat from ★ 10 times **more**, (ch 2, dc in next dc) twice, 2 dc in next ch-2 sp, dc in next dc, leave remaining 3 dc unworked: 223 sts.
Row 10: Turn; slip st in first 4 dc, ch 3, 2 dc in next ch-2 sp, (dc in next dc, ch 2) 3 times, ★ skip next 2 dc, (dc in next dc, ch 2) 6 times; repeat from ★ 10 times **more**, skip next 2 dc, dc in next dc, ch 2, dc in next dc, 2 dc in next ch-2 sp, dc in next dc, leave remaining 3 dc unworked: 217 sts.
Row 11: Turn; slip st in first 4 dc, ch 3, (2 dc in next ch-2 sp, dc in next dc) across to last 3 dc, leave remaining dc unworked: 211 dc.
Rows 12-91: Repeat Rows 2-11, 8 times.
Finish off.

Absolutely Gorgeous

This stunning mile-a-minute beauty features graceful swirls in each strip. A fanciful lace edging serves as the breathtaking finale.

Finished Size: 46" x 67"

MATERIALS

Red Heart Worsted Weight Yarn
[8 ounces (452 yards) per skein]: 5 skeins
Crochet hook, size H (5.00 mm) **or** size needed for gauge

GAUGE: Each Strip = 6½" wide

STITCH GUIDE

> **DOUBLE CROCHET CLUSTER**
> *(abbreviated dc Cluster)* (uses one sp)
> ★ YO, insert hook in sp indicated, YO and pull up a loop, YO and draw through 2 loops on hook; repeat from ★ once **more**, YO and draw through all 3 loops on hook.
>
> **TREBLE CROCHET CLUSTER**
> *(abbreviated tr Cluster)* (uses next 2 ch-5 sps)
> ★ YO twice, insert hook in **next** ch-5 sp, YO and pull up a loop, (YO and draw through 2 loops on hook) twice; repeat from ★ once **more**, YO and draw through all 3 loops on hook.

STRIP (Make 6)
CENTER

Ch 7; join with slip st to form a ring.
Row 1 (Right side): Ch 3 (**counts as first dc, now and throughout**), 12 dc in ring; do **not** join: 13 dc.
Note: Mark last row as **right** side and bottom edge.
Row 2: Ch 4 (**counts as first dc plus ch 1, now and throughout**), place marker around dc just made for st placement, **turn**; dc in next dc, (ch 1, dc in next dc) across: 12 ch-1 sps.
Row 3: Ch 3, turn; work dc Cluster in next ch-1 sp, (ch 2, work dc Cluster in next ch-1 sp) across, dc in last dc: 11 ch-2 sps.
Row 4: Ch 5, turn; (sc in next ch-2 sp, ch 5) 11 times, place marker around last ch-5 made for st placement, skip next dc Cluster, (sc, ch 1, dc) in sp **before** last dc to form last sp.
Row 5: Ch 3, do **not** turn; 8 dc in last sp made: 9 dc.
Row 6: Ch 3, slip st in beginning ring, ch 1, **turn**; dc in next dc, (ch 1, dc in next dc) 7 times: 8 ch-1 sps.
Row 7: Ch 3, turn; work dc Cluster in next ch-1 sp, (ch 2, work dc Cluster in next ch-1 sp) 7 times, slip st around post of marked dc (at end of Row 2): 7 ch-2 sps.
Row 8: Ch 3, do **not** turn; slip st in top of dc at end of next row (Row 3), ch 5, **turn**; (sc in next ch-2 sp, ch 5) 7 times, place marker around last ch-5 made for st placement, skip next dc Cluster, (sc, ch 1, dc) in sp **before** last dc to form last sp.

Row 9: Ch 3, do **not** turn; 8 dc in last sp made: 9 dc.
Row 10: Ch 3, skip next 2 rows, slip st around post of dc at end of next row, ch 1, **turn**; dc in next dc, (ch 1, dc in next dc) 7 times: 8 ch-1 sps.
Row 11: Ch 3, turn; work dc Cluster in next ch-1 sp, (ch 2, work dc Cluster in next ch-1 sp) 7 times, slip st in adjacent marked ch-5 sp: 7 ch-2 sps.
Row 12: Ch 5, turn; (sc in next ch-2 sp, ch 5) 7 times, place marker around last ch-5 made for st placement, skip next dc Cluster, (sc, ch 1, dc) in sp **before** last dc to form last sp.
Rows 13-88: Repeat Rows 9-12, 19 times.
Row 89: Ch 3, do **not** turn; 12 dc in last sp made: 13 dc.
Row 90: Ch 3, skip next 2 rows, slip st around post of dc at end of next row, ch 1, **turn**; dc in next dc, (ch 1, dc in next dc) 11 times, slip st in adjacent marked ch-5 sp: 12 ch-1 sps.
Row 91: Ch 3, turn; work dc Cluster in next ch-1 sp, (ch 2, work dc Cluster in next ch-1 sp) 11 times, slip st in marked ch-5 sp: 11 ch-2 sps.
Row 92: Ch 5, turn; (sc in next ch-2 sp, ch 5) 10 times, place marker around last ch-5 made for Border placement, sc in next ch-2 sp, ch 5, skip next dc Cluster, slip st in sp **before** last dc; finish off: 170 ch-5 sps around entire Center.

BORDER

Rnd 1: With **right** side facing, join yarn with sc in marked ch-5 sp *(see Joining With Sc, page 126)*; ch 3, (sc in next ch-5 sp, ch 3) 9 times, † work tr Cluster, ch 3, ★ (sc in next ch-5 sp, ch 3) 5 times, work tr Cluster, ch 3; repeat from ★ 9 times **more** †, (sc in next ch-5 sp, ch 3) 16 times, repeat from † to † once; join with slip st to first sc: 148 ch-3 sps.
Rnd 2: Slip st in first ch-3 sp, ch 1, (sc, ch 5, sc, ch 3, sc) in same sp, † (sc, ch 3, sc) in each of next 3 ch-3 sps, (sc, ch 3, sc, ch 5, sc) in next ch-3 sp, (sc, ch 3, sc) in each of next 69 ch-3 sps †, (sc, ch 5, sc, ch 3, sc) in next ch-3 sp, repeat from † to † once; join with slip st to first sc, finish off: 148 ch-3 sps and 4 ch-5 sps.

JOINING

Holding two Strips with **wrong** sides together and bottom edges to your right, join yarn with sc in first corner ch-5 sp on **front** Strip; ch 3, sc in corresponding corner ch-5 sp on **back** Strip, ch 2, ★ sc in next ch-3 sp on **front** Strip, ch 2, sc in next ch-3 sp on **back** Strip, ch 2; repeat from ★ across to next corner ch-5 sp on **front** Strip, sc in corner ch-5 sp, ch 3, sc in next corner ch-5 sp on **back** Strip; finish off.

Join remaining Strips in same manner.

EDGING

Rnd 1: With **right** side of one short edge facing, join yarn with sc in top right corner ch-5 sp; ch 7, (sc in same sp, ch 5) twice, ★ (sc in next sp, ch 5) across to next corner ch-5 sp, [sc, ch 7, (sc, ch 5) twice] in corner ch-5 sp; repeat from ★ 2 times **more**, sc in next ch-3 sp, (ch 5, sc in next sp) across, ch 2, dc in first sc to form last ch-5 sp: 236 ch-5 sps and 4 ch-7 sps.

Rnd 2: Ch 1, sc in same sp, ch 3, (sc, ch 5, sc) in next ch-7 sp, ch 3, ★ (sc in next ch-5 sp, ch 3) 3 times, (sc, ch 5, sc) in next sp, ch 3; repeat from ★ around to last 2 ch-5 sps, sc in next ch-5 sp, ch 3, sc in last ch-5 sp, ch 1, hdc in first sc to form last ch-3 sp: 240 ch-3 sps and 60 ch-5 sps.

Rnd 3: Ch 1, sc in same sp, ch 3, sc in next ch-3 sp, 9 dc in next ch-5 sp, sc in next ch-3 sp, ★ (ch 3, sc in next ch-3 sp) 3 times, 9 dc in next ch-5 sp, sc in next ch-3 sp; repeat from ★ around to last ch-3 sp, ch 3, sc in last ch-3 sp, ch 2, sc in first sc to form last ch-3 sp.

Rnd 4: Ch 1, sc in same sp and in next ch-3 sp, dc in next dc, (ch 1, dc in next dc) 8 times, ★ sc in next ch-3 sp, (sc, ch 3, sc) in next ch-3 sp, sc in next ch-3 sp, dc in next dc, (ch 1, dc in next dc) 8 times; repeat from ★ around to last ch-3 sp, sc in last ch-3 sp and in same sp as first sc, ch 1, hdc in first sc to form last ch-3 sp.

Rnd 5: Ch 1, sc in same sp and in next ch-1 sp, ch 5, (sc in next ch-1 sp, ch 5) 6 times, ★ sc in next 3 sps, ch 5, (sc in next ch-1 sp, ch 5) 6 times; repeat from ★ around to last ch-1 sp, sc in last ch-1 sp; join with slip st to first sc, finish off.

59

Appealing Aran

You'll love creating this crocheted version of a traditional knit Aran afghan! The elaborately textured wrap is made up of popcorn and zigzag panels.

Finished Size: 48" x 69"

MATERIALS

Red Heart Worsted Weight Yarn
[8 ounces (452 yards) per skein]: 8 skeins
Crochet hook, size I (5.50 mm) **or** size needed for gauge
Yarn needle

STITCH GUIDE

BACK POST TREBLE CROCHET
(abbreviated BPtr)
YO twice, insert hook from **back** to **front** around post of FPtr indicated **(Fig. 13, page 126)**, YO and pull up a loop, (YO and draw through 2 loops on hook) 3 times. Skip st in front of BPtr.

FRONT POST TREBLE CROCHET
(abbreviated FPtr)
YO twice, insert hook from **front** to **back** around post of st indicated **(Fig. 13, page 126)**, YO and pull up a loop, (YO and draw through 2 loops on hook) 3 times. Skip st behind FPtr.

FRONT POST DOUBLE TREBLE CROCHET
(abbreviated FPdtr)
YO 3 times, insert hook from **front** to **back** around post of st indicated **(Fig. 13, page 126)**, YO and pull up a loop, (YO and draw through 2 loops on hook) 4 times. Skip st behind FPdtr.

POPCORN
5 Dc in dc indicated, drop loop from hook, insert hook in first dc of 5-dc group, hook dropped loop and draw through.

POPCORN PANEL (Make 6)

GAUGE: Panel = 2³/₄" wide
In pattern, 5 sts = 1¹/₂"; 7 rows = 4¹/₄"

Ch 11 **loosely**.
Row 1: Dc in fourth ch from hook **(3 skipped chs count as first dc)** and in each ch across: 9 dc.
Row 2 (Right side): Ch 3 **(counts as first dc, now and throughout)**, turn; work FPtr around next dc, dc in next 2 dc, work Popcorn in next dc, dc in next 2 dc, work FPtr around next dc, dc in last dc.
Note: Mark last row as **right** side and bottom edge.
Row 3: Ch 3, turn; work BPtr around next FPtr, dc in next 5 sts, work BPtr around next FPtr, dc in last dc.

Row 4: Ch 3, turn; work FPtr around next BPtr, dc in next 2 dc, work Popcorn in next dc, dc in next 2 dc, work FPtr around next BPtr, dc in last dc.
Repeat Rows 3 and 4 until Panel measures approximately 68" from beginning ch, ending by working Row 3; finish off.

ZIGZAG PANEL (Make 5)

GAUGE: Panel = 6" wide
In pattern, 10 sts = 3"; 10 rows = 4"

Ch 21 **loosely**.
Row 1 (Right side): Hdc in second ch from hook and in each ch across: 20 hdc.
Note: Mark last row as **right** side and bottom edge.
Row 2: Ch 1, turn; hdc in each hdc across.
Row 3: Ch 1, turn; hdc in first hdc, work FPdtr around hdc one row **below** next hdc, hdc in next hdc, work FPdtr around hdc one row **below** each of next 3 hdc, hdc in next 4 hdc, work FPdtr around hdc one row **below** each of next 3 hdc, hdc in next 5 hdc, work FPdtr around hdc one row **below** next hdc, hdc in last hdc.
Row 4: Ch 1, turn; hdc in each st across.
Row 5: Ch 1, turn; hdc in first hdc, work FPdtr around FPdtr one row **below** next hdc, hdc in next 2 hdc, (work FPdtr around st one row **below** each of next 3 hdc, hdc in next 4 hdc) twice, work FPdtr around FPdtr one row **below** next hdc, hdc in last hdc.
Row 6: Ch 1, turn; hdc in each st across.
Row 7: Ch 1, turn; hdc in first hdc, work FPdtr around FPdtr one row **below** next hdc, hdc in next 3 hdc, work FPdtr around st one row **below** each of next 3 hdc, hdc in next 4 hdc, work FPdtr around st one row **below** each of next 3 hdc, hdc in next 3 hdc, work FPdtr around FPdtr one row **below** next hdc, hdc in last hdc.
Row 8: Ch 1, turn; hdc in each st across.
Row 9: Ch 1, turn; hdc in first hdc, work FPdtr around FPdtr one row **below** next hdc, (hdc in next 4 hdc, work FPdtr around st one row **below** each of next 3 hdc) twice, hdc in next 2 hdc, work FPdtr around FPdtr one row **below** next hdc, hdc in last hdc.
Row 10: Ch 1, turn; hdc in each st across.
Row 11: Ch 1, turn; hdc in first hdc, work FPdtr around FPdtr one row **below** next hdc, hdc in next 5 hdc, work FPdtr around st one row **below** each of next 3 hdc, hdc in next 4 hdc, work FPdtr around st one row **below** each of next 3 hdc, hdc in next hdc, work FPdtr around FPdtr one row **below** next hdc, hdc in last hdc.

Row 12: Ch 1, turn; hdc in each st across.

Row 13: Ch 1, turn; hdc in first hdc, work FPdtr around FPdtr one row **below** next hdc, (hdc in next 4 hdc, work FPdtr around st one row **below** each of next 3 hdc) twice, hdc in next 2 hdc, work FPdtr around FPdtr one row **below** next hdc, hdc in last hdc.

Row 14: Ch 1, turn; hdc in each st across.

Row 15: Ch 1, turn; hdc in first hdc, work FPdtr around FPdtr one row **below** next hdc, hdc in next 3 hdc, work FPdtr around st one row **below** each of next 3 hdc, hdc in next 4 hdc, work FPdtr around st one row **below** each of next 3 hdc, hdc in next 3 hdc, work FPdtr around FPdtr one row **below** next hdc, hdc in last hdc.

Row 16: Ch 1, turn; hdc in each st across.

Row 17: Ch 1, turn; hdc in first hdc, work FPdtr around FPdtr one row **below** next hdc, hdc in next 2 hdc, (work FPdtr around st one row **below** each of next 3 hdc, hdc in next 4 hdc) twice, work FPdtr around FPdtr one row **below** next hdc, hdc in last hdc.

Row 18: Ch 1, turn; hdc in each st across.

Row 19: Ch 1, turn; hdc in first hdc, work FPdtr around FPdtr one row **below** next hdc, hdc in next hdc, work FPdtr around st one row **below** each of next 3 hdc, hdc in next 4 hdc, work FPdtr around st one row **below** each of next 3 hdc, hdc in next 5 hdc, work FPdtr around FPdtr one row **below** next hdc, hdc in last hdc.

Repeat Rows 4-19 until Panel measures approximately 68" from beginning ch, ending by working Row 11; finish off.

ASSEMBLY

Alternating Panels and beginning and ending with Popcorn Panels, lay out Panels with **right** sides facing and marked edges at bottom; sew Panels together.

EDGING

Rnd 1: With **right** side facing, join yarn with sc in any st *(see Joining With Sc, page 126)*; sc evenly around entire Afghan working 3 sc in each corner and working an even number of sc; join with slip st to first sc.

Rnd 2: Ch 3, do **not** turn; working from **left** to **right**, skip next sc, ★ work reverse hdc in next sc *(Figs. 12a-d, page 126)*, ch 1, skip next sc; repeat from ★ around; join with slip st to st at base of beginning ch-3, finish off.

Sweetheart Wrap

*Brimming with filet hearts, this attractive cover-up
will show everyone your romantic side! Simple popcorns
and V-stitches make it super-easy to crochet.*

Finished Size: 47" x 64"

MATERIALS

Red Heart Worsted Weight Yarn
[8 ounces (452 yards) per skein]: 6 skeins
Crochet hook, size G (4.00 mm) **or** size needed for
gauge

GAUGE: In pattern, 5 V-Sts = 4"; 10 rows = 5½"

STITCH GUIDE

V-ST
(Dc, ch 2, dc) in ch or sp indicated.
POPCORN
4 Dc in sp indicated, drop loop from hook, insert hook
in first dc of 4-dc group, hook dropped loop and draw
through st. Push Popcorn to **right** side.
SCALLOP
Ch 4, dc in fourth ch from hook.

AFGHAN BODY

Ch 169 **loosely**, place marker in last ch made for st
placement, ch 2 **loosely**: 171 chs.
Row 1: Work V-St in sixth ch from hook, (skip next
2 chs, work V-St in next ch) across to last 3 chs, skip next
2 chs, dc in last ch: 55 V-Sts.
Row 2 (Right side): Ch 2, turn; work V-St in each of
next 6 ch-2 sps, ★ † ch 1, work Popcorn in next ch-2 sp,
ch 1 †, work V-St in each of next 13 ch-2 sps; repeat from
★ 2 times **more**, then repeat from † to † once, work V-St
in each of next 6 ch-2 sps, dc **between** last dc and turning
ch: 59 sps.
Row 3: Ch 2, turn; work V-St in each of next 5 ch-2 sps,
★ † ch 1, work Popcorn in next ch-2 sp, ch 1, dc in next
ch-1 sp, ch 2, dc in next ch-1 sp, ch 1, work Popcorn in
next ch-2 sp, ch 1 †, work V-St in each of next
11 ch-2 sps; repeat from ★ 2 times **more**, then repeat from
† to † once, work V-St in each of next 5 ch-2 sps, dc
between last dc and turning ch: 63 sps.
Row 4: Ch 2, turn; work V-St in each of next 4 ch-2 sps,
★ † ch 1, work Popcorn in next ch-2 sp, ch 1, dc in next
ch-1 sp, ch 2, (dc in next dc, ch 2) twice, skip next
Popcorn, dc in next ch-1 sp, ch 1, work Popcorn in next
ch-2 sp, ch 1 †, work V-St in each of next 9 ch-2 sps;
repeat from ★ 2 times **more**, then repeat from † to † once,
work V-St in each of next 4 ch-2 sps, dc **between** last dc
and turning ch.

Row 5: Ch 2, turn; work V-St in each of next 3 ch-2 sps,
★ † ch 1, work Popcorn in next ch-2 sp, ch 1, dc in next
ch-1 sp, ch 2, (dc in next dc, ch 2) 4 times, skip next
Popcorn, dc in next ch-1 sp, ch 1, work Popcorn in next
ch-2 sp, ch 1 †, work V-St in each of next 7 ch-2 sps;
repeat from ★ 2 times **more**, then repeat from † to † once,
work V-St in each of next 3 ch-2 sps, dc **between** last dc
and turning ch.
Row 6: Ch 2, turn; work V-St in each of next 2 ch-2 sps,
★ † ch 1, work Popcorn in next ch-2 sp, ch 1, dc in next
ch-1 sp, ch 2, (dc in next dc, ch 2) 6 times, skip next
Popcorn, dc in next ch-1 sp, ch 1, work Popcorn in next
ch-2 sp, ch 1 †, work V-St in each of next 5 ch-2 sps;
repeat from ★ 2 times **more**, then repeat from † to † once,
work V-St in each of next 2 ch-2 sps, dc **between** last dc
and turning ch.
Row 7: Ch 2, turn; work V-St in each of next 2 ch-2 sps,
★ † ch 1, work Popcorn in next ch-1 sp, ch 1, dc in next
dc, (ch 2, dc in next dc) 7 times, ch 1, skip next Popcorn,
work Popcorn in next ch-1 sp, ch 1 †, work V-St in each
of next 5 ch-2 sps; repeat from ★ 2 times **more**, then
repeat from † to † once, work V-St in each of next
2 ch-2 sps, dc **between** last dc and turning ch.
Row 8: Ch 2, turn; work V-St in each of next 2 ch-2 sps,
★ † ch 1, work Popcorn in next ch-1 sp, ch 1, dc in next
dc, (ch 2, dc in next dc) 3 times, ch 1, work Popcorn in
next ch-2 sp, ch 1, dc in next dc, (ch 2, dc in next dc) 3
times, ch 1, skip next Popcorn, work Popcorn in next
ch-1 sp, ch 1 †, work V-St in each of next 5 ch-2 sps;
repeat from ★ 2 times **more**, then repeat from † to † once,
work V-St in each of next 2 ch-2 sps, dc **between** last dc
and turning ch: 67 sps.
Row 9: Ch 2, turn; work V-St in each of next 2 ch-2 sps,
★ † ch 1, work Popcorn in next ch-1 sp, ch 1, dc in next
dc, (ch 2, dc in next dc) twice, ch 1, work Popcorn in
next ch-2 sp, ch 1, dc in next dc, ch 2, dc in next dc,
ch 1, work Popcorn in next ch-2 sp, ch 1, dc in next dc,
(ch 2, dc in next dc) twice, ch 1, skip next Popcorn, work
Popcorn in next ch-1 sp, ch 1 †, work V-St in each of
next 5 ch-2 sps; repeat from ★ 2 times **more**, then repeat
from † to † once, work V-St in each of next 2 ch-2 sps, dc
between last dc and turning ch: 71 sps.
Row 10: Ch 2, turn; work V-St in each of next 2 ch-2 sps,
★ † dc in next ch-1 sp, ch 2, dc in next dc, (ch 1, work
Popcorn in next ch-2 sp, ch 1, dc in next dc) twice, ch 2,
skip next dc, work V-St in next ch-2 sp, ch 2, skip next
Popcorn, dc in next dc, (ch 1, work Popcorn in next
ch-2 sp, ch 1, dc in next dc) twice, ch 2, skip next
Popcorn, dc in next ch-1 sp †, work V-St in each of next
5 ch-2 sps; repeat from ★ 2 times **more**, then repeat from

† to † once, work V-St in each of next 2 ch-2 sps, dc **between** last dc and turning ch.

Row 11: Ch 2, turn; work V-St in each of next 3 ch-2 sps, ★ † dc in next dc, (ch 2, dc in next dc) twice, work V-St in each of next 3 ch-2 sps, dc in next dc, (ch 2, dc in next dc) twice †, work V-St in each of next 7 ch-2 sps; repeat from ★ 2 times **more**, then repeat from † to † once, work V-St in each of next 3 ch-2 sps, dc **between** last dc and turning ch: 55 ch-2 sps.

Rows 12-111: Repeat Rows 2-11, 10 times.

Row 112: Ch 2, turn; work V-St in each ch-2 sp across, dc **between** last dc and turning ch; do **not** finish off.

EDGING

Rnd 1: Ch 1, do **not** turn; 2 sc in same st; working in end of rows, 3 sc in first row, 2 sc in each row across; 3 sc in marked ch, working in free loops of beginning ch **(Fig. 15b, page 127)** and in sps over beginning ch, work 162 sc evenly spaced across to last ch, 3 sc in last ch; working in end of rows, 3 sc in first row, 2 sc in each row across; working across Row 112, 3 sc in top of turning ch, work 162 sc evenly spaced across, sc in same st as first sc; join with slip st to first sc: 786 sc.

Rnd 2: Ch 7, dc in fourth ch from hook, (dc, work Scallop, dc) in same st at base of beginning ch-7, skip next 2 sc, [(dc, work Scallop, dc) in next sc, skip next 2 sc] across to center sc of next corner 3-sc group, ★ [dc, (work Scallop, dc) twice] in center sc, skip next 2 sc, [(dc, work Scallop, dc) in next sc, skip next 2 sc] across to center sc of next corner 3-sc group; repeat from ★ around; join with slip st to third ch of beginning ch-7, finish off.

Pineapple Dream

Our elegant afghan is as light as a dream! Crocheted with sparkling yarn for a lustrous look, the wrap features an airy pineapple pattern and a petite pineapple edging.

Finished Size: 48" x 73"

MATERIALS

Red Heart Worsted Weight Yarn
[2½ ounces (145 yards) per skein]: 14 skeins
Crochet hook, size G (4.00 mm) **or** size needed for gauge

GAUGE: In pattern, (ch 5, dc) 3 times = 3¾";
8 rows = 4¾"

STITCH GUIDE

> **PICOT**
> Ch 2, slip st in second ch from hook.
> **SHELL**
> (2 Hdc, dc, work Picot, dc, 2 hdc) in st indicated.

AFGHAN BODY

Ch 233 **loosely**.

Row 1: Slip st in eighth ch from hook, (ch 2, skip next 2 chs, dc in next ch, ch 2, skip next 2 chs, slip st in next ch) 3 times, skip next 2 chs, work Shell in next ch, skip next 2 chs, slip st in next ch, ★ (ch 2, skip next 2 chs, dc in next ch, ch 2, skip next 2 chs, slip st in next ch) 5 times, skip next 2 chs, work Shell in next ch, skip next 2 chs, slip st in next ch; repeat from ★ 4 times **more**, ch 2, skip next 2 chs, dc in next ch, (ch 2, skip next 2 chs, slip st in next ch, ch 2, skip next 2 chs, dc in next ch) 3 times: 6 Shells.

Row 2 (Right side): Ch 8 (**counts as first dc plus ch 5, now and throughout**), turn; (dc in next dc, ch 5) 3 times, slip st in next Picot, ch 5, ★ skip next ch-2 sp, (dc in next dc, ch 5) 5 times, slip st in next Picot, ch 5; repeat from ★ 4 times **more**, skip next ch-2 sp, (dc in next dc, ch 5) 3 times, skip next 5 sts, dc in next ch: 38 ch-5 sps.

Note: Mark last row as **right** side.

Row 3: Ch 5 (**counts as first dc plus ch 2, now and throughout**), turn; slip st in center ch of next ch-5, ch 2, (dc in next dc, ch 2, slip st in center ch of next ch-5, ch 2) twice, slip st in next dc, (work Shell in center ch of next ch-5, skip next 2 chs, slip st in next st) twice, ★ ch 2, slip st in center ch of next ch-5, ch 2, (dc in next dc, ch 2, slip st in center ch of next ch-5, ch 2) 3 times, slip st in next dc, (work Shell in center ch of next ch-5, skip next 2 chs, slip st in next st) twice; repeat from ★ across to last 3 dc, (ch 2, slip st in center ch of next ch-5, ch 2, dc in next dc) 3 times: 12 Shells.

Row 4: Ch 8, turn; (dc in next dc, ch 5) twice, skip next slip st, dc in next slip st, ch 2, slip st in next Picot, ch 5, slip st in next Picot, ch 2, dc in next slip st, ★ ch 5, (dc in next dc, ch 5) 3 times, skip next slip st, dc in next slip st, ch 2, slip st in next Picot, ch 5, slip st in next Picot, ch 2, dc in next slip st; repeat from ★ across to last 3 dc, (ch 5, dc in next dc) 3 times: 32 ch-5 sps and 12 ch-2 sps.

Row 5: Ch 5, turn; slip st in center ch of next ch-5, (ch 2, dc in next dc, ch 2, slip st in center ch of next ch-5) twice, work Shell in next dc, slip st in next slip st, ch 3, (dc, ch 2, dc) in center ch of next ch-5, ch 3, slip st in next slip st, work Shell in next dc, slip st in center ch of next ch-5, ★ (ch 2, dc in next dc, ch 2, slip st in center ch of next ch-5) 3 times, work Shell in next dc, slip st in next slip st, ch 3, (dc, ch 2, dc) in center ch of next ch-5, ch 3, slip st in next slip st, work Shell in next dc, slip st in center ch of next ch-5; repeat from ★ across to last 3 dc, ch 2, dc in next dc, (ch 2, slip st in center ch of next ch-5, ch 2, dc in next dc) twice: 46 ch-2 sps and 12 ch-3 sps.

Row 6: Ch 8, turn; (dc in next dc, ch 5) twice, slip st in next Picot, skip next ch-3 sp, 13 dc in next ch-2 sp, slip st in next Picot, ch 5, ★ skip next ch-2 sp, (dc in next dc, ch 5) 3 times, slip st in next Picot, skip next ch-3 sp, 13 dc in next ch-2 sp, slip st in next Picot, ch 5; repeat from ★ 4 times **more**, skip next ch-2 sp, dc in next dc, (ch 5, dc in next dc) twice: 6 13-dc groups and 26 ch-5 sps.

Row 7: Ch 5, turn; slip st in center ch of next ch-5, ch 2, dc in next dc, ch 2, slip st in center ch of next ch-5, ch 2, ★ slip st in next dc, work Shell in center ch of next ch-5, slip st in next slip st, sc in next dc, (ch 3, skip next dc, sc in next dc) 6 times, slip st in next slip st, work Shell in center ch of next ch-5, slip st in next dc, ch 2, slip st in center ch of next ch-5, ch 2, dc in next dc, ch 2, slip st in center ch of next ch-5, ch 2; repeat from ★ across to last dc, dc in last dc: 36 ch-3 sps and 28 ch-2 sps.

Row 8: Ch 8, turn; dc in next dc, ch 5, skip next slip st, dc in next slip st, ch 2, slip st in next Picot, ch 4, sc in next ch-3 sp, (ch 3, sc in next ch-3 sp) 5 times, ch 4, slip st in next Picot, ch 2, dc in next slip st, ★ ch 5, dc in next dc, ch 5, skip next slip st, dc in next slip st, ch 2, slip st in next Picot, ch 4, sc in next ch-3 sp, (ch 3, sc in next ch-3 sp) 5 times, ch 4, slip st in next Picot, ch 2, dc in next slip st; repeat from ★ across to last 2 dc, (ch 5, dc in next dc) twice: 68 sps.

Row 9: Ch 5, turn; slip st in center ch of next ch-5, ch 2, dc in next dc, ch 2, slip st in center ch of next ch-5, ★ work Shell in next dc, slip st in next slip st, ch 4, skip next ch-4 sp, sc in next ch-3 sp, (ch 3, sc in next ch-3 sp) 4 times, ch 4, slip st in next slip st, work Shell in next dc, slip st in center ch of next ch-5, ch 2, dc in next dc, ch 2, slip st in center ch of next ch-5; repeat from ★ across to last dc, ch 2, dc in last dc: 52 sps.

Row 10: Ch 8, turn; dc in next dc, ch 5, slip st in next Picot, ch 8, skip next ch-4 sp, sc in next ch-3 sp, (ch 3, sc in next ch-3 sp) 3 times, ch 8, slip st in next Picot, ch 5, skip next ch-2 sp, dc in next dc, ch 5, ★ slip st in next Picot, ch 8, skip next ch-4 sp, sc in next ch-3 sp, (ch 3, sc in next ch-3 sp) 3 times, ch 8, slip st in next Picot, ch 5, skip next ch-2 sp, dc in next dc, ch 5; repeat from ★ across to last dc, dc in last dc: 44 sps.

Row 11: Ch 5, turn; slip st in center ch of next ch-5, ch 2, dc in next dc, ch 2, slip st in center ch of next ch-5, ch 2, ★ slip st in next slip st, work Shell in third ch of next ch-8, skip next 2 chs, slip st in next ch, ch 2, sc in next ch-3 sp, (ch 3, sc in next ch-3 sp) twice, ch 2, skip next sc and next 2 chs, slip st in next ch, skip next 2 chs, work Shell in next ch, slip st in next slip st, ch 2, slip st in center ch of next ch-5, ch 2, dc in next dc, ch 2, slip st in center ch of next ch-5, ch 2; repeat from ★ across to last dc, dc in last dc: 52 sps.

Row 12: Ch 8, turn; dc in next dc, ch 5, skip next slip st, dc in next slip st, ch 2, slip st in next Picot, ch 8, skip next ch-2 sp, sc in next ch-3 sp, ch 3, sc in next ch-3 sp, ch 8, slip st in next Picot, ch 2, dc in next slip st, ★ ch 5, dc in next dc, ch 5, skip next slip st, dc in next slip st, ch 2, slip st in next Picot, ch 8, skip next ch-2 sp, sc in next ch-3 sp, ch 3, sc in next ch-3 sp, ch 8, slip st in next Picot, ch 2, dc in next slip st; repeat from ★ across to last 2 dc, (ch 5, dc in next dc) twice: 44 sps.

Row 13: Ch 5, turn; slip st in center ch of next ch-5, ch 2, dc in next dc, ch 2, slip st in center ch of next ch-5, ch 2, dc in next dc, ★ ch 2, slip st in next slip st, work Shell in third ch of next ch-8, skip next 2 chs, slip st in next ch, ch 2, sc in next ch-3 sp, ch 2, skip next sc and next 2 chs, slip st in next ch, skip next 2 chs, work Shell in next ch, slip st in next slip st, ch 2, dc in next dc, (ch 2, slip st in center ch of next ch-5, ch 2, dc in next dc) twice; repeat from ★ across: 52 sps.

Row 14: Ch 8, turn; (dc in next dc, ch 5) twice, slip st in next Picot, ch 5, dc in next sc, ch 5, slip st in next Picot, ch 5, ★ skip next ch-2 sp, (dc in next dc, ch 5) 3 times, slip st in next Picot, ch 5, dc in next sc, ch 5, slip st in next Picot, ch 5; repeat from ★ 4 times **more**, skip next ch-2 sp, dc in next dc, (ch 5, dc in next dc) twice: 38 ch-5 sps.

Continued on page 66.

Row 15: Ch 5, turn; slip st in center ch of next ch-5, ch 2, (dc in next dc, ch 2, slip st in center ch of next ch-5, ch 2) twice, slip st in next slip st, work Shell in center ch of next ch-5, slip st in next dc, work Shell in center ch of next ch-5, slip st in next slip st, ★ ch 2, slip st in center ch of next ch-5, ch 2, (dc in next dc, ch 2, slip st in center ch of next ch-5, ch 2) 3 times, slip st in next slip st, work Shell in center ch of next ch-5, slip st in next dc, work Shell in center ch of next ch-5, slip st in next slip st; repeat from ★ across to last 3 dc, (ch 2, slip st in center ch of next ch-5, ch 2, dc in next dc) 3 times: 52 ch-2 sps.

Row 16: Ch 8, turn; (dc in next dc, ch 5) twice, skip next slip st, dc in next slip st, ch 2, slip st in next Picot, ch 5, slip st in next Picot, ch 2, dc in next slip st, ★ ch 5, (dc in next dc, ch 5) 3 times, skip next slip st, dc in next slip st, ch 2, slip st in next Picot, ch 5, slip st in next Picot, ch 2, dc in next slip st; repeat from ★ across to last 3 dc, (ch 5, dc in next dc) 3 times: 32 ch-5 sps and 12 ch-2 sps.

Row 17: Ch 5, turn; (slip st in center ch of next ch-5, ch 2, dc in next dc, ch 2) 3 times, slip st in next slip st, work Shell in center ch of next ch-5, slip st in next slip st, ch 2, dc in next dc, ★ ch 2, (slip st in center ch of next ch-5, ch 2, dc in next dc, ch 2) 4 times, slip st in next slip st, work Shell in center ch of next ch-5, slip st in next slip st, ch 2, dc in next dc; repeat from ★ across to last 3 dc, (ch 2, slip st in center ch of next ch-5, ch 2, dc in next dc) 3 times: 64 ch-2 sps.

Row 18: Ch 8, turn; (dc in next dc, ch 5) 3 times, slip st in next Picot, ch 5, ★ skip next ch-2 sp, (dc in next dc, ch 5) 5 times, slip st in next Picot, ch 5; repeat from ★ 4 times **more**, skip next ch-2 sp, dc in next dc, (ch 5, dc in next dc) 3 times: 38 ch-5 sps.

Rows 19-114: Repeat Rows 3-18, 6 times; do **not** finish off.

EDGING
TOP
Row 1: Turn; slip st in first dc, ★ ch 3, skip next ch-5 sp, (dc, ch 2, dc) in next dc, ch 3, skip next ch-5 sp, slip st in next st; repeat from ★ across: 38 ch-3 sps and 19 ch-2 sps.

Row 2: Turn; slip st in first slip st, ch 5, slip st in next dc, (sc, 2 hdc, dc, tr, work Picot, tr, dc, 2 hdc, sc) in next ch-2 sp, slip st in next dc, ch 5, ★ skip next 2 ch-3 sps, slip st in next dc, (sc, 2 hdc, dc, tr, work Picot, tr, dc, 2 hdc, sc) in next ch-2 sp, slip st in next dc, ch 5; repeat from ★ across to last ch-3 sp, skip ch-3 sp, slip st in last slip st.

Row 3: Ch 3, turn; slip st in center ch of next ch-5, ch 3, ★ skip next 2 chs and next 2 sts, (sc in next st, ch 3, skip next st) twice, (sc, ch 5, sc) in next Picot, ch 3, (skip next st, sc in next st, ch 3) twice, slip st in center ch of next ch-5, ch 3; repeat from ★ across, slip st in last slip st; finish off.

BOTTOM
Row 1: With **wrong** side facing and working in free loops of beginning ch (*Fig. 15b, page 127*), join yarn with slip st in first ch; ★ ch 3, skip next 5 chs, (dc, ch 2, dc) in next ch, ch 3, skip next 5 chs, slip st in next ch; repeat from ★ 18 times **more**: 38 ch-3 sps and 19 ch-2 sps.

Rows 2 and 3: Work same as Top.

Captivating Crescents

This stunning afghan is surprisingly easy to make! The lacy spaces above and below each crescent create the illusion of strips, but the cover-up is actually crocheted all in one piece.

Finished Size: 48" x 62"

MATERIALS
Red Heart Worsted Weight Yarn
[6 ounces (325 yards) per skein]: 9 skeins
Crochet hook, size I (5.50 mm) **or** size needed for gauge

GAUGE: In pattern, one repeat and 8 rows = 5"

STITCH GUIDE

> **CLUSTER**
> ★ YO, insert hook in dc indicated, YO and pull up a loop, YO and draw through 2 loops on hook; repeat from ★ 3 times **more**, YO and draw through all 5 loops on hook.

AFGHAN BODY
Ch 151 **loosely**.

Row 1: Dc in fourth ch from hook (**3 skipped chs count as first dc**) and in next 3 chs, ★ ch 4, skip next 4 chs, sc in next ch, ch 3, skip next ch, sc in next ch, ch 4, skip next 4 chs, dc in next 5 chs; repeat from ★ across: 50 dc and 27 sps.

Row 2 (Right side): Ch 3 (**counts as first dc, now and throughout**), turn; dc in next 4 dc, ★ ch 2, sc in next ch-4 sp, ch 1, 7 dc in next ch-3 sp, ch 1, sc in next ch-4 sp, ch 2, dc in next 5 dc; repeat from ★ across: 113 dc.

Note: Mark last row as **right** side.

Row 3: Ch 3, turn; dc in next 4 dc, ★ ch 1, work Cluster in next dc, (ch 3, skip next dc, work Cluster in next dc) 3 times, ch 1, dc in next 5 dc; repeat from ★ across: 50 dc and 36 Clusters.

Row 4: Ch 3, turn; dc in next 4 dc, ★ ch 2, skip next ch-1 sp, sc in next ch-3 sp, (ch 3, sc in next ch-3 sp) twice, ch 2, dc in next 5 dc; repeat from ★ across: 36 sps.

Row 5: Ch 3, turn; dc in next 4 dc, ★ ch 4, skip next ch-2 sp, sc in next ch-3 sp, ch 3, sc in next ch-3 sp, ch 4, dc in next 5 dc; repeat from ★ across: 27 sps.

Row 6: Ch 3, turn; dc in next 4 dc, ★ ch 2, sc in next ch-4 sp, ch 1, 7 dc in next ch-3 sp, ch 1, sc in next ch-4 sp, ch 2, dc in next 5 dc; repeat from ★ across: 113 dc.

Rows 7-97: Repeat Rows 3-6, 22 times; then repeat Rows 3-5 once **more**; do **not** finish off.

EDGING

Rnd 1: Ch 1, do **not** turn; sc evenly around entire Afghan working 3 sc in each corner; join with slip st to first sc.

Rnd 2: Ch 1, turn; sc in same st and in each sc around working 3 sc in center sc of each corner 3-sc group; join with slip st to first sc, finish off.

Holding three 16" strands of yarn together for each fringe, add fringe across short edges of Afghan (*Figs. 20a & b, page 127*).

Just for Fun

Bright, colorful, and a little on the wild side, the afghans in this collection are one-of-a-kind! Stitch up a confetti-sprinkled wrap, sail across the sky with lively hot-air balloons, or get in touch with nature with an exotic leopard-spot pattern. You can't go wrong ... just express yourself!

69

It's a Party!

With its giant confetti-inspired flecks and party-streamer fringe, this afghan will bring fun to any room! Its rainbow of primary colors makes it especially nice for a child's playroom.

Finished Size: 47" x 67"

MATERIALS
Red Heart Worsted Weight Yarn
[3½ ounces (198 yards) per skein]:
White - 12 skeins
Red - 2 skeins
Orange - 2 skeins
Yellow - 2 skeins
Green - 2 skeins
Blue - 2 skeins
Lilac - 2 skeins
Crochet hook, size J (6.00 mm) **or** size needed for gauge

GAUGE: In pattern, 9 sts and 6 rows = 3"

STITCH GUIDE

Note: When working in chains on Twirls and Flecks, insert hook under top strand **and** back ridge of each chain (**Fig. 2c, page 125**).
BEGINNING TWIRL
Ch 20 **loosely**, 3 sc in second ch from hook and in each ch across.
FLECK
Ch 3, 6 sc in second ch from hook.
ENDING TWIRL
Ch 20 **loosely**, turn; 3 sc in second ch from hook and in each ch across, slip st in last sc on row.

COLOR SEQUENCE
Work one row **each**: White, Red, White, Orange, White, Yellow, White, ★ Green, White, Blue, White, Lilac, White, Red, White, Orange, White, Yellow, White; repeat from ★ throughout.

Note: Each row is worked across length of Afghan. When working a **right** side row, leave beginning and ending Twirls on previous row unworked.

AFGHAN BODY
With White, ch 201 **loosely**.
Row 1 (Right side): Dc in fourth ch from hook (**3 skipped chs count as first dc**) and in each ch across; finish off: 199 dc.
Note: Mark last row as **right** side.
Row 2: With next color, work beginning Twirl, with **wrong** side of Afghan facing, sc in first dc, ch 1, skip next st, sc in next dc, work Fleck, ★ skip next st, sc in next dc,

(ch 1, skip next st, sc in next dc) 3 times, work Fleck; repeat from ★ across to last 4 sts, skip next st, sc in next dc, ch 1, skip next st, sc in last dc, work ending Twirl; finish off: 25 Flecks.
Row 3: With **right** side facing, join White with slip st in first sc (same st as slip st); ch 3 (**counts as first dc, now and throughout**), working in **front** of next ch-1, tr in st one row **below** ch-1, dc in next sc, working **behind** next Fleck, tr in st one row **below** Fleck, dc in next sc, ★ (working in **front** of next ch-1, tr in st one row **below** ch-1, dc in next sc) 3 times, working **behind** next Fleck, tr in st one row **below** Fleck, dc in next sc; repeat from ★ across to last 2 sts, working in **front** of next ch-1, tr in st one row **below** ch-1, dc in last sc; finish off: 199 sts.
Row 4: With next color, work beginning Twirl, with **wrong** side of Afghan facing, sc in first dc, (ch 1, skip next tr, sc in next dc) 3 times, ★ work Fleck, skip next tr, sc in next dc, (ch 1, skip next tr, sc in next dc) 3 times; repeat from ★ across, work ending Twirl; finish off: 24 Flecks.
Row 5: With **right** side facing, join White with slip st in first sc (same st as slip st); ch 3, (working in **front** of next ch-1, tr in tr one row **below** ch-1, dc in next sc) 3 times, ★ working **behind** next Fleck, tr in tr one row **below** Fleck, dc in next sc, (working in **front** of next ch-1, tr in tr one row **below** ch-1, dc in next sc) 3 times; repeat from ★ across; finish off: 199 sts.
Repeat Rows 2-5 until Afghan measures approximately 46" from beginning ch, ending by working a **right** side row.

EDGING
FIRST SIDE
Row 1: With White, work beginning Twirl, with **wrong** side of Afghan facing, sc in first 2 sts on last row, ch 1, ★ skip next dc, sc in next tr, ch 1; repeat from ★ across to last 3 sts, skip next dc, sc in last 2 sts, work ending Twirl; do **not** finish off.
Row 2: Ch 2, (slip st in next ch-1 sp, ch 2) across to last 2 sc before beginning Twirl, skip next sc, slip st in last sc, leave beginning Twirl unworked; finish off.

SECOND SIDE
Row 1: With White, work beginning Twirl, with **wrong** side of Afghan facing and working in free loops of beginning ch, sc in first 2 chs (ch at base of first dc and next ch), ch 1, ★ skip next ch, sc in next ch, ch 1; repeat from ★ across to last 3 chs, skip next ch, sc in last 2 chs, work ending Twirl; do **not** finish off.
Row 2: Ch 2, (slip st in next ch-1 sp, ch 2) across to last 2 sc before beginning Twirl, skip next sc, slip st in last sc, leave beginning Twirl unworked; finish off.

Call of the wild

When you're lured by the call of the wild, be sure to take along this exotic afghan! Bold leopard spots are cross stitched on each strip for the untamed look of a rare jungle cat. Surprisingly, the striking throw is a pussycat to crochet!

Finished Size: 45" x 58"

MATERIALS

Red Heart Worsted Weight Yarn
[3½ ounces (198 yards) per skein]:
Light Brown - 10 skeins
Brown - 4 skeins
Black - 3 skeins
Crochet hook, size H (5.00 mm) **or** size needed for gauge
Yarn needle

GAUGE: Each Strip = 15" wide
12 sc and 14 rows = 4"

STRIP (Make 3)

With Light Brown, ch 40 **loosely**.
Row 1 (Wrong side)**:** Sc in second ch from hook and in each ch across: 39 sc.
Note: Mark **back** of any sc on last row as **right** side and bottom edge.
Rows 2-194: Ch 1, turn; sc in each sc across.
Row 195: Ch 1, turn; sc in first 4 sc, place marker around last sc made for cross stitch placement, sc in each sc across.
Rows 196-198: Ch 1, turn; sc in each sc across.
Finish off.

EDGING

Rnd 1: With **right** side facing, join Brown with sc in first sc *(see Joining With Sc, page 126)*; sc in same st and in each sc across to last sc, 3 sc in last sc; sc in end of each row across; working in free loops of beginning ch *(Fig. 15b, page 127)*, 3 sc in ch at base of first sc, sc in each ch across to last ch, 3 sc in last ch; sc in end of each row across and in same st as first sc; join with slip st to first sc: 482 sc.
Rnd 2: Ch 3, turn; (dc, ch 2, 2 dc) in same st, dc in next sc and in each sc across to center sc of next corner 3-sc group, ★ (2 dc, ch 2, 2 dc) in center sc, dc in each sc across to center sc of next corner 3-sc group; repeat from ★ 2 times **more**; join with slip st to top of beginning ch-3.
Rnd 3: Ch 1, turn; sc in same st and in each dc across to next corner ch-2 sp, 3 sc in corner ch-2 sp, ★ sc in each dc across to next corner ch-2 sp, 3 sc in corner ch-2 sp; repeat from ★ 2 times **more**, sc in last dc; join with slip st to first sc, finish off.

CROSS STITCH

Following instructions and chart, add cross stitch design to top of each Strip, repeat design vertically 5 times **more**; leaving 3 unworked rows at bottom of Strip. Each colored square on the chart represents one cross stitch. Each cross stitch is worked over one sc. To position design on Strip, use marked sc on Strip matched to the cross stitch marked with an X on chart. Using yarn needle and long strand of yarn, weave end under several stitches on **wrong** side of Strip to secure (do **not** tie knot). With **right** side facing and marked edge at top, work cross stitch as follows: bring needle up at 1, down at 2 (half cross made), up at 3, and down at 4 **(cross stitch completed, Fig. 1)**. All cross stitches should cross in the same direction. When working sts in a horizontal row, work sts from left to right and then back again; when working sts vertically, complete each before moving down to the next st. Finish off by weaving end under several sts on **wrong** side of Strip; cut yarn end close to work.

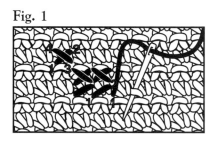

Fig. 1

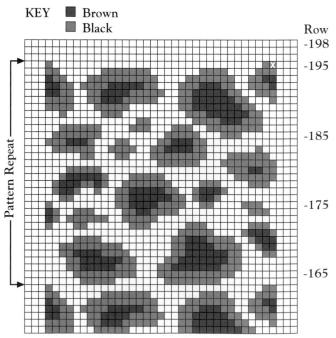

CHART

KEY ■ Brown
■ Black

Row
-198
-195
-185
-175
-165

Pattern Repeat

ASSEMBLY

Place two Strips with **wrong** sides together and bottom edges at same end. With Brown and working through **inside** loops of each stitch on both pieces, whipstitch Strips together *(Fig. 19a, page 127)*, beginning in center sc of first corner 3-sc group and ending in center sc of next corner 3-sc group.

Join last Strip in same manner, working in same direction.

TRIM

With **right** side facing, join Black with slip st in any sc; ch 1, working from **left** to **right**, work reverse sc *(Figs. 11a-d, page 126)* in each sc around working 3 reverse sc in center sc of each corner 3-sc group; join with slip st to first st, finish off.

Patriotic Diamonds

*Take along this patriotic-hued afghan to sit on during a
Fourth of July picnic or fireworks display! Strips of contrasting
red and blue diamond motifs make up the dazzling throw.*

Finished Size: 50" x 71"

MATERIALS
Red Heart Worsted Weight Yarn
[8 ounces (452 yards) per skein]:
Blue - 4 skeins
Red - 4 skeins
Crochet hook, size K (6.50 mm) **or** size needed for
gauge
Yarn needle

GAUGE: 6 sc and 7 rows = 2"

FOLLOWING CHARTS
Follow charts and the instructions given below to work
Strips. Each square on the charts represents one single
crochet, and each row of squares represents one row of
single crochets.

When changing colors, work the last sc to within one step
of completion, hook new yarn, and draw through both
loops on hook *(Fig. 16, page 127)*. Do not carry yarn
across large areas on back of work. Use a separate yarn for
each color change, and cut yarn when color is no longer
needed.

STRIP A (Make 4)
With Blue, ch 22 **loosely**.
Row 1 (Right side): Sc in second ch from hook and in
next 9 chs changing to Red in last sc made, sc in next ch
changing to Blue, sc in last 10 chs: 21 sc.
Note: Mark last row as **right** side and bottom edge.
Continue changing colors in same manner.
Rows 2-38: Follow Chart A.
Rows 39-209: Follow Rows 1-38 of Chart A, 4 times;
then follow Rows 1-19 once **more**; finish off.

STRIP B (Make 3)
With Red, ch 22 **loosely**.
Row 1 (Right side): Sc in second ch from hook and in
next 9 chs changing to Blue in last sc made, sc in next ch
changing to Red, sc in last 10 chs: 21 sc.
Note: Mark last row as **right** side and bottom edge.
Rows 2-38: Follow Chart B.
Rows 39-209: Follow Rows 1-38 of Chart B, 4 times;
then follow Rows 1-19 once **more**; finish off.

ASSEMBLY
With **wrong** sides together, bottom edges at the same end,
and using Blue, sew Strips together alternating Strip A
and Strip B.

TOP BORDER
Row 1: With **right** side facing and working in sc on last
row of each Strip, join Blue with sc in first sc *(see Joining
With Sc, page 126)*; sc in each sc across top edge: 147 sc.
Rows 2-10: Ch 1, turn; sc in each sc across.
Finish off.
Row 11: With **right** side facing, join Red with sc in first
sc; sc in each sc across.
Rows 12-20: Ch 1, turn; sc in each sc across.
Finish off.

BOTTOM BORDER
Row 1: With **right** side facing and working in free loops of
beginning ch on each Strip *(Fig. 15b, page 127)*, join Blue
with sc in first ch; sc in each ch across bottom edge: 147 sc.
Complete same as Top Border.

EDGING
With **right** side facing, join Blue with sc in any st; working
from **left** to **right**, work reverse sc *(Figs. 11a-d, page 126)*
in each st and in end of each row around entire Afghan;
join with slip st to first sc, finish off.

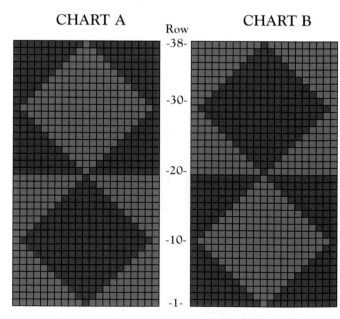

CHART A   Row   CHART B

-38-
-30-
-20-
-10-
-1-

Wrapped in Ruffles

Our irresistible baby wrap has ruffles all around! You add the soft frills as you complete each square, then our placement diagram makes assembly a breeze. A border of ruffles in all four pastels provides a festive finish.

Finished Size: 34" x 46"

MATERIALS

Red Heart Baby Sport Weight Pompadour Yarn [6 ounces (480 yards) per skein]:
White - 4 skeins
Green - 1 skein
Yellow - 1 skein
Pink - 1 skein
Blue - 1 skein
Crochet hook, size G (4.00 mm) **or** size needed for gauge
Yarn needle

GAUGE: Each Square = 3"

STITCH GUIDE

SCALLOP
Ch 3, dc in third ch from hook.

SQUARE

Referring to the diagram key, make the number of Squares specified with the ruffle colors indicated.
Rnd 1 (Right side)**:** With White, ch 5, in fifth ch from hook work [dc, ch 3, (dc, ch 1, dc, ch 3) 3 times]; join with slip st to fourth ch of beginning ch-5: 8 sts and 8 sps. *Note:* Mark last round as **right** side.
Rnd 2: Ch 4 (**counts as first dc plus ch 1, now and throughout**), dc in next dc, ch 1, (dc, ch 3, dc) in next ch-3 sp, ch 1, ★ (dc in next dc, ch 1) twice, (dc, ch 3, dc) in next ch-3 sp, ch 1; repeat from ★ around; join with slip st to first dc: 16 dc and 16 sps.
Rnd 3: Ch 4, (dc in next dc, ch 1) twice, (dc, ch 3, dc) in next ch-3 sp, ch 1, ★ (dc in next dc, ch 1) 4 times, (dc, ch 3, dc) in next ch-3 sp, ch 1; repeat from ★ 2 times **more**, dc in last dc, ch 1; join with slip st to first dc, finish off: 24 dc and 24 sps.

RUFFLE

With **right** side facing and working in sps on Rnd 2, join color indicated with sc in any corner ch-3 sp (**between** dc) (*see Joining With Sc, page 126*); work Scallop, (sc, work Scallop) twice in each of next 3 ch-1 sps, ★ sc in next ch-3 sp (**between** dc), work Scallop, (sc, work Scallop) twice in each of next 3 ch-1 sps; repeat from ★ around; join with slip st to first sc, finish off.

ASSEMBLY

With White, using Placement Diagram as a guide, and working through **both** loops, whipstitch Squares together forming 9 vertical strips of 13 Squares each (*Fig. 19b, page 127*), beginning in center ch of first corner ch-3 and ending in center ch of next corner ch-3; then whipstitch strips together in same manner.

PLACEMENT DIAGRAM

G	P	G	P	G	P	G	P	G
Y	B	Y	B	Y	B	Y	B	Y
G	P	G	P	G	P	G	P	G
Y	B	Y	B	Y	B	Y	B	Y
G	P	G	P	G	P	G	P	G
Y	B	Y	B	Y	B	Y	B	Y
G	P	G	P	G	P	G	P	G
Y	B	Y	B	Y	B	Y	B	Y
G	P	G	P	G	P	G	P	G
Y	B	Y	B	Y	B	Y	B	Y
G	P	G	P	G	P	G	P	G
Y	B	Y	B	Y	B	Y	B	Y
G	P	G	P	G	P	G	P	G

KEY

G Green (Make 35)
Y Yellow (Make 30)
P Pink (Make 28)
B Blue (Make 24)

EDGING

Rnd 1: With **right** side facing, join White with sc in any corner ch-3 sp; ch 2, sc in same sp, ch 1, (sc in next sp, ch 1) across to next corner ch-3 sp, ★ (sc, ch 2, sc) in corner ch-3 sp, ch 1, (sc in next sp, ch 1) across to next corner ch-3 sp; repeat from ★ around; join with slip st to first sc: 304 ch-1 sps and 4 ch-2 sps.
Rnd 2: Slip st in first ch-2 sp, ch 6 (**counts as first dc plus ch 3**), dc in same sp, ch 1, (dc in next ch-1 sp, ch 1) across to next corner ch-2 sp, ★ (dc, ch 3, dc) in corner ch-2 sp, ch 1, (dc in next ch-1 sp, ch 1) across to next corner ch-2 sp; repeat from ★ around; join with slip st to first dc: 308 ch-1 sps and 4 ch-3 sps.
Rnd 3: Ch 4, (dc, ch 3, dc) in next ch-3 sp, ch 1, ★ (dc in next dc, ch 1) across to next corner ch-3 sp, (dc, ch 3, dc) in corner ch-3 sp, ch 1; repeat from ★ 2 times **more**, (dc in next dc, ch 1) across; join with slip st to first dc: 316 ch-1 sps and 4 ch-3 sps.
Rnd 4: Ch 4, dc in next dc, ch 1, (dc, ch 3, dc) in next ch-3 sp, ch 1, ★ (dc in next dc, ch 1) across to next corner ch-3 sp, (dc, ch 3, dc) in corner ch-3 sp, ch 1; repeat from ★ 2 times **more**, (dc in next dc, ch 1) across; join with slip st to first dc: 324 ch-1 sps and 4 ch-3 sps.

Rnds 5-8: Ch 4, ★ (dc in next dc, ch 1) across to next corner ch-3 sp, (dc, ch 3, dc) in corner ch-3 sp, ch 1; repeat from ★ 3 times **more**, (dc in next dc, ch 1) across; join with slip st to first dc: 356 ch-1 sps and 4 ch-3 sps.

Rnd 9: Ch 1, sc in same st, ch 1, ★ (sc in next dc, ch 1) across to next corner ch-3 sp, (sc, ch 1) twice in corner ch-3 sp; repeat from ★ 3 times **more**, (sc in next dc, ch 1) across; join with slip st to first sc.

Rnd 10: Slip st in first ch-1 sp, ch 1, (slip st in next ch-1 sp, ch 1) around; join with slip st to first slip st, finish off.

RUFFLES

With **right** side facing and working in sps on Rnd 2, join Blue with sc in any corner ch-3 sp (**between** dc); work Scallop, (sc, work Scallop) twice in each ch-1 sp across to next corner ch-3 sp, ★ sc in corner ch-3 sp (**between** dc), work Scallop, (sc, work Scallop) twice in each ch-1 sp across to next corner ch-3 sp; repeat from ★ around; join with slip st to first sc, finish off.
With Yellow, repeat on Rnd 4.
With Green, repeat on Rnd 6.
With Pink, repeat on Rnd 8.

Tribal Spirit

This Southwestern-style throw honors our Native American heritage. Long double crochets worked in the hues of the desert after a refreshing rain form the afghan's diamond and stripe panels. Long fringe adds a spirited finishing touch.

Finished Size: 40" x 53"

MATERIALS
Red Heart Worsted Weight Yarn
[3½ ounces (198 yards) per skein]:
Teal - 7 skeins
Green - 6 skeins
Black - 3 skeins
Bronze - 3 skeins
Brown - 2 skeins
Crochet hook, size I (5.50 mm) **or** size needed for gauge

GAUGE: In pattern, 12 sts and 12 rows = 3½"

STITCH GUIDE

> **LONG DOUBLE CROCHET** *(abbreviated LDC)*
> YO, insert hook from **top** to **bottom** in free loop of st indicated *(Fig. 10, page 126)*, YO and pull up a loop even with last st made, (YO and draw through 2 loops on hook) twice.

Note: Each row is worked across length of Afghan. When joining yarn and finishing off, leave an 8" end to be worked into fringe.

AFGHAN
With Black, ch 182 **loosely**.
Row 1 (Right side): Sc in back ridge of second ch from hook and each ch across *(Fig. 2b, page 125)*; finish off: 181 sc.
Note: Mark last row as **right** side.
Row 2: With **right** side facing, join Bronze with sc in **both** loops of first sc *(see Joining With Sc, page 126)*; sc in Back Loop Only of each sc across to last sc *(Fig. 14, page 126)*, sc in **both** loops of last sc; finish off.
Row 3: With **right** side facing, join Brown with sc in **both** loops of first sc; sc in Back Loop Only of each sc across to last sc, sc in **both** loops of last sc; finish off.
Row 4: With **right** side facing, join Bronze with sc in **both** loops of first sc; sc in Back Loop Only of next sc, work LDC in st one row **below** each of next 2 sc, ★ sc in Back Loop Only of next 3 sts, work LDC in st one row **below** each of next 2 sc; repeat from ★ across to last 2 sc, sc in Back Loop Only of next sc, sc in **both** loops of last sc; finish off: 109 sc and 72 LDC.

Row 5: With **right** side facing, join Brown with sc in **both** loops of first sc; sc in Back Loop Only of next 3 sts, work LDC in sc one row **below** next sc, sc in Back Loop Only of next sc, work LDC in sc one row **below** next sc, ★ sc in Back Loop Only of next 2 LDC, work LDC in sc one row **below** next sc, sc in Back Loop Only of next sc, work LDC in sc one row **below** next sc; repeat from ★ across to last 4 sts, sc in Back Loop Only of next 3 sts, sc in **both** loops of last sc; finish off: 111 sc and 70 LDC.
Row 6: With **right** side facing, join Bronze with sc in **both** loops of first sc; sc in Back Loop Only of next sc, work LDC in st one row **below** each of next 2 sc, ★ sc in Back Loop Only of next 3 sts, work LDC in st one row **below** each of next 2 sc; repeat from ★ across to last 2 sc, sc in Back Loop Only of next sc, sc in **both** loops of last sc; finish off: 109 sc and 72 LDC.
Row 7: With **right** side facing, join Black with sc in **both** loops of first sc; sc in Back Loop Only of each st across to last sc, sc in **both** loops of last sc; finish off: 181 sc.
Row 8: With **right** side facing, join Teal with sc in **both** loops of first sc; sc in Back Loop Only of each sc across to last sc, sc in **both** loops of last sc; finish off.
Row 9: With **right** side facing, join Green with sc in **both** loops of first sc; sc in Back Loop Only of each sc across to last sc, sc in **both** loops of last sc; finish off.
Row 10: With **right** side facing, join Teal with sc in **both** loops of first sc; sc in Back Loop Only of next st, work LDC in sc one row **below** next sc, (sc in Back Loop Only of next 2 sts, work LDC in sc one row **below** next sc) twice, ★ sc in Back Loop Only of next 3 sts, work LDC in sc one row **below** next sc, (sc in Back Loop Only of next 2 sts, work LDC in sc one row **below** next sc) twice; repeat from ★ across to last 2 sts, sc in Back Loop Only of next st, sc in **both** loops of last sc; finish off: 127 sc and 54 LDC.
Row 11: With **right** side facing, join Green with sc in **both** loops of first sc; work LDC in st one row **below** next sc, sc in Back Loop Only of next 2 sts, work LDC in sc one row **below** next sc, sc in Back Loop Only of next st, work LDC in sc one row **below** next sc, sc in Back Loop Only of next 2 sts, ★ work LDC in st one row **below** each of next 3 sc, sc in Back Loop Only of next 2 sts, work LDC in sc one row **below** next sc, sc in Back Loop Only of next st, work LDC in sc one row **below** next sc, sc in Back Loop Only of next 2 sts; repeat from ★ across to last 2 sc, work LDC in st one row **below** next sc, sc in **both** loops of last sc; finish off: 92 sc and 89 LDC.

Row 12: With **right** side facing, join Teal with sc in **both** loops of first sc; sc in Back Loop Only of next 2 sts, work LDC in sc one row **below** next sc, sc in Back Loop Only of next 3 sts, work LDC in sc one row **below** next sc, ★ sc in Back Loop Only of next 5 sts, work LDC in sc one row **below** next sc, sc in Back Loop Only of next 3 sts, work LDC in sc one row **below** next sc; repeat from ★ across to last 3 sts, sc in Back Loop Only of next 2 sts, sc in **both** loops of last sc; finish off: 145 sc and 36 LDC.

Row 13: With **right** side facing, join Green with sc in **both** loops of first sc; work LDC in st one row **below** each of next 2 sc, sc in Back Loop Only of next 2 sts, work LDC in sc one row **below** next sc, sc in Back Loop Only of next 2 sts, work LDC in st one row **below** each of next 2 sc, ★ sc in Back Loop Only of next st, work LDC in st one row **below** each of next 2 sc, sc in Back Loop Only of next 2 sts, work LDC in sc one row **below** next sc, sc in Back Loop Only of next 2 sts, work LDC in st one row **below** each of next 2 sc; repeat from ★ across to last sc, sc in **both** loops of last sc; finish off: 91 sc and 90 LDC.

Row 14: With **right** side facing, join Teal with sc in **both** loops of first sc; sc in Back Loop Only of next 3 sts, work LDC in sc one row **below** next sc, sc in Back Loop Only of next st, work LDC in sc one row **below** next sc, ★ (sc in Back Loop Only of next 3 sts, work LDC in st one row **below** next sc) twice, sc in Back Loop Only of next st, work LDC in sc one row **below** next sc; repeat from ★ across to last 4 sts, sc in Back Loop Only of next 3 sts, sc in **both** loops of last sc; finish off: 128 sc and 53 LDC.

Row 15: With **right** side facing, join Green with sc in **both** loops of first sc; sc in Back Loop Only of next st, work LDC in st one row **below** each of next 2 sc, ★ sc in Back Loop Only of next 3 sts, work LDC in st one row **below** each of next 2 sc; repeat from ★ across to last 2 sts, sc in Back Loop Only of next st, sc in **both** loops of last sc; finish off: 109 sc and 72 LDC.

Row 16: With **right** side facing, join Teal with sc in **both** loops of first sc; (work LDC in st one row **below** next sc, sc in Back Loop Only of next 3 sts) twice, ★ work LDC in st one row **below** each of next 3 sc, sc in Back Loop Only of next 3 sts, work LDC in sc one row **below** next sc, sc in Back Loop Only of next 3 sts; repeat from ★ across to last 2 sc, work LDC in st one row **below** next sc, sc in **both** loops of last sc; finish off: 110 sc and 71 LDC.

Row 17: With **right** side facing, join Green with sc in **both** loops of first sc; sc in Back Loop Only of next 2 sts, work LDC in st one row **below** each of next 2 sc, sc in Back Loop Only of next st, work LDC in st one row **below** each of next 2 sc, ★ sc in Back Loop Only of next 5 sts, work LDC in st one row **below** each of next 2 sc, sc in Back Loop Only of next st, work LDC in st one row **below** each of next 2 sc; repeat from ★ across to last 3 sts, sc in Back Loop Only of next 2 sts, sc in **both** loops of last sc; finish off: 109 sc and 72 LDC.

Continued on page 80.

Row 18: With **right** side facing, join Teal with sc in **both** loops of first sc; work LDC in st one row **below** each of next 2 sc, sc in Back Loop Only of next 5 sts, work LDC in st one row **below** each of next 2 sc, ★ sc in Back Loop Only of next sc, work LDC in st one row **below** each of next 2 sc, sc in Back Loop Only of next 5 sts, work LDC in st one row **below** each of next 2 sc; repeat from ★ across to last sc, sc in **both** loops of last sc; finish off.

Row 19: Repeat Row 17.
Row 20: Repeat Row 16.
Row 21: Repeat Row 15.
Row 22: Repeat Row 14.
Row 23: Repeat Row 13.
Row 24: Repeat Row 12.
Row 25: Repeat Row 11.
Row 26: Repeat Row 10.
Row 27: Repeat Row 7.
Rows 28-33: Repeat Rows 2-7.
Row 34: With Green, repeat Row 8.
Row 35: With Teal, repeat Row 9.
Row 36: With Green, repeat Row 10.
Row 37: With Teal, repeat Row 11.
Row 38: With Green, repeat Row 12.

Row 39: With Teal, repeat Row 13.
Row 40: With Green, repeat Row 14.
Row 41: With Teal, repeat Row 15.
Row 42: With Green, repeat Row 16.
Row 43: With Teal, repeat Row 17.
Row 44: With Green, repeat Row 18.
Row 45: With Teal, repeat Row 17.
Row 46: With Green, repeat Row 16.
Row 47: With Teal, repeat Row 15.
Row 48: With Green, repeat Row 14.
Row 49: With Teal, repeat Row 13.
Row 50: With Green, repeat Row 12.
Row 51: With Teal, repeat Row 11.
Row 52: With Green, repeat Row 10.
Row 53: Repeat Row 7.
Rows 54-137: Repeat Rows 2-53 once, then repeat Rows 2-33 once **more**.

Holding six 16" strands of yarn together for each fringe, add additional fringe across short edges of Afghan (*Figs. 20a & b, page 127*).

Kaleidoscope

A kaleidoscope of color weaves its way through this decisively bold afghan. The striking contrast of the multicolored yarn against a black background is especially effective around the edges of each square in the wrap, where you catch tiny glimpses of color.

Finished Size: 49" x 65 "

MATERIALS
Red Heart Worsted Weight Yarn
[8 ounces (452 yards) per skein (Black) or 6 ounces (348 yards) per skein (Variegated)]:
Black - 5 skeins
Variegated - 4 skeins
Crochet hook, size G (4.00 mm) **or** size needed for gauge
Yarn needle

GAUGE: Each Square = 8"

STITCH GUIDE

FRONT POST TREBLE CROCHET
(abbreviated FPtr)
YO twice, insert hook from **front** to **back** around post of dc indicated (*Fig. 13, page 126*), YO and pull up a loop, (YO and draw through 2 loops on hook) 3 times.

SQUARE (Make 48)
With Variegated, ch 4; join with slip st to form a ring.
Rnd 1 (Right side): Ch 6 **(counts as first dc plus ch 3, now and throughout)**, (3 dc in ring, ch 3) 3 times, 2 dc in ring; join with slip st to first dc: 12 dc and 4 ch-3 sps.
Note: Mark last round as **right** side.
Rnds 2 and 3: Slip st in first ch-3 sp, ch 6, 2 dc in same sp, dc in each dc across to next ch-3 sp, ★ (2 dc, ch 3, 2 dc) in ch-3 sp, dc in each st across to next ch-3 sp; repeat from ★ around, dc in same sp as first dc; join with slip st to first dc: 44 dc.
Rnd 4: Slip st in first ch-3 sp, ch 4 **(counts as first hdc plus ch 2, now and throughout)**, 2 hdc in same sp, ch 1, skip next dc, (hdc in next dc, ch 1, skip next dc) across to next ch-3 sp, ★ (2 hdc, ch 2, 2 hdc) in ch-3 sp, ch 1, skip next dc, (hdc in next dc, ch 1, skip next st) across to next ch-3 sp; repeat from ★ around, hdc in same sp as first hdc; join with slip st to first hdc, finish off: 36 hdc and 28 sps.
Rnd 5: With **right** side facing, join Black with slip st in any ch-2 sp; ch 4, hdc in same sp and in next 2 hdc, ★ † work FPtr around dc one rnd **below** next ch-1, (hdc in next hdc, work FPtr around dc one rnd **below** next ch-1) 5 times, hdc in next 2 hdc †, (hdc, ch 2, hdc) in next ch-2 sp, hdc in next 2 hdc; repeat from ★ 2 times **more**, then repeat from † to † once; join with slip st to first hdc: 68 sts and 4 ch-2 sps.

Rnd 6: Slip st in first ch-2 sp, ch 4, hdc in same sp, working in Back Loops Only **(Fig. 14, page 126)**, hdc in each st across to next ch-2 sp, ★ (hdc, ch 2, hdc) in ch-2 sp, hdc in each st across to next ch-2 sp; repeat from ★ around; join with slip st to first hdc: 76 hdc.

Rnd 7: Ch 2 **(counts as first hdc, now and throughout)**, **turn**; working in both loops, ★ hdc in each hdc across to next ch-2 sp, (2 hdc, ch 2, 2 hdc) in ch-2 sp; repeat from ★ around; join with slip st to first hdc, finish off: 92 hdc.

Rnd 8: With **right** side facing, join Variegated with sc in any ch-2 sp **(see Joining With Sc, page 126)**; ch 2, sc in same sp, ch 1, skip next hdc, (sc in next hdc, ch 1, skip next hdc) across to next ch-2 sp, ★ (sc, ch 2, sc) in ch-2 sp, ch 1, skip next hdc, (sc in next hdc, ch 1, skip next hdc) across to next ch-2 sp; repeat from ★ around; join with slip st to first sc, finish off: 52 sc and 52 sps.

Rnd 9: With **right** side facing, join Black with slip st in any corner ch-2 sp; ch 2, (dc, 2 hdc) in same sp, 2 hdc in each ch-1 sp across to next corner ch-2 sp, ★ (2 hdc, dc, 2 hdc) in corner ch-2 sp, 2 hdc in each ch-1 sp across to next corner ch-2 sp; repeat from ★ around, hdc in same sp as first hdc; join with slip st to first hdc, finish off: 116 sts.

ASSEMBLY

With Black and working through **inside** loops, whipstitch Squares together forming 6 vertical strips of 8 Squares each **(Fig. 19a, page 127)**, beginning in dc at first corner and ending in dc at next corner; then whipstitch strips together in same manner.

EDGING

Rnd 1: With **right** side facing, join Black with sc in any st; sc evenly around entire Afghan working 3 sc in each corner dc; join with slip st to first sc.

Rnd 2: Ch 1, sc in same st and in each sc around working 3 sc in center sc of each corner 3-sc group; join with slip st to first sc, finish off.

Up, Up, and Away!

Balloons always inspire high spirits, and the colorful hot-air vessels on this uplifting afghan are no exception! The cover-up's sky-blue softness and lively motifs awaken the imagination and add a playful touch to junior's room.

Finished Size: 40" x 49"

MATERIALS

Red Heart Worsted Weight Yarn
[3 ounces (170 yards) per skein (Green) or
3½ ounces (198 yards) per skein (all other colors)]:
Blue - 8 skeins
Light Blue - 2 skeins
White - 2 skeins
Dark Blue - 1 skein
Brown - 1 skein
Yellow - 1 skein
Orange - 1 skein
Red - 1 skein
Green - 1 skein
Crochet hook, size H (5.00 mm) **or** size needed for gauge

GAUGE: Each Motif = 7" x 8¾ "

STITCH GUIDE

DC CLUSTER
★ YO, insert hook in sc indicated, YO and pull up a loop, YO and draw through 2 loops on hook; repeat from ★ once **more**, YO and draw through all 3 loops on hook.

TR CLUSTER (uses next 3 sc)
★ YO twice, insert hook in **next** sc, YO and pull up a loop, (YO and draw through 2 loops on hook) twice; repeat from ★ 2 times **more**, YO and draw through all 4 loops on hook.

LONG DOUBLE CROCHET (*abbreviated LDC*)
YO, insert hook in sp indicated, YO and pull up a loop even with last st made, (YO and draw through 2 loops on hook) twice (*Fig. 10, page 126*).

PUFF ST
YO, insert hook in st indicated, YO and pull up a loop, YO, insert hook in same st, YO and pull up a loop, YO and draw through all 5 loops on hook.

BEGINNING DECREASE
Pull up a loop in first 2 sts, YO and draw through all 3 loops on hook (**counts as one sc**).

SC DECREASE
Pull up a loop in next 2 sts, YO and draw through all 3 loops on hook (**counts as one sc**).

HDC DECREASE (uses next 2 sts)
★ YO, insert hook in **next** st, YO and pull up a loop; repeat from ★ once **more**, YO and draw through all 5 loops on hook (**counts as one hdc**).

DC DECREASE (uses next 2 sc)
★ YO, insert hook in **next** sc, YO and pull up a loop, YO and draw through 2 loops on hook; repeat from ★ once **more**, YO and draw through all 3 loops on hook (**counts as one dc**).

TR DECREASE (uses next 2 sc)
★ YO twice, insert hook in **next** sc, YO and pull up a loop, (YO and draw through 2 loops on hook) twice; repeat from ★ once **more**, YO and draw through all 3 loops on hook.

DOUBLE DECREASE
Pull up a loop in next 3 sts, YO and draw through all 4 loops on hook (**counts as one sc**).

BALLOON MOTIF (Make 13)

Referring to table for color sequence on Front and Back of each Balloon, make 3 Balloons **each** of A, B, and C, and make 2 **each** of D and E, working one row of each color listed from top to bottom.

Hint: Instead of weaving in yarn ends, tuck ends between Front and Back of Balloon, before working Joining Rnd.

A	B	C	D	E
Red	Orange	Yellow	Green	Dk Blue
Yellow	Green	Dk Blue	Orange	Red
Green	Yellow	Red	Dk Blue	Orange
Dk Blue	Red	Orange	Yellow	Green
Orange	Dk Blue	Green	Red	Yellow
Green	Yellow	Red	Dk Blue	Orange
Yellow	Green	Dk Blue	Orange	Red
Red	Orange	Yellow	Green	Dk Blue

FRONT

With first color, ch 4; join with slip st to form a ring.
Row 1 (Right side): Ch 4 (**counts as first tr, now and throughout**), 6 tr in ring; finish off: 7 tr.
Note: Mark last row as **right** side and bottom edge.
Row 2: With **wrong** side facing, join next color with slip st in first tr; ch 3 (**counts as first dc, now and throughout**), 2 dc in each of next 5 tr, dc in last tr; finish off: 12 dc.
Row 3: With **right** side facing, join next color with slip st in first dc; ch 2 (**counts as first hdc, now and throughout**), work Puff St in next 3 dc, work 2 Puff Sts in next dc, work Puff St in next 2 dc, work 2 Puff Sts in next dc, work

Puff St in next 3 dc, hdc in last dc; finish off: 14 sts.

Row 4: With **wrong** side facing, join next color with slip st in first hdc; ch 3, ★ (dc, ch 1, dc) in next Puff St, skip next Puff St; repeat from ★ 5 times **more**, dc in last hdc; finish off: 14 dc and 6 ch-1 sps.

Row 5: With **right** side facing, join next color with slip st in first dc; ch 3, dc in next ch-1 sp, ★ skip next dc, dc in sp **before** next dc, dc in next ch-1 sp; repeat from ★ 4 times **more**, skip next dc, dc in last dc; finish off: 13 dc.

Row 6: With **wrong** side facing, join next color with sc in first dc *(see Joining With Sc, page 126)*; sc in next dc and in each dc across; finish off.

Row 7: With **right** side facing, join next color with slip st in first sc; ch 3, dc decrease twice, work dc Cluster in next 3 sc, dc decrease twice, dc in last sc; finish off: 9 sts.

Row 8: With **wrong** side facing, join next color with slip st in first dc; ch 2, hdc decrease, work Puff St in next 3 Clusters, hdc decrease, hdc in last dc; finish off: 7 sts.

Continued on page 84.

BACK

With first color, ch 4; join with slip st to form a ring.
Row 1 (Right side): Ch 4, 6 tr in ring; finish off: 7 tr.
Note: Mark last row as **right** side and bottom edge.
Row 2: With **wrong** side facing, join next color with slip st in first tr; ch 3, (2 dc in each of next 2 tr, dc in next tr) twice; finish off: 11 dc.
Row 3: With **right** side facing, join next color with slip st in first dc; ch 2, work Puff St in next 3 dc, work 2 Puff Sts in each of next 2 dc, work Puff St in next 4 dc, hdc in last dc; finish off: 13 sts.
Row 4: With **wrong** side facing, join next color with slip st in first hdc; ch 3, skip next Puff St, ★ (dc, ch 1, dc) in next Puff St, skip next Puff St; repeat from ★ 4 times **more**, dc in last hdc; finish off: 12 dc and 5 ch-1 sps.
Row 5: With **right** side facing, join next color with slip st in first dc; ch 3, dc in next ch-1 sp, ★ skip next dc, dc in sp **before** next dc, dc in next ch-1 sp; repeat from ★ 3 times **more**, skip next dc, dc in last dc; finish off: 11 dc.
Row 6: With **wrong** side facing, join next color with sc in first dc; sc in next dc and in each dc across; finish off.
Row 7: With **right** side facing, join next color with slip st in first sc; ch 3, dc in next sc, dc decrease, work dc Cluster in next 3 sc, dc decrease twice; finish off: 8 sts.
Row 8: With **wrong** side facing, join next color with slip st in first dc; ch 2, hdc in next dc, work Puff St in next 3 Clusters, hdc decrease, hdc in last dc; do **not** finish off: 7 sts.
Joining Rnd: Ch 1, do **not** turn; with **wrong** sides of Front and Back together, Front facing you and working through **both** thicknesses and in end of rows, 2 sc in each of first 2 rows, sc in next row, 3 sc in each of next 2 rows, 2 sc in next row, sc in next row, place marker around sc just made for Border placement, 2 sc in same row, 4 sc in last row, 3 sc in beginning ring, 4 sc in first row, 3 sc in next row, 2 sc in next row, 3 sc in each of next 2 rows, sc in next row, 2 sc in each of last 2 rows; working across last row, skip first hdc, sc in next 6 sts; join with slip st to first sc, finish off: 49 sc.

BORDER

Foundation Row: With **right** side of Balloon Front facing, join Blue with slip st in marked sc; ch 5 (**counts as first dtr**), tr in same st, 2 dc in next sc, dc in next sc, hdc in next sc, sc decrease twice, sc in next sc, sc decrease twice, hdc in next sc, dc in next sc, 2 dc in next sc, (tr, dtr) in next sc, leave remaining 32 sc unworked: 17 sts.
Row 1: Ch 3, turn; dc in next tr and in each st across.
Row 2: Ch 3, turn; dc in next 4 dc changing to Brown in last dc made, work LDC in ring at base of Balloon, skip next dc, dc in next 5 dc, work LDC in ring at base of Balloon changing to Blue, skip next dc, dc in last 5 dc.
Row 3: Ch 3, turn; dc in next 4 dc changing to Brown in last dc made, dc in next 7 sts changing to Blue in last dc made; cut Brown, dc in last 5 dc.
Row 4: Ch 3, turn; dc in next 4 dc, dc in Back Loop Only of next 7 dc (***Fig. 14, page 126***), dc in **both** loops of last 5 dc; do **not** finish off.

EDGING

Rnd 1: Ch 1, do **not** turn; working in end of rows, work 2 sc in each of first 4 rows, (2 sc, hdc) in last row; tr in same st as last dtr on Foundation Row, working in remaining sc on Balloon, tr in next 2 sc, dc in next 4 sc, tr in next 3 sc, (2 tr, dtr) in next sc, (dtr, tr, dc) in next sc, dc in next sc, hdc in next sc, sc in next 6 sc, hdc in next sc, dc in next sc, (dc, tr, dtr) in next sc, (dtr, 2 tr) in next sc, tr in next 3 sc, dc in next 4 sc, tr in next 2 sc, tr in same sc as joining slip st on Foundation Row; working in end of rows, (hdc, 2 sc) in first row, 2 sc in each of last 4 rows; working across Row 4 of Border, 3 sc in first dc, sc in each dc across to last dc, 3 sc in last dc; join with slip st to first sc: 85 sts.
Rnd 2: Ch 1, sc in same st and in next 22 sts, 2 hdc in next dtr, sc in next 8 sts, 2 sc in next sc, sc in next 7 sts, 2 hdc in next dtr, sc in next 24 sts, 2 sc in next sc, sc in next 17 sc, 2 sc in next sc, sc in last sc; join with slip st to first sc: 90 sts.
Rnd 3: Ch 4, dc in same st, skip next 2 sc, [(dc, ch 1, dc) in next sc, skip next 2 sts] 7 times, † dc in next st, (ch 1, dc in same st) 3 times, skip next 2 sc, [(dc, ch 1, dc) in next sc, skip next 2 sc] 5 times, dc in next st, (ch 1, dc in same st) 3 times, skip next 2 sts †, [(dc, ch 1, dc) in next sc, skip next 2 sc] 8 times, repeat from † to † once; join with slip st to third ch of beginning ch-4, finish off: 38 ch-1 sps.

SKY MOTIF (Make 12)

With Blue, ch 20 **loosely**.
Row 1: Sc in second ch from hook and in each ch across: 19 sc
Row 2 (Right side): Ch 1, turn; sc in first sc, ★ hdc in next sc, dc in next sc, 3 tr in next sc, dc in next sc, hdc in next sc, sc in next sc; repeat from ★ across: 25 sts.
Note: Mark last row as **right** side and bottom edge.
Row 3: Ch 1, turn; work beginning decrease, sc in next 2 sts, 3 sc in next tr, sc in next 2 sts, ★ double decrease, sc in next 2 sts, 3 sc in next tr, sc in next 2 sts; repeat from ★ once **more**, sc decrease; finish off: 25 sc.
Row 4: With **right** side facing, join White with slip st in first sc; ch 1, pull up a loop in same st and in next sc, YO and draw through all 3 loops on hook (**counts as first sc**), sc in next 2 sts, 3 sc in next sc, sc in next 2 sts, ★ double decrease, sc in next 2 sts, 3 sc in next sc, sc in next 2 sc; repeat from ★ once **more**, sc decrease.
Row 5: Ch 3, turn; tr in next sc (**ch 3 and tr counts as first tr decrease**), dc in next sc, hdc in next sc, sc in next sc, hdc in next sc, dc in next sc, ★ work tr Cluster, dc in next sc, hdc in next sc, sc in next sc, hdc in next sc, dc in next sc; repeat from ★ once **more**, tr decrease; finish off: 19 sts.
Row 6: With **right** side facing, join Light Blue with sc in first st; sc in each st across.
Row 7: Ch 1, turn; sc in each sc across; finish off.

Row 8: With **right** side facing, join Blue with sc in first sc; ★ hdc in next sc, dc in next sc, 3 tr in next sc, dc in next sc, hdc in next sc, sc in next sc; repeat from ★ across: 25 sts.

Rows 9-17: Repeat Rows 3-8 once, then repeat Rows 3-5 once **more**: 19 sts.

Row 18: With **right** side facing, join Blue with sc in first st; sc in next st and in each st across.

Row 19: Ch 1, turn; sc in each sc across; do **not** finish off.

EDGING

Rnd 1: Ch 1, turn; 3 sc in first sc, sc in each sc across to last sc, 3 sc in last sc; work 26 sc evenly spaced across end of rows; working in free loops of beginning ch, 3 sc in ch at base of first sc, sc in each ch across to last ch, 3 sc in last ch; work 26 sc evenly spaced across end of rows; join with slip st to first sc: 98 sc.

Rnd 2: Ch 1, do **not** turn; sc in same st, 3 sc in next sc, ★ sc in each sc across to center sc of next corner 3-sc group, 3 sc in center sc; repeat from ★ 2 times **more**, sc in each sc across; join with slip st to first sc, finish off: 106 sc.

ASSEMBLY

Using Placement Diagram as a guide and following instructions for Motif and Strip Joining, join Motifs forming 5 vertical strips of 5 Motifs each

PLACEMENT DIAGRAM

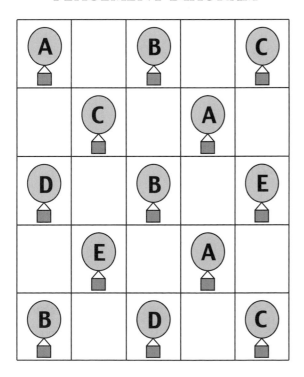

MOTIF JOINING

Holding Motifs with **wrong** sides together, having Balloon Motif facing toward you, and matching top of first Motif to bottom of second Motif, join Blue with slip st in first corner ch-1 sp on **Balloon Motif**; ch 2, sc in first corner sc on **Sky Motif**, ch 2, skip next dc on **Balloon Motif**, sc in next ch-1 sp, ch 2, skip next sc on **Sky Motif**, sc in next sc, ch 2, ★ skip next 2 dc on **Balloon Motif**, sc in next ch-1 sp, ch 2, skip next 2 sc on **Sky Motif**, sc in next sc, ch 2; repeat from ★ 5 times **more**, skip next dc on **Balloon Motif**, sc in last corner ch-1 sp, ch 2, skip next sc on **Sky Motif**, slip st in corner sc; finish off.
Repeat for remaining Motifs.

STRIP JOINING

Place 2 strips with **wrong** sides together; with Balloon Motif to right and facing toward you, join Blue with slip st in first corner ch-1 sp on **Balloon Motif**; ch 2, sc in first corner sc on **Sky Motif**, ch 2, skip next dc on **Balloon Motif**, sc in next ch-1 sp, ch 2, skip next sc on **Sky Motif**, sc in next sc, ★ † ch 2, [skip next 2 dc on **Balloon Motif**, sc in next ch-1 sp, ch 2, skip next 2 sc on **Sky Motif**, sc in next sc, ch 2] 9 times, skip next dc on **Balloon Motif** †, sc in next ch-2 sp of joining, ch 2, sc in ch-2 sp of opposite joining, ch 2, skip first sc from corner sc of next **Sky Motif**, sc in next sc, ch 2, skip first dc on next **Balloon Motif**, sc in next ch-1 sp, ch 2, [skip next 2 sc on **Sky Motif**, sc in next sc, ch 2, skip next 2 dc on **Balloon Motif**, sc in next ch-1 sp, ch 2] 9 times, skip next sc on **Sky Motif**, sc in next ch-2 sp of joining, ch 2, sc in ch-2 sp of opposite joining, ch 2, skip first dc on next **Balloon Motif**, sc in next ch-1 sp, ch 2, skip first sc from corner sc on next **Sky Motif**, sc in next sc; repeat from ★ once **more**, then repeat from † to † once, sc in last corner ch-1 sp, ch 2, skip next sc on **Sky Motif**, slip st in last corner sc; finish off.
Repeat for remaining strips.

TRIM

Rnd 1: With **right** side facing, join Blue with sc in top right corner ch-1 sp; sc in same sp, † sc in each dc and in each ch-1 sp across to next joining, 5 sc in joining, ♥ sc in each sc across to next joining, 4 sc in joining, sc in each dc and in each ch-1 sp across to next joining, 4 sc in joining ♥, sc in each sc across to next joining, 5 sc in joining, sc in each dc and in each ch-1 sp across to next corner ch-1 sp, 3 sc in corner ch-1 sp, sc in each dc and in each ch-1 sp across to next joining, 3 sc in joining, repeat from ♥ to ♥ once, sc in each sc across to next joining, 4 sc in joining, sc in each dc and in each ch-1 sp across to next corner ch-1 sp †, 3 sc in corner ch-1 sp, repeat from † to † once, sc in same sp as first sc; join with slip st to first sc: 588 sc.

Rnd 2: Ch 4, 2 tr in same st, dc in next sc, hdc in next sc, sc in next sc, hdc in next sc, dc in next sc, ★ 3 tr in next sc, dc in next sc, hdc in next sc, sc in next sc, hdc in next sc, dc in next sc; repeat from ★ around; join with slip st to first tr, finish off.

American Homecoming

This afghan honors the American tradition of displaying yellow ribbons until loved ones in the military return home safe and sound. To make it, you simply whipstitch granny squares together following our color diagram and add an effortless edging.

Finished Size: 40" x 58"

MATERIALS
Red Heart Worsted Weight Yarn
[3½ ounces (198 yards) per skein (Gold) or 3 ounces (170 yards) per skein (all other colors)]:
Red - 4 skeins
White - 4 skeins
Blue - 3 skeins
Gold - 2 skeins
Crochet hook, size I (5.50 mm) **or** size needed for gauge
Yarn needle

GAUGE: Each Square = 3"

SQUARE A (Make 231)
Make 21 with Gold, 46 with Blue, 77 with White, and 87 with Red.
With color indicated, ch 4; join with slip st to form a ring.
Rnd 1 (Right side): Ch 3 **(counts as first dc, now and throughout)**, 2 dc in ring, ch 2, (3 dc in ring, ch 2) 3 times; join with slip st to first dc: 12 dc and 4 ch-2 sps.
Note: Mark last round as **right** side.
Rnd 2: Slip st in next 2 dc and in next ch-2 sp, ch 3, (2 dc, ch 2, 3 dc) in same sp, ch 1, ★ (3 dc, ch 2, 3 dc) in next ch-2 sp, ch 1; repeat from ★ around; join with slip st to first dc, finish off: 24 dc and 8 sps.

SQUARE B (Make 16)
Make 2 with Gold and White, and 14 with Gold and Blue.
With first color indicated, ch 4; join with slip st to form a ring.
Rnd 1 (Right side): Ch 5 **(counts as first dc plus ch 2)**, 3 dc in ring, cut first color; with second color indicated, YO and draw through, ch 1, 3 dc in ring, ch 2, 3 dc in ring, cut second color; with first color, YO and draw through, ch 1, 2 dc in ring; join with slip st to first dc: 12 dc and 4 ch-2 sps.
Note: Mark last round as **right** side.
Rnd 2: Slip st in first ch-2 sp, ch 3, (2 dc, ch 2, 3 dc) in same sp, ch 1, 3 dc in next ch-2 sp, cut first color; with second color, YO and draw through, ch 1, 3 dc in same sp, ch 1, (3 dc, ch 2, 3 dc) in next ch-2 sp, ch 1, 3 dc in next ch-2 sp, cut second color; with first color, YO and draw through, ch 1, 3 dc in same sp, ch 1; join with slip st to first dc, finish off: 24 dc and 8 sps.

ASSEMBLY
With matching colors, using Placement Diagram as a guide, and working through **inside** loops only, whipstitch Squares together forming 13 horizontal strips of 19 Squares each *(Fig. 19a, page 127)*, beginning in second ch of first corner ch-2 and ending in first ch of next corner ch-2; then whipstitch strips together in same manner.

PLACEMENT DIAGRAM

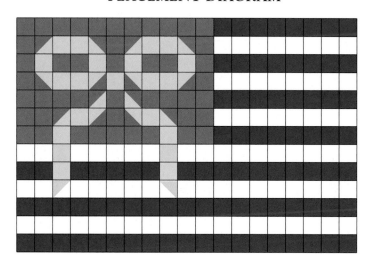

EDGING
Rnd 1: With **right** side facing, join Gold with sc in any corner ch-2 sp *(see Joining With Sc, page 126)*; ch 2, sc in same sp, sc in each dc and in each sp and each joining across to next corner ch-2 sp, ★ (sc, ch 2, sc) in corner ch-2 sp, sc in each dc and in each sp and each joining across to next corner ch-2 sp; repeat from ★ around; join with slip st to first sc: 636 sc and 4 ch-2 sps.
Rnd 2: Slip st in first ch-2 sp, ch 1, (sc, ch 3) twice in same sp, skip next sc, (sc in next sc, ch 3, skip next sc) across to next corner ch-2 sp, ★ (sc, ch 3) twice in corner ch-2 sp, skip next sc, (sc in next sc, ch 3, skip next sc) across to next corner ch-2 sp; repeat from ★ around; join with slip st to first sc, finish off.

Noah's Ark

This prize-winning afghan captured our hearts! The Bible-story shapes are crocheted separately and attached to the finished panels.

Finished Size: 45" x 61"

MATERIALS
Red Heart Worsted Weight Yarn
[8 ounces (452 yards) per skein]:
Green - 3 skeins
Dark Blue - 2 skeins
Blue - 2 skeins
Tan, Brown, White, and Rose - 1 skein **each**
[3½ ounces (198 yards) per skein]:
Gold, Purple, and Grey - 1 skein **each**
Crochet hook, size H (5.00 mm) **or** size needed for gauge
Yarn needle
Sewing needle and thread
¾" Buttons for Giraffes' spots - 12
1" Buttons for Stars - 4
6 mm Round black beads for eyes - 16
Safety pins

GAUGE: On Panels, in pattern,
3 Shells and 8 rows = 4";
(sc, dc) 6 times and 12 rows = 4"
On all other pieces, 7 sc and 7 rows = 2"

STITCH GUIDE

SHELL
Dc in st indicated, (ch 1, dc in same st) twice.

CLUSTER
★ YO, insert hook in st indicated, YO and pull up a loop, YO and draw through 2 loops on hook; repeat from ★ 2 times **more**, YO and draw through all 4 loops on hook.

BEGINNING DECREASE
Pull up a loop in first 2 sc, YO and draw through all 3 loops on hook (**counts as one sc**).

DECREASE
Pull up a loop in next 2 sc, YO and draw through all 3 loops on hook (**counts as one sc**).

STRAIGHT STITCH
Straight Stitch is just what the name implies, a single, straight stitch. Bring needle up at 1 and go down at 2 (**Fig. 1**). Continue in same manner.

Fig. 1

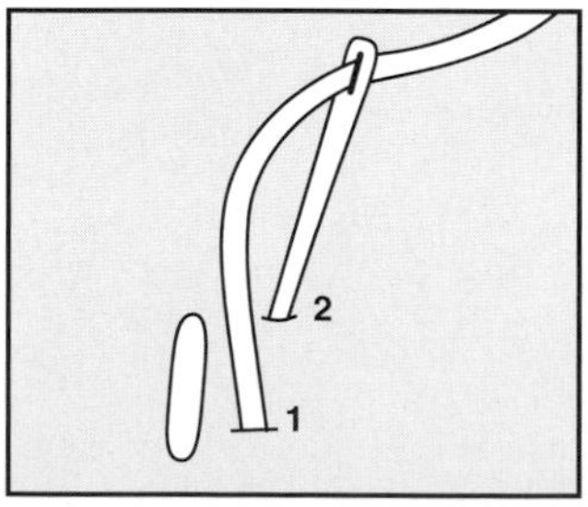

FRENCH KNOT
Bring needle up at 1. Wrap yarn desired number of times around needle and go down at 2, holding end of yarn with non-stitching fingers (**Fig. 2**). Tighten knot; then pull needle through, holding yarn until it must be released.

Fig. 2
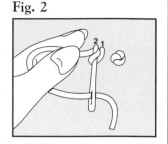

AFGHAN BODY
CENTER PANEL
With Dark Blue, ch 78 **loosely**.

Row 1: Sc in second ch from hook, ★ skip next ch, work Shell in next ch, skip next ch, sc in next ch; repeat from ★ across: 19 Shells and 20 sc.

Row 2 (Right side): Ch 4 (**counts as first dc plus ch 1**), turn; working in Back Loops Only (**Fig. 14, page 126**), dc in same st, skip next dc, sc in next dc, ★ skip next dc, work Shell in next sc, skip next dc, sc in next dc; repeat from ★ across to last 3 sts, skip next ch and next dc, (dc, ch 1, dc) in last sc: 18 Shells and 19 sc.

Note: Mark last row as **right** side.

Row 3: Ch 1, turn; working in both loops, sc in first dc, ★ skip next dc, work Shell in next sc, skip next dc, sc in next dc; repeat from ★ across: 19 Shells and 20 sc.

Rows 4-34: Repeat Rows 2 and 3, 15 times; then repeat Row 2 once **more**.

Row 35: Ch 1, turn; working in both loops, sc in first dc, ★ skip next dc, work Shell in next sc, skip next dc, sc in next dc; repeat from ★ across changing to Blue in last sc (**Fig. 16, page 127**).

Row 36: Ch 1, turn; working in Back Loops Only, sc in first sc, place marker around sc just made for Edging placement, dc in same st, ★ sc in next dc, skip next ch, dc in next dc, skip next ch, sc in next dc, dc in next sc; repeat from ★ across: 78 sts.

Rows 37-110: Ch 1, turn; working in both loops, sc in first dc, dc in next sc, (sc in next dc, dc in next sc) across. Finish off.

EDGING
Rnd 1: With **right** side facing and working in end of rows, join Blue with sc in marked row (first Blue row) (**see Joining With Sc, page 126**); sc in each row across; working across Row 110, 3 sc in first sc, sc in each st across to last dc, 3 sc in last dc; sc in end of first 75 rows changing to Dark Blue in last sc; work 50 sc evenly spaced across end of rows; working in free loops of beginning ch (**Fig. 15b, page 127**), 3 sc in first ch (base of first sc), work 76 sc evenly spaced across to last ch, 3 sc in last ch; work 50 sc evenly spaced across end of rows; join with slip st to first sc, finish off: 414 sc.

Rnd 2: With **right** side facing, join Tan with sc in any sc; sc in next sc and in each sc around working 3 sc in center sc of each corner 3-sc group; join with slip st to first sc, finish off: 422 sc.

SIDE PANEL (Make 2)
With Green, ch 23 **loosely**.

Row 1 (Right side): Sc in second ch from hook, dc in next ch, (sc in next ch, dc in next ch) across: 22 sts.

Note: Mark last row as **right** side.

Rows 2-125: Ch 1, turn; sc in first dc, dc in next sc, (sc in next dc, dc in next sc) across; do **not** finish off.

EDGING
Rnd 1: Ch 1, do **not** turn; sc in end of each row across; working in free loops of beginning ch, 3 sc in first ch, sc in next 20 chs, 3 sc in next ch; sc in end of each row across; working across Row 125, 3 sc in first sc, sc in each st across to last dc, 3 sc in last dc; join with slip st to first sc, finish off: 302 sc.

Rnd 2: With **right** side facing, join Tan with sc in any sc; sc in each sc around working 3 sc in center sc of each corner 3-sc group; join with slip st to first sc, finish off: 310 sc.

Continued on page 90.

TOP/BOTTOM PANEL (Make 2)

With Green, ch 79 **loosely**.

Row 1 (Right side): Sc in second ch from hook, dc in next ch, (sc in next ch, dc in next ch) across: 78 sts.

Note: Mark last row as **right** side.

Rows 2-20: Ch 1, turn; sc in first dc, dc in next sc, (sc in next dc, dc in next sc) across; do **not** finish off.

EDGING

Rnd 1: Ch 1, turn; 3 sc in first dc, sc in each st across to last sc, 3 sc in last sc; sc in end of each row across; working in free loops of beginning ch, 3 sc in first ch, sc in next 76 chs, 3 sc in next ch; sc in end of each row across; join with slip st to first sc, finish off: 204 sc.

Rnd 2: With **right** side facing, join Tan with sc in any sc; sc in each sc around working 3 sc in center sc of each corner 3-sc group; join with slip st to first sc, finish off: 212 sc.

CORNER PANEL (Make 4)

Make 2 **each** of Dark Blue and Blue.

Ch 23 **loosely**.

Row 1 (Right side): Sc in second ch from hook, dc in next ch, (sc in next ch, dc in next ch) across: 22 sts.

Note: Mark last row as **right** side.

Rows 2-20: Ch 1, turn; sc in first dc, dc in next sc, (sc in next dc, dc in next sc) across; do **not** finish off.

EDGING

Rnd 1: Ch 1, turn; 3 sc in first dc, sc in each st across to last sc, 3 sc in last sc; sc in end of each row across; working in free loops of beginning ch, 3 sc in first ch, sc in next 20 chs, 3 sc in next ch; sc in end of each row across; join with slip st to first sc, finish off: 92 sc.

Rnd 2: With **right** side facing, join Tan with sc in any sc; sc in each sc around working 3 sc in center sc of each corner 3-sc group; join with slip st to first sc, finish off: 100 sc.

ASSEMBLY

Using photo as a guide for placement, Panels should be joined in the following order: Side Panels to Center Panel, Dark Blue Corner Panels to Top Panel, Blue Corner Panels to Bottom Panel, Top Panel section to Center Panel section, and Bottom Panel section to Center Panel section. To join first two Panels, place Panels with **wrong** sides together. Working through **inside** loop of each stitch on **both** pieces, join Tan with slip st in center sc of first corner 3-sc group; (ch 1, slip st in next sc) across working last slip st in center sc of next corner 3-sc group; finish off. Join remaining Panels in same manner.

BORDER

With **right** side facing and working in Back Loops Only, join Tan with slip st in center sc of any corner 3-sc group; ch 1, (slip st in same st, ch 1) twice, (slip st in next sc, ch 1) around working (slip st, ch 1) 3 times in center sc of each corner 3-sc group; join with slip st to first slip st, finish off.

ADDITIONAL PIECES
ARK
BOTTOM

With Brown, ch 41 **loosely**.

Row 1 (Right side): Sc in back ridge of second ch from hook and each ch across (*Fig. 2b, page 125*): 40 sc.

Note: Mark last row as **right** side.

Rows 2-8: Ch 1, turn; 2 sc in first sc, sc in each sc across to last sc, 2 sc in last sc: 54 sc.

Row 9: Ch 1, turn; sc in each sc across.

Row 10 (Increase row): Ch 1, turn; 2 sc in first sc, sc in each sc across to last sc, 2 sc in last sc: 56 sc.

Rows 11-20: Repeat Rows 9 and 10, 5 times: 66 sc.

Rows 21-37: Ch 1, turn; sc in each sc across. Finish off.

Waves: With **right** side facing and working in free loops of beginning ch, join Dark Blue with slip st in first ch; ch 1, (sc, ch 3) twice in same st and in next 38 chs, [(sc, ch 3) twice, slip st] in next ch; finish off.

ROOF

With Brown, ch 51 **loosely**.

Row 1: Sc in back ridge of second ch from hook and each ch across: 50 sc.

Row 2 (Right side): Ch 1, turn; sc in each sc across.

Note: Mark last row as **right** side.

Row 3 (Decrease row): Ch 1, turn; work beginning decrease, sc in each sc across to last 2 sc, decrease: 48 sc.

Row 4: Ch 1, turn; sc in each sc across.

Rows 5-20: Repeat Rows 3 and 4, 8 times: 32 sc. Finish off.

HOUSE

With Tan and leaving a 20" end for sewing, ch 16 **loosely**.

Row 1 (Wrong side): Sc in back ridge of second ch from hook and each ch across: 15 sc.

Note: Mark **back** of any stitch on last row as **right** side.

Rows 2-40: Ch 1, turn; sc in each sc across. Finish off leaving a 20" end for sewing.

LARGE HEART

Row 1 (Right side): With Rose, ch 2, 3 sc in second ch from hook: 3 sc.

Note: Mark last row as **right** side.

Row 2: Ch 1, turn; 2 sc in first sc, sc in next sc, 2 sc in last sc: 5 sc.

Row 3: Ch 1, turn; sc in each sc across.

Row 4 (Increase row): Ch 1, turn; 2 sc in first sc, sc in each sc across to last sc, 2 sc in last sc: 7 sc.

Rows 5-9: Repeat Rows 3 and 4 twice, then repeat Row 3 once **more**; do **not** finish off: 11 sc.

FIRST SIDE

Row 1: Ch 1, turn; work beginning decrease, sc in next 3 sc, leave remaining 6 sc unworked: 4 sc.

Row 2: Ch 1, turn; sc in each sc across.

Row 3: Ch 1, turn; work beginning decrease, decrease; finish off: 2 sc.

SECOND SIDE

Row 1: With **wrong** side facing, skip next sc from First Side and join Rose with sc in next sc; sc in next 2 sc, decrease: 4 sc.

Row 2: Ch 1, turn; sc in each sc across.

Row 3: Ch 1, turn; work beginning decrease, decrease; do **not** finish off: 2 sc.

EDGING

Ch 1, turn; sc evenly around entire Heart working 3 sc at bottom point; join with slip st to first sc, finish off leaving a long end for sewing.

Using photo, page 89, as a guide for placement:
Sew Large Heart to House.
Sew House to Bottom and Roof.
Sew Ark to Center Panel.

RIGHT DOVE

BODY

With White, ch 13 **loosely**, place marker in sixth ch from hook for Wing placement.

Row 1: Sc in back ridge of second ch from hook and each ch across: 12 sc.

Row 2 (Right side): Ch 2, turn; 2 sc in first sc, (sc, slip st) in next sc, skip next sc, 2 dc in next sc, 2 tr in each of next 2 sc, 2 dc in next sc, skip next 2 sc, sc in next 2 sc, 2 sc in last sc: 17 sts.

Note: Mark last row as **right** side.

Row 3: Ch 2, turn; 2 dc in first sc, 2 tr in next sc, leave remaining 15 sts unworked; finish off.

FIRST WING

Row 1: With **right** side facing and working in free loops of beginning ch, join White with sc in marked ch; sc in next 2 chs, leave remaining 5 chs unworked: 3 sc.

Row 2: Ch 1, turn; sc in first 2 sc, 2 sc in last sc: 4 sc.

Row 3: Ch 1, turn; 2 sc in first sc, sc in last 3 sc: 5 sc.

Row 4: Ch 1, turn; work beginning decrease, sc in next 2 sc, 2 sc in last sc: 5 sc.

Row 5: Ch 1, turn; work beginning decrease, sc in next sc, decrease: 3 sc.

Row 6: Ch 1, turn; sc in first sc, decrease: 2 sc.

Row 7: Ch 1, turn; work beginning decrease: one sc.

Row 8: Ch 1, turn; sc in next sc; finish off.

SECOND WING

Row 1: With **right** side facing and working in free loops of beginning ch, join White with sc in next ch from First Wing; sc in next ch, leave remaining 3 chs unworked: 2 sc.

Row 2: Ch 1, turn; 2 sc in first sc, sc in last sc: 3 sc.

Row 3: Ch 1, turn; sc in first 2 sc, 2 sc in last sc: 4 sc.

Row 4: Ch 1, turn; 2 sc in first sc, sc in next sc, decrease: 4 sc.

Row 5: Ch 1, turn; work beginning decrease, decrease: 2 sc.

Row 6: Ch 1, turn; work beginning decrease: one sc.

Row 7: Ch 1, turn; sc in next sc; finish off.

Using photo as a guide for placement, sew eye to Right Dove and sew Dove to Center Panel, lapping First Wing over Second Wing.

LEFT DOVE

BODY

With White, ch 13 **loosely**, place marker in tenth ch from hook for Wing placement.

Row 1 (Right side): Sc in back ridge of second ch from hook and each ch across: 12 sc.

Note: Mark last row as **right** side.

Row 2: Ch 2, turn; 2 sc in first sc, (sc, slip st) in next sc, skip next sc, 2 dc in next sc, 2 tr in each of next 2 sc, 2 dc in next sc, skip next 2 sc, sc in next 2 sc, 2 sc in last sc: 17 sts.

Row 3: Ch 2, turn; 2 dc in first sc, 2 tr in next sc, leave remaining 15 sts unworked; finish off.

FIRST WING

Row 1: With **right** side facing and working in free loops of beginning ch, join White with sc in marked ch; sc in next ch, leave remaining 8 chs unworked: 2 sc.

Row 2: Ch 1, turn; sc in first sc, 2 sc in last sc: 3 sc.

Row 3: Ch 1, turn; 2 sc in first sc, sc in last 2 sc: 4 sc.

Row 4: Ch 1, turn; work beginning decrease, sc in next sc, 2 sc in last sc: 4 sc.

Row 5: Ch 1, turn; work beginning decrease, decrease: 2 sc.

Row 6: Ch 1, turn; work beginning decrease: one sc.

Row 7: Ch 1, turn; sc in next sc; finish off.

SECOND WING

Row 1: With **right** side facing and working in free loops of beginning ch, join White with sc in next ch from First Wing; sc in next 2 chs, leave remaining 5 chs unworked: 3 sc.

Row 2: Ch 1, turn; 2 sc in first sc, sc in last 2 sc: 4 sc.

Row 3: Ch 1, turn; sc in first 3 sc, 2 sc in last sc: 5 sc.

Row 4: Ch 1, turn; 2 sc in first sc, sc in next 2 sc, decrease: 5 sc.

Row 5: Ch 1, turn; work beginning decrease, sc in next sc, decrease: 3 sc.

Row 6: Ch 1, turn; work beginning decrease, sc in last sc: 2 sc.

Row 7: Ch 1, turn; work beginning decrease: one sc.

Row 8: Ch 1, turn; sc in next sc; finish off.

Using photo as a guide for placement, sew eye to Left Dove and sew Dove to Center Panel, lapping Second Wing over First Wing.

NOAH

BODY

With Purple, ch 11 **loosely**.

Row 1: Sc in second ch from hook and in each ch across: 10 sc.

Row 2 (Right side): Ch 1, turn; sc in each sc across.

Note: Mark last row as **right** side.

Row 3 (Decrease row): Ch 1, turn; work beginning decrease, sc in each sc across to last 2 sc, decrease: 8 sc.

Rows 4-6: Ch 1, turn; sc in each sc across.

Rows 7-11: Repeat Rows 3-6 once, then repeat Row 3 once **more**: 4 sc.

Row 12: Ch 1, turn; sc in each sc across.

Continued on page 92.

Edging: Ch 1, do **not** turn; sc evenly across end of rows; working in free loops of beginning ch, 3 sc in first ch (base of first sc), sc in each ch across to last ch, 3 sc in last ch; sc evenly across end of rows; working across Row 12, 3 sc in first sc, sc in last 3 sc, place marker around last sc made for Head placement, 2 sc in same st; join with slip st to first sc, finish off leaving a long end for sewing.

HEAD

Row 1: With **wrong** side of Body facing, join Tan with sc in marked sc; sc in next 3 sc, leave remaining sc unworked: 4 sc.
Row 2: Ch 1, turn; working in Back Loops Only, 2 sc in first sc, sc in next sc, place marker around sc just made for Mustache placement, sc in next sc, 2 sc in last sc: 6 sc.
Rows 3 and 4: Ch 1, turn; sc in **both** loops of each sc across.
Row 5: Ch 1, turn; work beginning decrease, sc in next 2 sc, decrease: 4 sc.
Row 6: Ch 1, turn; sc in each sc across; finish off.
Edging: With **right** side facing, join Tan with slip st in right end of Row 1; work 15 sc evenly spaced around Head, slip st in opposite end of Row 1; finish off leaving a long end for sewing: 17 sts.

HAIR

First Side: With **right** side facing, skip first 3 sts on Head Edging and join White with slip st in next sc; sc in same st and in next 2 sc, slip st in next sc, leave remaining 10 sts unworked; finish off.
Second Side: With **right** side facing, skip next 3 sc from First Side and join White with slip st in next sc; sc in next 2 sc, (sc, slip st) in next sc, leave remaining 3 sts unworked; finish off.

BEARD

Row 1: With **right** side facing, Head toward you, and working in free loops on Row 1 (*Fig. 15a, page 127*), join White with sc in first sc; sc in last 3 sc: 4 sc.
Row 2: Ch 1, turn; work beginning decrease, decrease: 2 sc.
Row 3: Ch 1, turn; sc in next 2 sc.
Row 4: Ch 1, turn; work beginning decrease: one sc.
Row 5: Ch 1, turn; sc in next sc; finish off leaving a long end for sewing.
Sew bottom of Beard to Body.

Moustache: With **right** side facing and body toward you, join White with slip st in right end of Row 1 on Beard; ch 2, slip st around post of marked sc on Head, ch 2, slip st in opposite end of Row 1 on Beard; finish off.

Using photo as a guide for placement, sew eyes to Head.

ARM (Make 2)

Row 1 (Right side): With Purple, ch 2, sc in second ch from hook: one sc.
Note: Mark last row as **right** side.
Rows 2-5: Ch 1, turn; sc in next sc.
Edging: Ch 1, do **not** turn; sc evenly around entire Arm; join with slip st to first sc, finish off leaving a long end for sewing.

HAND (Make 2)

With Tan, ch 2, 3 sc in second ch from hook, slip st in same ch; finish off leaving a long end for sewing.

Using photo as a guide for placement, sew Arms to Body, then sew Hands to ends of Arms.

MRS. NOAH

Work same as Noah through Row 1 of Head: 4 sc.
Row 2: Ch 1, turn; 2 sc in first sc, sc in next 2 sc, 2 sc in last sc: 6 sc.
Rows 3 and 4: Ch 1, turn; sc in each sc across.
Row 5: Ch 1, turn; work beginning decrease, sc in next 2 sc, decrease: 4 sc.
Row 6: Ch 1, turn; sc in each sc across; finish off.
Edging: With **right** side facing, join Tan with slip st in right end of Row 1; work 15 sc evenly spaced around Head, slip st in opposite end of Row 1; finish off leaving a long end for sewing: 17 sts.

HAIR

With **right** side facing, skip first slip st on Head Edging and join White with slip st in next sc; ch 3, sc in same st, ch 3, (sc, ch 3) twice in each sc around to last 2 sts, (sc, ch 3, slip st) in next sc, leave remaining slip st unworked; finish off.

Using photo as a guide for placement, sew eyes to Head.

ARMS AND HANDS

Work same as Noah.

SMALL HEART

Row 1 (Right side): With Rose, ch 2, sc in second ch from hook: one sc.
Note: Mark last row as **right** side.
Row 2: Ch 1, turn; 3 sc in next sc.
Row 3: Ch 1, turn; 2 sc in first sc, sc in next sc, 2 sc in last sc; do **not** finish off: 5 sc.

FIRST SIDE

Row 1: Ch 1, turn; work beginning decrease, leave remaining 3 sc unworked: one sc.
Row 2: Ch 1, turn; sc in next sc; finish off.

SECOND SIDE

Row 1: With **wrong** side facing, skip next sc from First Side and join Rose with slip st in next sc; ch 1, pull up a loop in same st and in last sc, YO and draw through all 3 loops on hook: one st.
Row 2: Ch 1, turn; sc in next st; do **not** finish off.

EDGING

Ch 1, do **not** turn; sc evenly around entire Heart working 3 sc in bottom point; join with slip st to first sc, finish off leaving a long end for sewing.

With White and using photo as a guide, use straight stitches (*Fig. 1, page 88*) and French knots (*Fig. 2, page 88*) to add the word "by" to Heart.

WORDS

T (Make 2)
Horizontal Line
With Rose, ch 10 **loosely**.
Row 1: (Work Cluster, slip st) in second ch from hook, slip st in each ch across to last ch, (work Cluster, slip st) in last ch; finish off leaving a long end for sewing.

Vertical Line
With Rose, ch 20 **loosely**.
Row 1: (Work Cluster, slip st) in second ch from hook, slip st in each ch across to last ch, (work Cluster, slip st) in last ch; finish off leaving a long end for sewing.

W (Make 2)
With Rose, ch 36 **loosely**.
Row 1: (Work Cluster, slip st) in second ch from hook, slip st in next 16 chs, (work Cluster, slip st) in next ch, slip st in next 16 chs, (work Cluster, slip st) in last ch; finish off leaving a long end for sewing.

O (Make 2)
With Rose, ch 23 **loosely**.
Row 1: (Work Cluster, slip st) in second ch from hook, slip st in each ch across; join with slip st to top of first Cluster, finish off leaving a long end for sewing.

Using photo as a guide for placement, sew Noah, Mrs. Noah, Small Heart, and Words to Bottom Panel.

ELEPHANT (Make 2)
BODY
With Grey, ch 13 **loosely**.
Row 1 (Right side): Sc in second ch from hook and in next ch, 2 sc in each of next 2 chs, sc in each ch across: 14 sc.
Note: Mark last row as **right** side.
Row 2: Ch 1, turn; 2 sc in first sc, sc in next 6 sc, slip st in next sc, leave remaining 6 sc unworked: 9 sts.
Row 3: Ch 1, turn; skip first slip st, slip st in next sc, sc in next 6 sc, 2 sc in last sc: 9 sts.
Row 4: Ch 1, turn; 2 sc in first sc, sc in next 5 sc, decrease, leave remaining slip st unworked: 8 sc.
Row 5: Ch 1, turn; sc in first sc, sc in Back Loop Only of each sc across to last sc, sc in **both** loops of last sc.
Row 6: Ch 1, turn; sc in both loops of each sc across.
Row 7: Ch 8 **loosely**, turn; sc in second ch from hook and in next 6 chs, sc in next 6 sc, decrease: 14 sc.
Row 8: Ch 1, turn; work beginning decrease, sc in each sc across: 13 sc.
Row 9: Ch 1, turn; sc in each sc across to last sc, 2 sc in last sc: 14 sc.
Row 10: Ch 1, turn; sc in first 11 sc, leave remaining 3 sc unworked.
Row 11: Ch 1, turn; sc in each sc across to last sc, 2 sc in last sc: 12 sc.
Row 12: Ch 1, turn; sc in each sc across.
Row 13: Ch 1, turn; sc in each sc across to last sc, 2 sc in last sc: 13 sc.
Rows 14-16: Ch 1, turn; sc in each sc across.
Row 17: Ch 4 **loosely**, turn; sc in second ch from hook and in next 2 chs, sc in each sc across: 16 sc.

Row 18: Ch 1, turn; work beginning decrease, sc in each sc across: 15 sc.
Row 19: Ch 1, turn; sc in each sc across to last 2 sc, decrease: 14 sc.
Row 20: Ch 1, turn; work beginning decrease, sc in next 6 sc, decrease, leave remaining 4 sc unworked: 8 sc.
Row 21: Ch 1, turn; work beginning decrease, sc in next 4 sc, decrease: 6 sc.
Row 22: Ch 1, turn; work beginning decrease, sc in next sc, slip st in last 3 sc, ch 3; finish off leaving a 1" end for tail.

Unravel tail and trim ends as desired.

EAR
Row 1: With **right** side facing, head toward you, and working in free loops on Row 4, join Grey with sc in first sc; sc in same st and in next 5 sc: 7 sc.
Row 2: Ch 1, turn; 2 sc in first sc, sc in next 5 sc, 2 sc in last sc: 9 sc.
Row 3: Ch 1, turn; 2 sc in first sc, sc in each sc across: 10 sc.
Row 4: Ch 1, turn; work beginning decrease, sc in each sc across: 9 sc.
Row 5: Ch 1, turn; work beginning decrease, sc in next 5 sc, decrease: 7 sc.
Row 6: Ch 1, turn; work beginning decrease, sc in next 3 sc, decrease; finish off: 5 sc.

CAMEL (Make 2)
Row 1 (Right side): With Gold, ch 2, 2 sc in second ch from hook: 2 sc.
Note: Mark last row as **right** side.
Row 2: Ch 1, turn; sc in next 2 sc.
Row 3: Ch 1, turn; 2 sc in first sc, leave remaining sc unworked: 2 sc.
Row 4: Ch 1, turn; 2 sc in first sc, sc in next sc: 3 sc.
Row 5: Ch 3, turn; slip st in third ch from hook (ear), 2 sc in first sc, sc in next 2 sc: 4 sc.
Row 6: Ch 8 **loosely**, turn; 2 sc in second ch from hook, sc in next 6 chs and in next 2 sc, decrease, leave ear unworked: 11 sc.
Row 7: Ch 1, turn; work beginning decrease, sc in each sc across to last sc, 2 sc in last sc: 11 sc.
Row 8: Ch 1, turn; 2 sc in first sc, sc in next 4 sc, slip st in last 6 sc: 12 sts.
Row 9: Turn; skip first slip st, working **around** Row 8 (*Fig. 18, page 127*), slip st in next sc on Row 7, sc in next 4 sc; working in sc on Row 8, sc in next 5 sc, 2 sc in last sc: 12 sts.
Row 10: Ch 1, turn; 2 sc in first sc, sc in next 3 sc, decrease, leave remaining 6 sts unworked: 6 sc.
Row 11: Ch 1, turn; sc in each sc across.
Row 12: Ch 9 **loosely**, turn; sc in second ch from hook and in next 7 chs, sc in next 5 sc, 2 sc in last sc: 15 sc.
Row 13: Ch 1, turn; 2 sc in first sc, sc in each sc across: 16 sc.
Row 14: Ch 1, turn; sc in each sc across to last sc, 2 sc in last sc: 17 sc.
Row 15: Ch 1, turn; 2 sc in first sc, sc in next 6 sc, decrease, leave remaining 8 sc unworked: 9 sc.

Continued on page 94.

Row 16: Ch 1, turn; work beginning decrease, sc in each sc across to last sc, 2 sc in last sc: 9 sc.
Row 17: Ch 1, turn; 2 sc in first sc, sc in each sc across: 10 sc.
Row 18: Ch 1, turn; sc in each sc across.
Row 19: Ch 1, turn; work beginning decrease, sc in each sc across: 9 sc.
Row 20: Ch 1, turn; 2 sc in first sc, sc in next 6 sc, decrease: 9 sc.
Row 21: Ch 1, turn; work beginning decrease, sc in each sc across to last sc, 2 sc in last sc: 9 sc.
Row 22: Ch 9 **loosely**, turn; sc in second ch from hook and in next 7 chs, sc in next 7 sc, decrease: 16 sc.
Row 23: Ch 1, turn; work beginning decrease, sc in each sc across: 15 sc.
Row 24: Ch 1, turn; sc in each sc across to last 2 sc, decrease: 14 sc.
Row 25: Ch 1, turn; work beginning decrease, sc in next 3 sc, decrease, leave remaining 7 sc unworked: 5 sc.
Row 26: Ch 1, turn; work beginning decrease, sc in next sc, decrease: 3 sc.
Row 27: Turn; slip st in first sc, ch 3, leave remaining 2 sc unworked; finish off leaving a 1" end for tail.

Unravel tail and trim ends as desired.

SHEEP (Make 2)
BODY
With White, ch 11 **loosely**, place marker in third ch from hook for Leg placement.
Row 1: Tr in second ch from hook, sc in next ch, (tr in next ch, sc in next ch) across: 10 sts.
Row 2 (Right side): Ch 1, turn; sc in each st across.
Note: Mark last row as **right** side.
Row 3: Ch 1, turn; sc in first sc, (tr in next sc, sc in next sc) across to last sc, (tr, slip st) in last sc: 11 sts.
Row 4: Ch 1, turn; skip first slip st, sc in each st across: 10 sts.
Row 5: Ch 1, turn; tr in first sc, sc in next sc, (tr in next sc, sc in next sc) across.
Row 6: Ch 2, turn; 2 sc in second ch from hook (tail), sc in each st across Body, ch 3, 2 sc in second ch from hook (ear), fold ear down over Body, slip st in last sc made on Body (sc before ch-3); finish off.

FACE
Row 1: With **right** side facing and working in end of rows, join Brown with sc in Row 6 at ear; 2 sc in next row, leave remaining 4 rows unworked: 3 sc.
Row 2: Ch 1, turn; pull up a loop in next 3 sc, YO and draw through all 4 loops on hook: one st.
Row 3: Ch 1, turn; sc in next st; finish off.

FIRST LEG
Row 1: With **right** side facing and working in free loops of beginning ch, join Brown with sc in marked ch; sc in next ch, leave remaining 7 chs unworked: 2 sc.
Rows 2 and 3: Ch 1, turn; sc in each sc across.
Finish off.

NEXT LEG
Row 1: With **right** side facing and working in free loops of beginning ch, skip next 4 chs from First Leg and join Brown with sc in next ch; sc in next ch, leave remaining ch unworked: 2 sc.
Rows 2 and 3: Ch 1, turn; sc in each sc across.
Finish off.

GIRAFFE (Make 2)
Row 1 (Right side): With Gold, ch 2, 3 sc in second ch from hook.
Note: Mark last row as **right** side.
Row 2: Ch 1, turn; sc in first 2 sc, 2 sc in last sc: 4 sc.
Row 3: Ch 1, turn; sc in each sc across.
Row 4: Ch 1, turn; sc in each sc across to last sc, 2 sc in last sc: 5 sc.
Row 5: Ch 2, turn; sc in second ch from hook (ear) and in each sc across: 6 sc.
Row 6: Ch 25 **loosely**, turn; sc in second ch from hook and in each ch across, sc in next 3 sc, decrease, leave ear unworked: 28 sc.
Row 7: Ch 1, turn; work beginning decrease, sc in each sc across: 27 sc.
Row 8: Ch 1, turn; sc in first 16 sc, slip st in each sc across.
Row 9: Turn; working **around** Row 8, slip st in first 2 sc on Row 7, sc in next 9 sc; sc in next 8 sc on Row 8, leave remaining 8 sc unworked: 19 sts.
Row 10: Ch 1, turn; 2 sc in first sc, sc in next 5 sc, decrease, leave remaining 11 sts unworked: 8 sc.
Row 11: Ch 1, turn; work beginning decrease, sc in next 5 sc, 2 sc in last sc: 8 sc.
Row 12: Ch 1, turn; 2 sc in first sc, sc in next 5 sc, decrease: 8 sc.
Row 13: Ch 1, turn; work beginning decrease, sc in next 5 sc, 2 sc in last sc: 8 sc.
Row 14: Ch 7 **loosely**, turn; sc in second ch from hook and in next 5 chs, sc in next 6 sc, decrease: 13 sc.
Row 15: Ch 1, turn; work beginning decrease, sc in each sc across: 12 sc.
Row 16: Ch 1, turn; sc in each sc across to last 2 sc, decrease: 11 sc.
Row 17: Turn; slip st in first sc, ch 4, leave remaining 10 sc unworked; finish off leaving a 1" end for tail.
Unravel tail and trim ends as desired.

Using photo as a guide for placement:
Sew six spots to Giraffe.
For each spot, thread ends of a 5" length of Gold up from back of Giraffe through holes in button and knot ends to secure. Unravel ends and trim as desired.

HIPPO (Make 2)
With Grey and leaving a ¹/₂" end for tail, ch 9 **loosely**.
Row 1 (Right side): Sc in second ch from hook and in next 5 chs, leave remaining 2 chs unworked (tail): 6 sc.
Note: Mark last row as **right** side.
Row 2: Ch 1, turn; 2 sc in first sc, sc in next 4 sc, 2 sc in last sc: 8 sc.
Row 3: Ch 1, turn; 2 sc in first sc, sc in each sc across: 9 sc.

Row 4: Ch 4 loosely, turn; sc in second ch from hook and in next 2 chs, sc in next 8 sc, 2 sc in last sc: 13 sc.

Rows 5 and 6: Ch 1, turn; sc in each sc across.

Row 7: Ch 1, turn; sc in first 10 sc, leave remaining 3 sc unworked.

Rows 8-12: Ch 1, turn; sc in each sc across.

Row 13: Ch 1, turn; work beginning decrease, sc in each sc across: 9 sc.

Row 14: Ch 4 loosely, turn; sc in second ch from hook and in next 2 chs, sc in next 7 sc, decrease: 11 sc.

Row 15: Ch 1, turn; sc in each sc across.

Row 16: Ch 1, turn; sc in each sc across to last 2 sc, decrease: 10 sc.

Row 17: Ch 3, turn; slip st in second ch from hook and in next ch (ear), sc in next 7 sc, leave remaining 3 sc unworked: 7 sc.

Row 18: Ch 1, turn; 2 sc in first sc, sc in next 6 sc, leave ear unworked: 8 sc.

Row 19: Ch 1, turn; work beginning decrease, sc in next 5 sc, 2 sc in last sc: 8 sc.

Row 20: Ch 1, turn; 2 sc in first sc, sc in each sc across: 9 sc.

Row 21: Ch 1, turn; work beginning decrease, sc in next 5 sc, decrease: 7 sc.

Row 22: Ch 1, turn; work beginning decrease, sc in each sc across: 6 sc.

Row 23: Ch 1, turn; work beginning decrease, sc in next 2 sc, decrease: 4 sc.

Row 24: Ch 1, turn; work beginning decrease, decrease; finish off: 2 sc.

Unravel tail and trim ends as desired.

Using photo as a guide for placement:
Sew an eye to each animal, then sew animals to Side Panels.

RAINBOW
COLOR SEQUENCE
Work 2 rows of **each** color: Purple, Dark Blue, Blue, Green, Gold, Rose.

With Purple, ch 30 loosely.

Row 1 (Right side): Working in back ridge, sc in second ch from hook and in next 3 chs, (2 sc in next ch, sc in next 4 chs) across: 34 sc.

Note: Mark last row as **right** side.

Row 2: Ch 1, turn; 2 sc in first sc, sc in each sc across to last sc, 2 sc in last sc changing to next color in last sc: 36 sc.

Row 3: Ch 1, turn; 2 sc in first sc, sc in each sc across to last sc, 2 sc in last sc: 38 sc.

Rows 4-11: Repeat Rows 2 and 3, 4 times: 54 sc.

Row 12: Ch 1, turn; 2 sc in first sc, sc in each sc across to last sc, 2 sc in last sc; finish off leaving a long end for sewing.

CLOUD (Make 2)
With White, ch 28 loosely.

Row 1: Sc in second ch from hook and in each ch across: 27 sc.

Row 2 (Right side): Ch 1, turn; work beginning decrease, sc in each sc across to last 2 sc, decrease: 25 sc.

Note: Mark last row as **right** side.

Rows 3-7: Ch 1, turn; skip first sc, decrease, sc in each sc across to last 3 sc, decrease, leave remaining sc unworked: 5 sc.

Row 8: Ch 1, turn; 2 sc in first sc, sc in next 3 sc, 2 sc in last sc: 7 sc.

Row 9: Ch 1, turn; work beginning decrease, sc in next 3 sc, decrease: 5 sc.

Row 10: Ch 1, turn; work beginning decrease, sc in next sc, decrease: 3 sc.

Edging: Ch 1, do **not** turn; working in end of rows, skip first row, sc in next 2 rows, (5 dc in next row, skip next row, sc in next row) twice, 3 dc in last row; working in free loops of beginning ch, 3 sc in first ch (base of first sc), sc in each ch across to last ch, 3 sc in last ch; working in end of rows, 3 dc in first row, (sc in next row, skip next row, 5 dc in next row) twice, sc in next 2 rows, skip last row; working across Row 10, sc in first sc, 3 dc in next sc, sc in last sc; join with slip st to first sc, finish off leaving a long end for sewing.

Center and sew Rainbow and Clouds to Top Panel.

STAR (Make 4)
CENTER
Rnd 1 (Right side): With Gold, ch 2, 5 sc in second ch from hook; join with slip st to first sc.

Note: Mark last round as **right** side.

Rnd 2: Ch 1, 2 sc in same st and in each sc around; join with slip st to first sc: 10 sc.

Rnd 3: Ch 1, sc in same st, 2 sc in next sc, (sc in next sc, 2 sc in next sc) around; join with slip st to first sc: 15 sc.

Rnd 4: Ch 1, 2 sc in same st and in each sc around; join with slip st to first sc, do **not** finish off: 30 sc.

FIRST POINT
Row 1: Ch 1, sc in same st and in next 5 sc, leave remaining 24 sc unworked: 6 sc.

Row 2: Ch 1, turn; work beginning decrease, sc in next 2 sc, decrease: 4 sc.

Row 3: Ch 1, turn; sc in each sc across.

Row 4: Ch 1, turn; work beginning decrease, decrease: 2 sc.

Row 5: Ch 1, turn; sc in each sc across.

Row 6: Ch 1, turn; work beginning decrease: one sc.

Row 7: Ch 1, turn; sc in next sc; finish off.

NEXT THREE POINTS
Row 1: With **right** side facing, join Gold with sc in next sc on Rnd 4 of Center from last Point made; sc in next 5 sc, leave remaining sc unworked: 6 sc.

Rows 2-7: Work same as First Point.

LAST POINT
Row 1: With **right** side facing, join Gold with sc in next sc on Rnd 4 of Center from last Point made; sc in last 5 sc: 6 sc.

Rows 2-6: Work same as First Point.

Row 7: Ch 1, turn; sc in next sc; do **not** finish off.

EDGING
Ch 1, do **not** turn; sc evenly around entire Star working 3 sc in end of each Point; join with slip st to first sc, finish off.

Using photo as a guide for placement:
Sew button to center of Star.
Thread ends of a 5" length of Gold up from back of Star through holes in button and knot ends to secure. Unravel ends and trim as desired.
Sew one Star to each Corner Panel.

Christmas Stripes

This handsome afghan will make a wonderful Christmas accent. Its holiday stripes are made from front post double crochet stitches, and the sides are edged with reverse single crochets. The throw is finished with a festive fringe.

Finished Size: 50" x 65"

MATERIALS
Red Heart Worsted Weight Yarn
[3½ ounces (198 yards) per skein]:
Dark Green - 7 skeins
Green - 5 skeins
Tan - 5 skeins
Red - 5 skeins
Crochet hook, size H (5.00 mm) **or** size needed for gauge

GAUGE: In pattern, 12 sts and 12 rows = 4"

STITCH GUIDE

FRONT POST DOUBLE CROCHET
(abbreviated FPdc)
YO, insert hook from **front** to **back** around post of dc one row **below** next sc *(Fig. 13, page 126)*, YO and pull up a loop even with loops on hook, (YO and draw through 2 loops on hook) twice. Skip sc behind FPdc.

AFGHAN BODY
With Dark Green, ch 148 **loosely**.
Row 1: Sc in second ch from hook and in each ch across: 147 sc.
Row 2 (Right side): Ch 3 **(counts as first dc)**, turn; dc in next sc and in each sc across.
Note: Mark last row as **right** side.
Row 3: Ch 1, turn; sc in each st across changing to Green in last sc *(Fig. 16, page 127)*.

Row 4: Ch 2 **(counts as first hdc, now and throughout)**, turn; work FPdc, (dc in next sc, work FPdc) across to last sc, hdc in last sc: 73 FPdc.
Row 5: Ch 1, turn; sc in each st across changing to Tan in last sc: 147 sc.
Row 6: Ch 2, turn; dc in next sc, (work FPdc, dc in next sc) across to last sc, hdc in last sc: 72 FPdc.
Row 7: Ch 1, turn; sc in each st across changing to Red in last sc: 147 sc.
Row 8: Ch 2, turn; work FPdc, (dc in next sc, work FPdc) across to last sc, hdc in last sc: 73 FPdc.
Row 9: Ch 1, turn; sc in each st across changing to Dark Green in last sc: 147 sc.
Row 10: Ch 2, turn; dc in next sc, (work FPdc, dc in next sc) across to last sc, hdc in last sc: 72 FPdc.

Repeat Rows 3-10 until Afghan measures approximately 64" from beginning ch, ending by working Row 10.
Last Row: Ch 1, turn; sc in each st across; finish off.

EDGING
Row 1: With **right** side of one long edge facing, join Dark Green with sc in end of first row *(see Joining With Sc, page 126)*; sc evenly across end of rows.
Row 2: Ch 1, do **not** turn; working from **left** to **right**, work reverse sc *(Figs. 11a-d, page 126)* in each sc across; finish off.

Repeat across opposite edge of Afghan.

Holding six 20" strands of Dark Green together for each fringe, add fringe across short edges of Afghan *(Figs. 20a & b, page 127)*.

Garden Gathering

Even if you don't have a green thumb, you can enjoy the beautiful blossoms on these colorful afghans! Whether you choose darling daisies, pretty pansies, or cascading petals, your needlework "garden" will bloom all year 'round.

Flower Patch Silhouette

With these bold and beautiful blooms, you can sow an entire flower garden without "sewing." Our colorful motifs are joined as you crochet this distinctive cover-up.

Finished Size: 47" x 58"

MATERIALS
Red Heart Worsted Weight Yarn
[8 ounces (452 yards) per skein]:
Black - 7 skeins
Yellow - 1 skein
Green - 1 skein
Rose - 1 skein
Lavender - 1 skein
Crochet hook, size G (4.00 mm) **or** size needed for gauge

GAUGE: Each Motif = 2⅝" square

FIRST MOTIF
With Black, ch 4; join with slip st to form a ring.
Rnd 1 (Right side): Ch 1, 16 sc in ring; join with slip st to first sc.
Note: Mark last round as **right** side.
Rnd 2: Ch 1, sc in same st, ch 4, skip next sc, sc in next sc, ch 6, skip next sc, ★ sc in next sc, ch 4, skip next sc, sc in next sc, ch 6, skip next sc; repeat from ★ 2 times **more**; join with slip st to first sc: 8 sps.
Rnd 3: 5 Dc in first ch-4 sp, slip st in next sc, 7 dc in next corner ch-6 sp, ★ slip st in next sc, 5 dc in next ch-4 sp, slip st in next sc, 7 dc in next corner ch-6 sp; repeat from ★ 2 times **more**; join with slip st to joining slip st, finish off: 48 dc.

ADDITIONAL MOTIFS
Note: Follow Placement Diagram to make and join Motifs, using color indicated for Rnds 2 and 3 on each Two Color Motif. When joining to a Motif that has been previously joined, work into same dc.

PLACEMENT DIAGRAM

G	R		Y	L		G	R		Y	L
Y	L		G	R		Y	L		G	R

KEY
- **G** Green
- **R** Rose
- **Y** Yellow
- **L** Lavender
- ☐ Solid Motif

SOLID COLOR MOTIF
Work same as First Motif through Rnd 2: 8 sps.
Rnd 3 (Joining rnd): Work One Side or Two Side Joining.

TWO COLOR MOTIF
With Black, ch 4; join with slip st to form a ring.
Rnd 1 (Right side): Ch 1, 16 sc in ring; join with slip st to first sc, finish off.
Note: Mark last round as **right** side.
Rnd 2: With **right** side facing, join color indicated with sc in same st as joining (*see Joining With Sc, page 126*); ch 4, skip next sc, sc in next sc, ch 6, skip next sc, ★ sc in next sc, ch 4, skip next sc, sc in next sc, ch 6, skip next sc; repeat from ★ 2 times **more**; join with slip st to first sc: 8 sps.
Rnd 3 (Joining rnd): Work One Side or Two Side Joining.

ONE SIDE JOINING
Rnd 3 (Joining rnd): 5 Dc in first ch-4 sp, slip st in next sc, ★ 7 dc in next corner ch-6 sp, slip st in next sc, 5 dc in next ch-4 sp, slip st in next sc; repeat from ★ once **more**, 3 dc in next corner ch-6 sp, holding Motifs with **right** sides facing, † drop loop from hook, insert hook from **front** to **back** in center dc of corresponding corner 7-dc group on **adjacent Motif** (*Fig. 17, page 127*), hook dropped loop and draw through st, 4 dc in same sp on **new Motif** †, slip st in next sc, 2 dc in next ch-4 sp, drop loop from hook, insert hook from **front** to **back** in center dc of next 5-dc group on **adjacent Motif**, hook dropped loop and draw through st, 3 dc in same sp on **new Motif**, slip st in next sc, 3 dc in next corner ch-6 sp, repeat from † to † once; join with slip st to joining slip st, finish off.

TWO SIDE JOINING
Rnd 3 (Joining rnd): 5 Dc in first ch-4 sp, slip st in next sc, 7 dc in next corner ch-6 sp, slip st in next sc, 5 dc in next ch-4 sp, slip st in next sc, 3 dc in next corner ch-6 sp, holding Motifs with **right** sides facing, ★ † drop loop from hook, insert hook from **front** to **back** in center dc of corresponding corner 7-dc group on **adjacent Motif**, hook dropped loop and draw through st, 4 dc in same sp on **new Motif** †, slip st in next sc, 2 dc in next ch-4 sp, drop loop from hook, insert hook from **front** to **back** in center dc of next 5-dc group on **adjacent Motif**, hook dropped loop and draw through st, 3 dc in same sp on **new Motif**, slip st in next sc, 3 dc in next corner ch-6 sp; repeat from ★ once **more**, then repeat from † to † once; join with slip st to joining slip st, finish off.

Spring Fantasy

This afghan is a dream come true! Post stitches and clusters produce texture, while shades of spring give it a light and airy appearance. Fashioned in strips and then joined, this captivating cover-up will keep you comfortable in the season's cool breezes!

Finished Size: 46" x 64"

MATERIALS
Red Heart Worsted Weight Yarn
[3½ ounces (198 yards) per skein]:
White - 8 skeins
Lavender - 5 skeins
Green - 2 skeins
Crochet hook, size I (5.50 mm) **or** size needed for gauge
Yarn needle

GAUGE: Each Strip = 5¾" wide

STITCH GUIDE

FRONT POST SINGLE CROCHET
(abbreviated FPsc)
Insert hook from **front** to **back** around st indicated *(Fig. 13, page 126)*, YO and pull up a loop even with last st made, YO and draw through both loops on hook **(counts as one sc)**.

HDC CLUSTER (uses next 3 sc)
★ YO, insert hook in **next** sc, YO and pull a loop; repeat from ★ 2 times **more**, YO and draw through all 7 loops on hook.

DC CLUSTER
★ YO, insert hook in sp indicated, YO and pull up a loop, YO and draw through 2 loops on hook; repeat from ★ once **more**, YO and draw through all 3 loops on hook.

FRONT POST CLUSTER *(abbreviated FP Cluster)*
YO, working in **front** of sts at end of rows *(Fig. 18, page 127)*, insert hook from **front** to **back** around first st indicated *(Fig. 13, page 126)*, YO and pull up a loop even with last st made, YO and draw through 2 loops on hook, YO, insert hook from **front** to **back** around next st indicated, YO and pull up a loop even with last st made, YO and draw through 2 loops on hook, YO and draw through all 3 loops on hook.

STRIP (Make 8)
CENTER
With White, ch 16 **loosely**.
Row 1: Sc in second ch from hook and in next ch, ch 3, skip next 3 chs, ★ sc in next ch, ch 3, skip next 3 chs; repeat from ★ once **more**, sc in last 2 chs: 6 sc and 3 ch-3 sps.

Row 2 (Right side): Ch 1, turn; sc in first 2 sc, ch 1, skip next ch-3 sp, work dc Cluster in next ch-3 sp, (ch 3, work dc Cluster in same sp) 4 times, ch 1, skip next ch-3 sp, sc in last 2 sc: 9 sts and 6 sps.
Note: Mark last row as **right** side and bottom edge.
Row 3: Ch 4 **(counts as first tr, now and throughout)**, turn; tr in next sc, ch 3, skip next 2 sps, (sc in next ch-3 sp, ch 3) twice, skip next 2 sps, tr in last 2 sc: 6 sts and 3 ch-3 sps.
Row 4: Ch 1, turn; sc in first 2 tr, ch 1, skip next ch-3 sp, work dc Cluster in next ch-3 sp, (ch 3, work dc Cluster in same sp) 4 times, ch 1, skip next ch-3 sp, sc in last 2 tr: 9 sts and 6 sps.
Rows 5-81: Repeat Rows 3 and 4, 38 times; then repeat Row 3 once **more**.
Finish off.

BORDER
Rnd 1: With **right** side facing, join Lavender with slip st in center ch-3 sp on Row 81; ch 4, 3 tr in same sp, working in ch-3 sp **and** around posts of 2 tr at end of same row at the same time, 7 dc in next sp, ★ work FP Cluster around ch-1 **below** 2 sc on next row and around ch-3 **below** 2 tr on next row, 5 dc around posts of 2 tr at end of same row; repeat from ★ 38 times **more**, work FP Cluster around ch-1 **below** 2 sc on next row and around ch-3 **below** 2 sc on last row; working over beginning ch, 7 dc in first sp, 7 tr in next sp, 7 dc in next sp; work FP Cluster around ch-3 **below** 2 sc on same row and around ch-1 **below** 2 sc on next row, † 5 dc around posts of 2 tr at end of next row, work FP Cluster around ch-3 **below** 2 tr on same row and around ch-1 **below** 2 sc on next row †; repeat from † to † 38 times **more**; working around posts of 2 tr at end of last row and in ch-3 sp at the **same** time, 7 dc in last sp, 3 tr in same sp as first tr; join with slip st to first tr, finish off: 512 sts.
Rnd 2: With **right** side facing and working in Back Loops Only *(Fig. 14, page 126)*, join Green with sc in same st as joining *(see Joining With Sc, page 126)*; ch 1, sc in same st and in next 5 sts, 2 sc in next dc, sc in next 4 dc, work FPsc around next FP Cluster, † sc in next 5 dc, work FPsc around next FP Cluster †, repeat from † to † 38 times **more**, sc in next 4 dc, 2 sc in next dc, sc in next 5 sts, (sc, ch 1, sc) in next tr, sc in next 5 sts, 2 sc in next dc, sc in next 4 dc, work FPsc around next FP Cluster; repeat from † to † 39 times, sc in next 4 dc, 2 sc in next dc, sc in last 5 sts; join with slip st to **both** loops of first sc, finish off: 518 sc and 2 ch-1 sps.

Rnd 3: With **right** side facing and working in Back Loops Only, join White with sc in first ch-1 sp; ch 1, sc in same sp, ✝ skip next sc, sc in next 10 sc, place marker around last sc made for joining placement, work hdc Cluster, (sc in next 3 sc, work hdc Cluster) 39 times, sc in next 2 sc, place marker around last sc made for joining placement, sc in next 8 sc ✝, skip next sc, (sc, ch 1, sc) in next ch-1 sp, repeat from ✝ to ✝ once, skip last st; join with slip st to **both** loops of first sc, finish off.

ASSEMBLY

Place two Strips with **wrong** sides together and bottom edges at the same end. With White and working through **both** loops of each stitch on **both** pieces, whipstitch Strips together *(Fig. 19b, page 127)*, beginning in first marked sc and ending in next marked sc.

Join remaining Strips in same manner, always working in the same direction.

103

Country Baskets

A tisket, a tasket, an afghan full of baskets! The prize-winning latticework design on this wrap is created by weaving strips into bordered squares, which are then whipstitched together.

Finished Size: 44" x 60"

MATERIALS
Red Heart Worsted Weight Yarn
[3 ounces (170 yards) per skein]:
White - 7 skeins
Blue - 5 skeins
Yellow - 5 skeins
Pink - 4 skeins
Green - 4 skeins
Crochet hook, size H (5.00 mm) **or** size needed for gauge
Safety pins
Yarn needle

GAUGE: Each Lattice Strip = 7" x 1¼"
Each Square = 8¼"

SQUARE (Make 35)
LATTICE STRIP
Make 3 **each** with Blue and Yellow; make 2 **each** with Pink and Green.
Ch 26 **loosely.**
Row 1 (Right side): Sc in back ridge of second ch from hook and each ch across *(Fig. 2b, page 125)*: 25 sc.
Note: Mark last row as **right** side.
Row 2: Ch 4 **(counts as first dc plus ch 1, now and throughout)**, turn; skip next sc, dc in next sc, ★ ch 1, skip next sc, dc in next sc; repeat from ★ across: 13 dc and 12 ch-1 sps.
Row 3: Ch 1, turn; sc in each dc and in each ch across; finish off: 25 sc.

With **right** sides facing, using photo as a guide for placement, and using safety pins to hold Strips in place, weave Lattice Strips together to form Square.

BORDER
Rnd 1 of Border is worked in end of rows on short edges of Lattice Strips; be careful not to catch stitches on long edges of Strips as you work.
Rnd 1: With **right** side facing, join White with sc in first row on Strip at top right corner *(see Joining With Sc, page 126)*; work 3 sc evenly spaced across Strip, (ch 1, work 4 sc evenly spaced across next Strip) 4 times, ch 3, ★ work 4 sc evenly spaced across next Strip, (ch 1, work 4 sc evenly spaced across next Strip) 4 times, ch 3; repeat from ★ around; join with slip st to first sc: 80 sc and 28 chs.

Rnd 2: Ch 1, working in Back Loops Only of sc *(Fig. 14, page 126)* and in top loop and back ridge of chs, sc in same st and in each st around working 3 sc in center ch of each corner ch-3; join with slip st to first sc: 116 sc.
Rnd 3: Ch 1, sc in Back Loop Only of same st and each sc around working 3 sc in center sc of each corner 3-sc group; join with slip st to **both** loops of first sc, finish off: 124 sc.

ASSEMBLY
With White and working through **inside** loops only, whipstitch Squares together forming 5 vertical strips of 7 Squares each *(Fig. 19a, page 127)*, beginning in center sc of first corner 3-sc group and ending in center sc of next corner 3-sc group; then whipstitch strips together in same manner.

EDGING
Rnd 1: With **right** side facing and working in Back Loops Only, join White with sc in center sc of any corner 3-sc group; sc in same st, 2 sc in next sc, sc in next 29 sc, (sc in same st as joining on same Square and in same st as joining on next Square, sc in next 30 sc) across to center sc of next corner 3-sc group, ★ 3 sc in center sc, 2 sc in next sc, sc in next 29 sc, (sc in same st as joining on same Square and in same st as joining on next Square, sc in next 30 sc) across to center sc of next corner 3-sc group; repeat from ★ around, sc in same st as first sc; join with slip st to **both** loops of first sc: 776 sc.
Rnd 2: Ch 4, turn; skip next sc, working in both loops, (dc in next sc, ch 1, skip next sc) across to center sc of next corner 3-sc group, ★ (dc, ch 1, tr, ch 1, dc) in center sc, ch 1, skip next sc, (dc in next sc, ch 1, skip next sc) across to center sc of next corner 3-sc group; repeat from ★ around, (dc, ch 1, tr) in same st as first dc, ch 1; join with slip st to first dc: 396 sts and 396 ch-1 sps.
Rnd 3: Ch 1, turn; sc in same st and in each ch and each dc around working 3 sc in each corner tr; join with slip st to first sc: 800 sc.
Rnd 4: Ch 1, do **not** turn; (slip st in next sc, ch 1) around; join with slip st to first slip st, finish off.

Easter Basket

Inspired by colors you'd find in an Easter basket, this pretty throw captures the splendor of spring. Each motif begins with a circular center but ends up forming a square. The wrap is finished with a coordinating striped edging.

Finished Size: 44" x 62"

MATERIALS
Red Heart Worsted Weight Yarn
[3 ounces (170 yards) per skein]:
Ecru - 5 skeins
Blue - 4 skeins
Yellow - 1 skein
Green - 4 skeins
Pink - 5 skeins
Crochet hook, size H (5.00 mm) **or** size needed for gauge
Yarn needle

GAUGE: Each Square = 9¼ "

STITCH GUIDE

FRONT POST DOUBLE CROCHET
(abbreviated FPdc)
YO, insert hook from **front** to **back** around post of st indicated *(Fig. 13, page 126)*, YO and pull up a loop, (YO and draw through 2 loops on hook) twice. Skip st behind FPdc.

FRONT POST TREBLE CROCHET
(abbreviated FPtr)
YO twice, insert hook from **front** to **back** around post of dc indicated *(Fig. 13, page 126)*, YO and pull up a loop, (YO and draw through 2 loops on hook) 3 times. Skip st behind FPtr.

SQUARE (Make 24)
With Yellow, ch 6; join with slip st to form a ring.
Rnd 1 (Right side): Ch 4 **(counts as first dc plus ch 1, now and throughout)**, (dc in ring, ch 1) 11 times; join with slip st to first dc, finish off: 12 ch-1 sps.
Note: Mark last round as **right** side.
Rnd 2: With **right** side facing, join Green with slip st in any ch-1 sp; ch 4, dc in same sp, (dc, ch 1, dc) in each ch-1 sp around; join with slip st to first dc, finish off.
Rnd 3: With **right** side facing, join Ecru with sc in any ch-1 sp *(see Joining With Sc, page 126)*; sc in same sp, work FPtr around corresponding dc on Rnd 1, (2 sc in next ch-1 sp on Rnd 2, work FPtr around next dc on Rnd 1) around; join with slip st to first sc, finish off: 24 sc and 12 FPtr.

Rnd 4: With **right** side facing, join Pink with slip st in same st as joining; ch 3 **(counts as first dc, now and throughout)**, (dc, ch 2, 2 dc) in same st, dc in next 8 sts, ★ (2 dc, ch 2, 2 dc) in next sc, dc in next 8 sts; repeat from ★ around; join with slip st to first dc, finish off: 48 dc and 4 ch-2 sps.
Rnd 5: With **right** side facing, join Blue with slip st in any corner ch-2 sp; ch 3, (dc, ch 2, 2 dc) in same sp, dc in each dc across to next ch-2 sp, ★ (2 dc, ch 2, 2 dc) in ch-2 sp, dc in each dc across to next ch-2 sp; repeat from ★ around; join with slip st to first dc, finish off: 64 dc.
Rnd 6: With **right** side facing, join Green with slip st in any corner ch-2 sp; ch 3, (dc, ch 2, 2 dc) in same sp, dc in each dc across to next ch-2 sp, ★ (2 dc, ch 2, 2 dc) in ch-2 sp, dc in each dc across to next ch-2 sp; repeat from ★ around; join with slip st to first dc, finish off: 80 dc.
Rnd 7: With **right** side facing, join Ecru with slip st in any corner ch-2 sp; ch 3, (dc, ch 2, 2 dc) in same sp, dc in next 2 dc, work FPtr around dc one rnd **below** next dc, (dc in next 4 dc, work FPtr around dc one rnd **below** next dc) 3 times, dc in next 2 dc, ★ (2 dc, ch 2, 2 dc) in next ch-2 sp, dc in next 2 dc, work FPtr around dc one rnd **below** next dc, (dc in next 4 dc, work FPtr around dc one rnd **below** next dc) 3 times, dc in next 2 dc; repeat from ★ around; join with slip st to first dc, finish off: 80 dc and 16 FPtr.
Rnd 8: With **right** side facing, join Blue with slip st in any corner ch-2 sp; ch 3, (dc, ch 2, 2 dc) in same sp, dc in next 4 dc, (work FPdc around next FPtr, dc in next 4 dc) 4 times, ★ (2 dc, ch 2, 2 dc) in next ch-2 sp, dc in next 4 dc, (work FPdc around next FPtr, dc in next 4 dc) 4 times; repeat from ★ around; join with slip st to first dc, finish off: 96 dc and 16 FPdc.
Rnd 9: With **right** side facing, join Pink with slip st in any corner ch-2 sp; ch 3, 4 dc in same sp, dc in next 6 dc, work FPdc around next FPdc, (dc in next 4 dc, work FPdc around next FPdc) 3 times, dc in next 6 dc, ★ 5 dc in next ch-2 sp, dc in next 6 dc, work FPdc around next FPdc, (dc in next 4 dc, work FPdc around next FPdc) 3 times, dc in next 6 dc; repeat from ★ around; join with slip st to first dc, finish off: 116 dc and 16 FPdc.

ASSEMBLY
With Pink and working through **inside** loops, whipstitch Squares together forming 4 vertical strips of 6 Squares each *(Fig. 19a, page 127)*, beginning in center dc of first corner 5-dc group and ending in center dc of next corner 5-dc group; then whipstitch strips together in same manner.

EDGING

Rnd 1: With **right** side facing, join Ecru with slip st in center dc of any corner 5-dc group; ch 3, dc in next 8 dc, work FPdc around next FPdc, (dc in next 4 dc, work FPdc around next FPdc) 3 times, dc in next 8 dc, † dc in same st as joining on **same** Square and in same st as joining on **next** Square, dc in next 8 dc, work FPdc around next FPdc, (dc in next 4 dc, work FPdc around next FPdc) 3 times, dc in next 8 dc †; repeat from † to † across to center dc of next corner 5-dc group, ★ 3 dc in center dc, dc in next 8 dc, work FPdc around next FPdc, (dc in next 4 dc, work FPdc around next FPdc) 3 times, dc in next 8 dc, repeat from † to † across to center dc of next corner 5-dc group; repeat from ★ around, 2 dc in same st as first dc; join with slip st to first dc, do **not** finish off: 684 sts.

Rnd 2: Ch 3, dc in next dc and in each st around working 5 dc in center dc of each corner 3-dc group; join with slip st to first dc, finish off: 700 dc.

Rnd 3: With **right** side facing, join Pink with slip st in any dc; ch 3, dc in next dc and in each dc around working 3 dc in center dc of each corner 5-dc group; join with slip st to first dc, finish off: 708 dc.

Rnd 4: With **right** side facing, join Ecru with slip st in any dc; ch 3, dc in next dc and in each dc around working 5 dc in center dc of each corner 3-dc group; join with slip st to first dc, finish off: 724 dc.

Rnd 5: With **right** side facing, join Green with slip st in any dc; ch 3, dc in next dc and in each dc around working 3 dc in center dc of each corner 5-dc group; join with slip st to first dc, do **not** finish off: 732 dc.

Rnd 6: Ch 3, dc in next dc and in each dc around working 5 dc in center dc of each corner 3-dc group; join with slip st to first dc, finish off.

Braided Miles

*It's worth going the extra mile to create this captivating
cover-up! The prize-winning mile-a-minute afghan features
a fascinating woven design in complementary colors.*

Finished Size: 45" x 64"

MATERIALS
Red Heart Worsted Weight Yarn
[8 ounces (452 yards) per skein]:
Ecru - 4 skeins
Dark Green - 2 skeins
Green - 2 skeins
Crochet hook, size H (5.00 mm) **or** size needed for
gauge
Safety pins - 2

GAUGE: Each Panel = 4½ " wide; 14 dc = 4"

STITCH GUIDE

CLUSTER (uses next 5 chs)
★ YO, insert hook in **next** ch, YO and pull up a loop, YO
and draw through 2 loops on hook; repeat from ★ 4 times
more, YO and draw through all 6 loops on hook.

PANEL (Make 10)
STRIP A
With Dark Green, ch 294 **loosely**, place marker in third ch
from hook for st placement.
Row 1 (Right side): Working in back ridges of beginning
ch *(Fig. 2a, page 125)*, dc in fourth ch from hook
(3 skipped chs count as first dc, now and throughout)
and in next 2 chs, place marker around last dc made to
mark **right** side and bottom edge, 5 dc in next ch, dc in
next 7 chs, ★ work Cluster, dc in next 7 chs, 5 dc in next
ch, dc in next 7 chs; repeat from ★ across; finish off:
296 sts.

STRIP B
With Green, ch 298 **loosely**, place marker in ninth ch from
hook for st placement.
Row 1 (Right side): Working in back ridges of beginning
ch, dc in fourth ch from hook and in next 5 chs, place
marker around last dc made to mark **right** side and bottom
edge, work Cluster, ★ dc in next 7 chs, 5 dc in next ch, dc
in next 7 chs, work Cluster; repeat from ★ across to last
4 chs, dc in last 4 chs; finish off: 292 sts.

STRIP C
With Ecru, ch 289 **loosely**, place marker in third ch from
hook for st placement.

Row 1 (Right side): Working in back ridges of beginning
ch, dc in fourth ch from hook and in next 5 chs, place
marker around last dc made to mark **right** side and bottom
edge, ★ 5 dc in next ch, dc in next 7 chs, work Cluster, dc
in next 7 chs; repeat from ★ across; finish off: 287 sts.

BRAIDING
With **right** sides facing and bottom edges at same end,
braid Strips together, overlapping bottom edges of Strips,
matching marked chs on Strips B and C *(Fig. 1a)*, and
overlapping top edges of Strips *(Fig. 1b)*. Use safety pins
on each end to hold braid together.

Fig. 1a   Fig. 1b

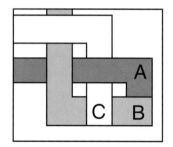 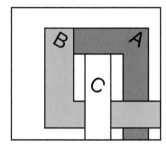

BORDER
Rnd 1: With **right** side facing and working across first dc
on Strip C **and** in free loops of beginning ch on Strip B
(through **both** thicknesses) *(Fig. 15b, page 127)*, join
Ecru with sc in marked chs *(see Joining With Sc,
page 126)*; sc in next 2 chs, sc in next ch on Strip B only;
working in free loops of beginning ch on Strip B **and**
across first dc on Strip A, sc in next ch on Strip B **and**
marked ch on Strip A, sc in next ch; working across first
dc on Strip B **and** dc on Strip A, 3 sc in next st, sc in next
2 sts; sc in next 3 dc on Strip A only, 3 sc in next dc
(center dc of 5-dc group), ch 4, (sc in center dc of
5-dc group on next Strip, ch 4) across to center dc of last
5-dc group on Strip A, 3 sc in center dc, sc in next 2 dc;
working through Strip A **and** Strip C, sc in next dc on
Strip A **and** last dc on Strip C, sc in next dc on Strip A
and side of same dc on Strip C, sc in next dc on Strip A
and free loop of ch at base of same dc on Strip C, sc in
next dc on Strip A only; working through Strip B **and**
Strip A, sc in last dc on Strip B **and** next dc on Strip A, sc
in side of same dc on Strip B **and** next dc on Strip A, 3 sc
in ch at base of same dc on Strip B **and** last dc on Strip A,
sc in free loop of next ch on Strip B and side of same dc
on Strip A, sc in free loop of ch on Strip B **and** free loop
of ch at base of same dc on Strip A; working in beginning

ch, sc in free loops of next 3 chs on Strip B only, 3 sc in next ch (center ch at base of Cluster), ch 4, (sc in center ch at base of next Cluster on next Strip, ch 4) across to last Cluster on Strip B, 3 sc in center ch, sc in last 2 chs; join with slip st to first sc: 126 sc and 84 ch-4 sps.

Rnd 2: Ch 3, dc in next 6 sc, 3 dc in next sc, dc in next 7 sc, 3 dc in next sc, ✝ dc in next sc and in next ch-4 sp, place marker around last dc made for joining placement, 3 dc in same sp, (dc in next sc, 4 dc in next ch-4 sp) 41 times, place marker around last dc made for joining placement, dc in next sc, 3 dc in next sc ✝, dc in next 10 sc, 3 dc in next sc, dc in next 7 sc, 3 dc in next sc, repeat from ✝ to ✝ once, dc in last 3 sc; join with slip st to top of beginning ch-3, finish off.

ASSEMBLY

With **wrong** sides of two Panels together, bottom edges at same end, and working through **inside** loops of each stitch on **both** pieces, join Dark Green with slip st in **second** marked dc; ch 1, working from **left** to **right**, work reverse sc (*Figs. 11a-d, page 126*) in each dc across to next marked dc; finish off.

Join remaining Panels in same manner, always working in same direction.

EDGING

With **right** side facing and working in Back Loops Only (*Fig. 14, page 126*), join Dark Green with slip st in any st; ch 1, working from **left** to **right**, work reverse sc in each st around; join with slip st to first st, finish off.

Autumn Splendor

*You won't be able to resist wrapping yourself in the lush folds
of this traditional afghan. Rows of bobbles create a pleasing texture,
and the lovely fall flowers are cross stitched onto the throw.*

Finished Size: 51" x 61"

MATERIALS

Red Heart Worsted Weight Yarn
[3 ounces (170 yards) per skein]:
Brown - 10 skeins
Ecru - 8 skeins
Rose - 1 skein
Dark Rose - 1 skein
Spruce - 1 skein
Teal - 1 skein
Crochet hook, size I (5.50 mm) **or** size needed for gauge
Yarn needle

GAUGE: 12 sc = 4"; Rows 1-10 = 3³/₄ "

STITCH GUIDE

CLUSTER
★ YO, insert hook in sp indicated, YO and pull up a
loop, YO and draw through 2 loops on hook; repeat from
★ 2 times **more**, YO and draw through 3 loops on hook,
YO and draw through remaining 2 loops on hook.

AFGHAN BODY

With Brown, ch 176 **loosely**.
Row 1 (Right side): Sc in second ch from hook and in
each ch across: 175 sc.
Note: Mark last sc on last row as **right** side and top edge.
Row 2: Ch 3 **(counts as first dc, now and throughout)**,
turn; dc in next sc, skip next sc, (dc, ch 1, dc) in next sc,
★ skip next sc, dc in next sc, skip next sc, (dc, ch 1, dc) in
next sc; repeat from ★ across to last 3 sc, skip next sc, dc
in last 2 sc: 132 dc and 43 ch-1 sps.
Row 3: Ch 1, turn; sc in first 3 dc, (work Cluster in next
ch-1 sp, sc in next 3 dc) across: 43 Clusters.
Row 4: Ch 3, turn; dc in next sc, skip next sc, (dc, ch 1,
dc) in next Cluster, ★ skip next sc, dc in next sc, skip
next sc, (dc, ch 1, dc) in next Cluster; repeat from ★
across to last 3 sc, skip next sc, dc in last 2 sc: 132 dc and
43 ch-1 sps.
Rows 5 and 6: Repeat Rows 3 and 4.
Row 7: Ch 1, turn; sc in each dc and in each ch-1 sp
across: 175 sc.
Rows 8-10: Ch 1, turn; sc in each sc across changing to
Ecru in last sc on last row.
Rows 11-18: Ch 1, turn; sc in each sc across.

Row 19: Ch 1, turn; sc in first 17 sc, place marker around
last sc made for cross stitch placement, (sc in next 68 sc,
place marker around last sc made for cross stitch
placement) twice, sc in each sc across.
Rows 20-27: Ch 1, turn; sc in each sc across changing to
Brown in last sc on last row *(Fig. 16, page 127)*.
Rows 28-31: Ch 1, turn; sc in each sc across.
Row 32: Ch 3, turn; dc in next sc, skip next sc, (dc, ch 1,
dc) in next sc, ★ skip next sc, dc in next sc, skip next sc,
(dc, ch 1, dc) in next sc; repeat from ★ across to last 3 sc,
skip next sc, dc in last 2 sc: 132 dc and 43 ch-1 sps.
Row 33: Ch 1, turn; sc in first 3 dc, (work Cluster in next
ch-1 sp, sc in next 3 dc) across: 43 Clusters.
Row 34: Ch 3, turn; dc in next sc, skip next sc, (dc, ch 1,
dc) in next Cluster, ★ skip next sc, dc in next sc, skip
next sc, (dc, ch 1, dc) in next Cluster; repeat from ★
across to last 3 sc, skip next sc, dc in last 2 sc: 132 dc and
43 ch-1 sps.
Rows 35 and 36: Repeat Rows 33 and 34.
Row 37: Ch 1, turn; sc in each dc and in each ch-1 sp
across: 175 sc.
Rows 38-40: Ch 1, turn; sc in each sc across changing to
Ecru in last sc on last row.
Rows 41-48: Ch 1, turn; sc in each sc across.
Row 49: Ch 1, turn; sc in first 50 sc, place marker around
last sc made for cross stitch placement, sc in next 69 sc,
place marker around last sc made for cross stitch
placement, sc in each sc across.
Rows 50-78: Repeat Rows 20-48.
Row 79: Ch 1, turn; sc in first 17 sc, place marker around
last sc made for cross stitch placement, (sc in next 68 sc,
place marker around last sc made for cross stitch
placement) twice, sc in each sc across.
Rows 80-87: Ch 1, turn; sc in each sc across changing to
Brown in last sc on last row.
Rows 88-91: Ch 1, turn; sc in each sc across.
Rows 92-157: Repeat Rows 32-91 once, then repeat
Rows 32-37 once **more**; do **not** finish off.

EDGING

Rnd 1: Ch 1, do **not** turn; sc evenly around entire Afghan
working 3 sc in each corner and working an even number
of sc; join with slip st to first sc.
Rnds 2 and 3: Ch 1, **turn;** sc in same st and in each sc
around working 3 sc in center sc of each corner
3-sc group; join with slip st to first sc.
Rnd 4: Ch 3, do **not** turn; working from **left** to **right**, skip
next sc, ★ work reverse hdc in next sc *(Figs. 12a-d,
page 126)*, ch 1, skip next sc; repeat from ★ around; join
with slip st to st at base of beginning ch-3, finish off.

CHART

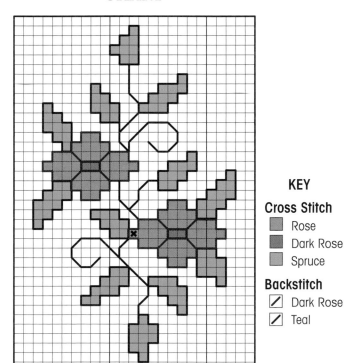

KEY

Cross Stitch

- ▨ Rose
- ▨ Dark Rose
- ▨ Spruce

Backstitch

- ⁄ Dark Rose
- ⁄ Teal

CROSS STITCH

Following Chart, add cross stitch designs to Afghan as follows:

Each colored square on the chart represents one cross stitch and each thick straight line represents one backstitch. Each cross stitch or backstitch is worked over one sc. To position each design on Afghan, use marked sc on Afghan matched to the cross stitch marked with an **X** on chart. Using yarn needle and long strand of yarn, weave end under several stitches on **wrong** side of Afghan to secure (do **not** tie knot). With **right** side facing and marked short edge of Afghan at top, work cross stitch as follows: bring needle up at 1, down at 2 (half cross made), up at 3, and down at 4 **(cross stitch completed, *Fig. 1*)**. All cross stitches should cross in the same direction. Finish off by weaving end under several sts on **wrong** side of Afghan; cut yarn end close to work. When cross stitch is complete, work backstitch as follows: bring needle up at 1, down at 2, and up at 3; to continue, go down at 4 and come up at 5 **(*Fig. 2*)**.

Fig. 1

Fig. 2

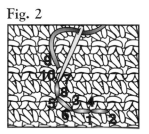

111

Pansy Perfection

*The perfect beauty of pansies inspired our gorgeous afghan.
"Planted" on squares that are joined diagonally, the three-
dimensional flower motifs are blooming with irresistible
color! A dainty shell edging completes the graceful look.*

Finished Size: 49" x 77"

MATERIALS

Red Heart Worsted Weight Yarn
[3½ ounces (198 yards) per skein]:
White - 16 skeins
Green - 2 skeins
Black - 1 skein
Yellow - 1 skein
Rose - 1 skein
Red - 1 skein
Blue - 1 skein
Light Lavender - 1 skein
Lavender - 1 skein
Crochet hook, size H (5.00 mm) **or** size needed for
gauge

GAUGE: Each Pansy Motif (through Rnd 11) and
each Solid Motif (through Rnd 7) = 6"

STITCH GUIDE

LEAF
Ch 8 **loosely**, sc in third ch from hook, dc in next ch, tr
in last 4 chs.

CLUSTER
★ YO, insert hook in ring, YO and pull up a loop, YO
and draw through 2 loops on hook; repeat from ★ once
more, YO and draw through all 3 loops on hook.

DECREASE
Pull up a loop in next 2 sps, YO and draw through all
3 loops on hook.

CENTER DECREASE
Pull up a loop in **same** sp and in **next** ch-2 sp, YO and
draw through all 3 loops on hook.

SHELL
Dc in sp indicated, (ch 1, dc in same sp) twice.

CORNER SHELL
Dc in sp indicated, (ch 1, dc in same sp) 4 times.

PLACEMENT DIAGRAM

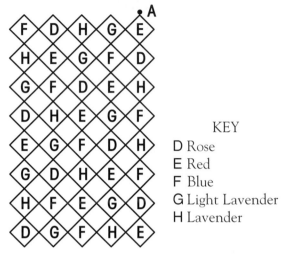

KEY
D Rose
E Red
F Blue
G Light Lavender
H Lavender

FIRST MOTIF

With Black, ch 4; join with slip st to form a ring.
Rnd 1 (Right side)**:** Ch 3 **(counts as first dc)**, 2 dc in
ring, (ch 3, 3 dc in ring) 3 times changing to Yellow in
last dc, ch 5, place marker around ch-5 just made for
stitch placement, sc around bottom of center ring **between**
second and third 3-dc groups, ch 5; join with slip st to first
dc, finish off: 3 ch-3 sps and 2 ch-5 sps.
Note: Mark last round as **right** side.
Refer to Placement Diagram for pansy color used on
Rnds 2-4.
Rnd 2: With **right** side facing, join Pansy color with sc in
marked ch-5 sp *(see Joining With sc, page 126)*; ch 4, in
same sp work [dc, ch 1, (tr, ch 1) 7 times, dc, ch 4, sc], sc
in next sc, in next ch-5 sp work [sc, ch 4, dc, ch 1, (tr,
ch 1) 7 times, dc, ch 4, sc], sc in center dc of next
3-dc group, ★ (5 dc, ch 1, 5 dc) in next ch-3 sp, sc in
center dc of next 3-dc group; repeat from ★ around; join
with slip st to first sc: 5 Petals.
Rnd 3: Ch 3, (sc in next sp, ch 3) 10 times, skip next sc,
sc in next sc, ch 3, (sc in next sp, ch 3) 10 times, slip st in
next sc, leave remaining Petals unworked.
Rnd 4: Slip st in next sc, ch 4, working **behind** Petals, (sc
in st between next 2 Petals, ch 4) 3 times, ★ working
behind Rnd 3, slip st in center tr on Rnd 2 of next Petal,
ch 4; repeat from ★ once **more**; join with slip st to first
slip st, finish off: 6 ch-4 sps.

Rnd 5: With **right** side facing, join Green with slip st in same st as joining; work Leaf, slip st in next ch-4 sp, ch 3, slip st in next ch-4 sp, (work Leaf, slip st in next ch-4 sp) twice; finish off: 3 Leaves.

Rnd 6: With **right** side facing and working **behind** Leaves, join White with sc in same sp on Rnd 4 as first Leaf made; 5 sc in same sp, 6 sc in each ch-4 sp around; join with slip st to first sc: 36 sc.

Rnd 7: Ch 4 (**counts as first hdc plus ch 2**), (hdc in next 9 sc, ch 2) 3 times, hdc in last 8 sc; join with slip st to first hdc: 36 hdc and 4 ch-2 sps.

Rnd 8: Slip st in first ch-2 sp, ch 1, sc in same sp, ch 3, skip next hdc, (sc in next hdc, ch 3, skip next hdc) 4 times, ★ (sc, ch 5, sc) in next ch-2 sp, ch 3, skip next hdc, (sc in next hdc, ch 3, skip next hdc) 4 times; repeat from ★ around, sc in same sp as first sc, ch 2, dc in first sc to form last ch-5 sp: 20 ch-3 sps and 4 ch-5 sps.

Rnd 9: Ch 1, 3 sc in same sp, sc in next ch-3 sp, 2 sc in each of next 4 ch-3 sps, ★ 5 sc in next ch-5 sp, sc in next ch-3 sp, 2 sc in each of next 4 ch-3 sps; repeat from ★ around, 2 sc in same sp as first sc; join with slip st to first sc: 56 sc.

Continued on page 114.

Rnd 10: Ch 5 (**counts as first dc plus ch 2, now and throughout**), 2 dc in same st, dc in next 13 sc, ★ (2 dc, ch 2, 2 dc) in next sc, dc in next 13 sc; repeat from ★ around, dc in same st as first dc; join with slip st to first dc: 68 dc and 4 ch-2 sps.

Rnd 11: Slip st in first ch-2 sp, ch 1, (sc in same sp, ch 3) twice, skip next dc, (sc in next dc, ch 3, skip next dc) across to next ch-2 sp, ★ (sc, ch 3) twice in ch-2 sp, skip next dc, (sc in next dc, ch 3, skip next dc) across to next ch-2 sp; repeat from ★ around; join with slip st to first sc: 40 ch-3 sps.

Rnd 12: Slip st in first ch-3 sp, ch 1, (sc, ch 5, sc) in same sp, ch 3, (sc in next ch-3 sp, ch 3) across to next corner ch-3 sp, ★ (sc, ch 5, sc) in corner ch-3 sp, ch 3, (sc in next ch-3 sp, ch 3) across to next corner ch-3 sp; repeat from ★ around; join with slip st to first sc, finish off: 44 sps.

ADDITIONAL MOTIFS
SOLID MOTIF

With White, ch 4; join with slip st to form a ring.

Rnd 1 (Right side): Ch 2, dc in ring, ch 3, (work Cluster, ch 3) 5 times; join with slip st to first dc: 6 ch-3 sps.

Note: Mark last round as **right** side.

Rnd 2: Slip st in first ch-3 sp, ch 1, 4 sc in same sp and in each ch-3 sp around; join with slip st to first sc: 24 sc.

Rnd 3: Ch 5, 2 dc in same st, dc in next 5 sc, ★ (2 dc, ch 2, 2 dc) in next sc, dc in next 5 sc; repeat from ★ around, dc in same st as first dc; join with slip st to first dc: 36 dc and 4 ch-2 sps.

Rnd 4: Slip st in first ch-2 sp, ch 1, sc in same sp, ch 3, skip next dc, (sc in next dc, ch 3, skip next dc) 4 times, ★ (sc, ch 5, sc) in next ch-2 sp, ch 3, skip next dc, (sc in next dc, ch 3, skip next dc) 4 times; repeat from ★ around, sc in same sp as first sc, ch 2, dc in first sc to form last ch-5 sp: 20 ch-3 sps and 4 ch-5 sps.

Rnds 5-7: Work same as Rnds 9-11 of First Motif; finish off: 40 ch-3 sps.

Rnd 8: Work One or Two Side Joining.

PANSY MOTIF

Work same as First Motif through Rnd 11; finish off: 40 ch-3 sps.

Rnd 12: Work One or Two Side Joining.

ONE SIDE JOINING

With **right** side facing, join White with sc in corner ch-3 sp; ch 2, holding Motifs with **wrong** sides together, slip st in third ch of ch-5 sp on **adjacent Motif**, ch 2, sc in same sp on **new Motif** (*Fig. 17, page 127*), ★ ch 1, slip st in second ch of next ch-3 sp on **adjacent Motif**, ch 1, sc in next ch-3 sp on **new Motif**; repeat from ★ 9 times **more**, ch 2, slip st in third ch of next ch-5 sp on **adjacent Motif**, ch 2, sc in same sp on **new Motif**, ch 3, (sc in next ch-3 sp, ch 3) across to next corner ch-3 sp, † (sc, ch 5, sc) in corner ch-3 sp, ch 3, (sc in next ch-3 sp, ch 3) across to next corner ch-3 sp †; repeat from † to † once **more**; join with slip st to first sc, finish off: 44 sps.

TWO SIDE JOINING

With **right** side facing, join White with sc in corner ch-3 sp; ch 2, holding Motifs with **wrong** sides together, slip st in third ch of ch-5 sp on **adjacent Motif**, ch 2, sc in same sp on **new Motif**, † ★ ch 1, slip st in second ch of next ch-3 sp on **adjacent Motif**, ch 1, sc in next ch-3 sp on **new Motif**; repeat from ★ 9 times **more**, ch 2, slip st in third ch of next ch-5 sp on **adjacent Motif**, ch 2, sc in same sp on **new Motif** †; repeat from † to † once **more**, ch 3, (sc in next ch-3 sp, ch 3) across to next corner ch-3 sp, (sc, ch 5, sc) in corner ch-3 sp, ch 3, (sc in next ch-3 sp, ch 3) across; join with slip st to first sc, finish off: 44 sps.

EDGING

Rnd 1: With **right** side facing, join Green with sc in top right corner ch-5 sp at Point A on diagram; ch 2, sc in same sp, ch 2, † (sc in next ch-3 sp, ch 2) 10 times, decrease, ch 2, (sc in next ch-3 sp, ch 2) 10 times, (sc, ch 2) twice in next corner ch-5 sp †; repeat from † to † 3 times **more**, (sc in next ch-3 sp, ch 2) 10 times, (sc, ch 2) twice in next corner ch-5 sp, repeat from † to † 7 times, (sc in next ch-3 sp, ch 2) 10 times, (sc, ch 2) twice in next corner ch-5 sp, repeat from † to † 4 times, (sc in next ch-3 sp, ch 2) 10 times, (sc, ch 2) twice in next corner ch-5 sp, repeat from † to † 7 times, (sc in next ch-3 sp, ch 2) 10 times; join with slip st to first sc, finish off: 554 ch-2 sps.

Rnd 2: With **right** side facing, join White with sc in first ch-2 sp; ch 1, sc in same sp, (sc, ch 1, sc) in next 10 ch-2 sps, sc in next ch-2 sp, ch 1, work center decrease, ch 1, sc in same sp, † (sc, ch 1, sc) in next 21 ch-2 sps, sc in next ch-2 sp, ch 1, work center decrease, ch 1, sc in same sp †; repeat from † to † 2 times **more**, (sc, ch 1, sc) in next 33 ch-2 sps, sc in next ch-2 sp, ch 1, work center decrease, ch 1, sc in same sp, repeat from † to † 6 times, (sc, ch 1, sc) in next 33 ch-2 sps, sc in next ch-2 sp, ch 1, work center decrease, ch 1, sc in same sp, repeat from † to † 3 times, (sc, ch 1, sc) in next 33 ch-2 sps, sc in next ch-2 sp, ch 1, work center decrease, ch 1, sc in same sp, repeat from † to † 6 times, (sc, ch 1, sc) in last 22 ch-2 sps; join with slip st to first sc: 554 ch-1 sps.

Rnd 3: Slip st in first ch-1 sp, ch 4, dc in same sp, (ch 1, dc in same sp) 3 times, † (sc in next ch-1 sp, work Shell in next ch-1 sp) 5 times, decrease, (work Shell in next ch-1 sp, sc in next ch-1 sp) 5 times, work corner Shell in next ch-1 sp †; repeat from † to † 3 times **more**, sc in next ch-1 sp, (work Shell in next ch-1 sp, sc in next ch-1 sp) 5 times, work corner Shell in next ch-1 sp, repeat from † to † 7 times, sc in next ch-1 sp, (work Shell in next ch-1 sp, sc in next ch-1 sp) 5 times, work corner Shell in next ch-1 sp, repeat from † to † 4 times, sc in next ch-1 sp, (work Shell in next ch-1 sp, sc in next ch-1 sp) 5 times, work corner Shell in next ch-1 sp, repeat from † to † 7 times, sc in next ch-1 sp, (work Shell in next ch-1 sp, sc in next ch-1 sp) 5 times; join with slip st to third ch of beginning ch-4, finish off.

Bargello Blanket

Drape this eye-catching afghan over a patio chair, sofa, or bed to add dazzle to your decor! Radiant bands of pinks and greens contrast vividly with black to capture the classic look of bargello needlepoint.

Finished Size: 48" x 64"

MATERIALS
Red Heart Worsted Weight Yarn
[3 ounces (170 yards) per skein]:
Black - 9 skeins
Dark Green - 4 skeins
Green - 4 skeins
Pink - 4 skeins
Rose - 4 skeins
Crochet hook, size I (5.50 mm) **or** size needed for gauge

GAUGE: In pattern, 15 sts and 13 rows = 4"

Note: Each row is worked across length of Blanket. When joining yarn and finishing off, leave an 8" end to be worked into fringe.

COLOR SEQUENCE
Work 5 rows of Black, work 2 rows of **each** color: Rose, Pink, ★ Black, Dark Green, Green, Black, Rose, Pink; repeat from ★ 11 times **more**, then work 4 rows of Black.

AFGHAN BODY
With Black, ch 240 **loosely**.
Row 1 (Right side)**:** Sc in second ch from hook and in each ch across; finish off: 239 sc.
Note: Mark last row as **right** side.
Row 2: With **wrong** side facing, join Black with sc in first sc (*see Joining With Sc, page 126*); sc in next 2 sc, ch 3, ★ skip next 3 sc, sc in next 2 sc, ch 3; repeat from ★ across to last 6 sc, skip next 3 sc, sc in last 3 sc; finish off: 98 sc and 47 ch-3 sps.
Row 3: With **right** side facing, join Black with sc in first sc; ch 2, ★ skip next 2 sc, working in **front** of next ch-3 (*Fig. 18, page 127*), dc in each of 3 skipped sc one row below ch-3, ch 2; repeat from ★ across to last 3 sc, skip next 2 sc, sc in last sc; finish off: 143 sts and 48 ch-2 sps.

Continued on page 116.

Row 4: With **wrong** side facing, join next color with sc in first sc; working **behind** next ch-2, dc in each of 2 skipped sts one row **below** ch-2, ★ ch 3, skip next 3 dc, working **behind** next ch-2, dc in each of 2 skipped sts one row **below** ch-2; repeat from ★ across to last sc, sc in last sc; finish off: 98 sts and 47 ch-3 sps.

Row 5: With **right** side facing, join same color with sc in first sc; ch 2, ★ skip next 2 dc, working in **front** of next ch-3, dc in each of 3 skipped dc one row **below** ch-3, ch 2; repeat from ★ across to last 3 sts, skip next 2 dc, sc in last sc; finish off: 143 sts and 48 ch-2 sps.

Rows 6-156: Repeat Rows 4 and 5, 75 times; then repeat Row 4 once **more**: 98 sts and 47 ch-3 sps.

Row 157: With **right** side facing, join Black with sc in first sc; ★ sc in next 2 dc, working in **front** of next ch-3, dc in each of 3 skipped dc one row **below** ch-3; repeat from ★ across to last 3 sts, sc in last 3 sts; finish off.

EDGING
FIRST SIDE
With **right** side facing, join Black with slip st in first sc on Row 157; ★ ch 1, skip next st, slip st in next st; repeat from ★ across; finish off.

SECOND SIDE
With **right** side facing and working in free loops of beginning ch (**Fig. 15b, page 127**), join Black with slip st in first ch; ★ ch 1, skip next ch, slip st in next ch; repeat from ★ 118 times **more**; finish off.

Holding nine 18" strands of yarn together for each fringe, add additional fringe across short edges of Blanket (**Figs. 20a & b, page 127**).

Daisy Blanket

This little baby afghan reminds us of a field of daisies waving in the summer breeze! With picturesque petals and a snuggly texture, the blanket will fascinate wee ones and wrap them in warmth.

Finished Size: 32¹/₂ " x 45"

MATERIALS
Red Heart Baby Sport Weight Pompadour Yarn [6 ounces (480 yards) per skein]:
Yellow - 2 skeins
Blue - 1 skein
Green - 1 skein
Pink - 1 skein
White - 1 skein
Crochet hook, size G (4.00 mm) **or** size needed for gauge
Yarn needle

GAUGE: Each Square = 4¹/₄ "

STITCH GUIDE

> **PICOT**
> Ch 3, sc in third ch from hook.

SQUARE (Make 70)
With Yellow, ch 5; join with slip st to form a ring.
Rnd 1 (Right side): Ch 1, 12 sc in ring; join with slip st to first sc, finish off: 12 sc.
Note: Mark last round as **right** side.
Using the following colors for Rnd 2, make 24 flowers with White, 23 flowers **each** with Pink and Blue.

Rnd 2: With **right** side facing, join next color with slip st in same st as joining; ★ ch 6 **loosely**, working in top loop only of each ch, dc in third ch from hook and in last 3 chs (**Petal made**), slip st in next sc; repeat from ★ around working last slip st in same st as joining; finish off: 12 Petals.

Rnd 3: With **right** side facing, join Green with slip st in ch-2 sp at tip of any Petal; ch 3 (**counts as first dc, now and throughout**), (2 dc, ch 3, 3 dc) in same sp, ch 1, sc in ch-2 sp at tip of next Petal, ch 2, sc in ch-2 sp at tip of next Petal, ch 1, ★ (3 dc, ch 3, 3 dc) in ch-2 sp at tip of next Petal, ch 1, sc in ch-2 sp at tip of next Petal, ch 2, sc in ch-2 sp at tip of next Petal, ch 1; repeat from ★ 2 times **more**; join with slip st to first dc, finish off: 16 sps.

Rnd 4: With **right** side facing, join Yellow with slip st in any ch-3 sp; ch 3, (2 dc, ch 3, 3 dc) in same sp, ch 1, 2 dc in next ch-1 sp, hdc in next sc, ch 1, 2 hdc in next ch-2 sp, ch 1, hdc in next sc, 2 dc in next ch-1 sp, ch 1, ★ (3 dc, ch 3, 3 dc) in next ch-3 sp, ch 1, 2 dc in next ch-1 sp, hdc in next sc, ch 1, 2 hdc in next ch-2 sp, ch 1, hdc in next sc, 2 dc in next ch-1 sp, ch 1; repeat from ★ 2 times **more**; join with slip st to first dc, finish off: 56 sts and 20 sps.

ASSEMBLY
Using Placement Diagram as a guide, with Yellow, and working through **both** loops of each stitch on **both** pieces, whipstitch Squares together (**Fig. 19b, page 127**), beginning in center ch of first corner ch-3 and ending in center ch of next corner ch-3; then whipstitch strips together in same manner.

PLACEMENT DIAGRAM

EDGING

Rnd 1: With **right** side facing, join Pink with slip st in top right corner ch-3 sp; ch 3, (2 dc, ch 3, 3 dc) in same sp, ch 2, (dc in next sp, ch 2) across to next corner ch-3 sp, ★ (3 dc, ch 3, 3 dc) in corner ch-3 sp, ch 2, (dc in next sp, ch 2) across to next corner ch-3 sp; repeat from ★ 2 times **more**; join with slip st to first dc, finish off: 220 dc and 204 sps.

Rnd 2: With **right** side facing, join Green with slip st in top right corner ch-3 sp; ch 3, (2 dc, ch 3, 3 dc) in same sp, ★ 3 dc in each ch-2 sp across to next corner ch-3 sp, (3 dc, ch 3, 3 dc) in corner ch-3 sp; repeat from ★ 2 times **more**, 3 dc in each ch-2 sp across; join with slip st to first dc, finish off: 624 dc and 4 ch-3 sps.

Rnd 3: With **right** side facing, join Blue with sc in top right corner ch-3 sp; work Picot, (sc in same sp, work Picot) twice, ★ † skip next 3 dc, sc in sp **before** next dc, work Picot †; repeat from † to † across to within 3 dc of next corner ch-3 sp, skip next 3 dc, (sc, work Picot) 3 times in corner ch-3 sp; repeat from ★ 2 times **more**, then repeat from † to † across to last 3 dc, skip last 3 dc; join with slip st to first sc, finish off.

117

Floral Cascade

Cascading flowers take center stage on this romantic afghan. The center floral panel is bordered by alternating panels of leaves and berries. We used post and popcorn stitches to create the three-dimensional motifs; reverse single crochets join the panels.

Finished Size: 54" x 67"

MATERIALS

Red Heart Worsted Weight Yarn,
[8 ounces (452 yards) per skein]:
Pink - 6 skeins
White - 4 skeins
Crochet hook, size J (6.00 mm) **or** size needed for gauge

GAUGE: 11 dc and 7 rows = 4"
Each Leaf Panel = 4 ³/₄ "
Each Berry Panel = 9 ³/₄ "
Floral Panel = 15 ¹/₂ "

STITCH GUIDE

BACK POST TREBLE CROCHET (abbreviated BPtr)
YO twice, insert hook from **back** to **front** around post of st indicated **(Fig. 13, page 126)**, YO and pull up a loop, (YO and draw through 2 loops on hook) 3 times. Skip st in front of BPtr unless otherwise indicated.

FRONT POST TREBLE CROCHET (abbreviated FPtr)
YO twice, insert hook from **front** to **back** around post of st indicated **(Fig. 13, page 126)**, YO and pull up a loop, (YO and draw through 2 loops on hook) 3 times. Skip st behind FPtr unless otherwise indicated.

RIGHT LARGE LEAF
YO 6 times, working in **front** of previous rows, insert hook around post of center FPtr 2 rows **below (Fig. 18, page 127)**, YO and pull up a loop, (YO and draw through 2 loops on hook) 6 times, YO 5 times, insert hook around same post **above** leg just made, YO and pull up a loop, (YO and draw through 2 loops on hook) 5 times, ★ YO 4 times, insert hook around same post **above** leg just made, YO and pull up a loop, (YO and draw through 2 loops on hook) 4 times; repeat from ★ once **more**, YO and draw through all 5 loops on hook.

LEFT LARGE LEAF
YO 4 times, working in **front** of previous rows, insert hook around post of center FPtr 2 rows **below (Fig. 8, page 127)**, YO and pull up a loop, (YO and draw through 2 loops on hook) 4 times, YO 4 times, insert hook around same post **below** leg just made, YO and pull up a loop, (YO and draw through 2 loops on hook) 4 times, YO 5 times, insert hook around same post **below** leg just made, YO and pull up a loop, (YO and draw through 2 loops on hook) 5 times, YO 6 times, insert hook around same post

below leg just made, YO and pull up a loop, (YO and draw through 2 loops on hook) 6 times, YO and draw through all 5 loops on hook.

BACK POPCORN
6 Dc in st indicated, drop loop from hook, insert hook from the **back** in first dc of 6-dc group, hook dropped loop and draw through.

FRONT POPCORN
6 Dc in st indicated, drop loop from hook, insert hook from the **front** in first dc of 6-dc group, hook dropped loop and draw through.

RIGHT SMALL LEAF
YO 5 times, working in **front** of previous row, insert hook around post of next BPtr one row **below (Fig. 18, page 127)**, YO and pull up a loop, (YO and draw through 2 loops on hook) 5 times, YO 4 times, insert hook around same post **above** leg just made, YO and pull up a loop, (YO and draw through 2 loops on hook) 4 times, YO and draw through all 3 loops on hook.

LEFT SMALL LEAF
YO 4 times, working in **front** of previous row, insert hook around post of previous BPtr one row **below** (working **below** st already around post, if any) **(Fig. 18, page 127)**, YO and pull up a loop, (YO and draw through 2 loops on hook) 4 times, YO 5 times, insert hook around same post **below** leg just made, YO and pull up a loop, (YO and draw through 2 loops on hook) 5 times, YO and draw through all 3 loops on hook.

LOWER PETALS
YO 5 times, working **behind** previous row, insert hook around post of first marked dc **(Fig. 18, page 127)**, † YO and pull up a loop, (YO and draw through 2 loops on hook) 5 times, ★ YO 4 times, insert hook around same post **below** leg just made, YO and pull up a loop, (YO and draw through 2 loops on hook) 4 times; repeat from ★ once **more**, YO 5 times, insert hook around same post **below** leg just made, YO and pull up a loop, (YO and draw through 2 loops on hook) 5 times †, YO 5 times, insert hook around post of **next** marked dc, repeat from † to † once working each leg **above** leg just made, YO and draw through all 9 loops on hook, remove markers.

LEFT PETAL
YO 5 times, working **behind** previous rows, insert hook in top of next BPtr 2 rows **below** (next to Lower Petals), YO and pull up a loop, (YO and draw through 2 loops on hook) 5 times, ★ YO 4 times, insert hook in **same** st, YO and pull up a loop, (YO and draw through 2 loops on

Continued on page 120.

hook) 4 times; repeat from ★ once **more**, YO 5 times, insert hook in **same** st, YO and pull up a loop, (YO and draw through 2 loops on hook) 5 times, YO and draw through all 5 loops on hook.

RIGHT PETAL
YO 5 times, working **behind** previous rows, insert hook in **same** BPtr as Left Petal, YO and pull up a loop, (YO and draw through 2 loops on hook) 5 times, ★ YO 4 times, insert hook in **same** st, YO and pull up a loop, (YO and draw through 2 loops on hook) 4 times; repeat from ★ once **more**, YO 5 times, insert hook in **same** st, YO and pull up a loop, (YO and draw through 2 loops on hook) 5 times, YO and draw through all 5 loops on hook.

TOP PETAL
YO 5 times, working in **front** of previous rows and working **between** Left and Right Petals, insert hook in **same** BPtr as Petals, YO and pull up a loop, (YO and draw through 2 loops on hook) 5 times, ★ YO 4 times, insert hook in **same** st, YO and pull up a loop, (YO and draw through 2 loops on hook) 4 times; repeat from ★ once **more**, YO 5 times, insert hook in **same** st, YO and pull up a loop, (YO and draw through 2 loops on hook) 5 times, YO and draw through all 5 loops on hook.

LEAF PANEL (Make 4)
With White, ch 15 **loosely**.

Row 1 (Right side): Dc in fourth ch from hook **(3 skipped chs count as first dc, now and throughout)** and in each ch across: 13 dc.

Note: Mark last row as **right** side and bottom edge.

Row 2: Ch 3 **(counts as first dc, now and throughout)**, turn; dc in next 5 dc, work BPtr around next dc, dc in last 6 dc.

Row 3: Ch 3, turn; dc in next 5 dc, work FPtr around next BPtr, dc in last 6 dc.

Row 4: Ch 3, turn; dc in next 5 dc, work BPtr around next FPtr, dc in last 6 dc.

Row 5: Ch 3, turn; dc in next 2 dc, work Right Large Leaf, skip next dc, dc in next 2 dc, work FPtr around next BPtr, dc in last 6 dc.

Row 6: Ch 3, turn; dc in next 5 dc, work BPtr around next FPtr, dc in last 6 sts.

Row 7: Ch 3, turn; dc in next 5 dc, work FPtr around next BPtr, dc in next 2 dc, work Left Large Leaf, skip next dc, dc in last 3 dc.

Row 8: Ch 3, turn; dc in next 5 sts, work BPtr around next FPtr, dc in last 6 dc.

Rows 9-113: Repeat Rows 5-8, 26 times; then repeat Row 5 once **more**.

Row 114: Ch 3, turn; dc in next dc and in each st across.

Row 115: Ch 3, turn; dc in next 8 dc, work Left Large Leaf, skip next dc, dc in last 3 dc.

Rows 116 and 117: Ch 3, turn; dc in next dc and in each st across.

Finish off.

BERRY PANEL (Make 2)
With Pink, ch 29 **loosely**.

Row 1: Dc in fourth ch from hook and in each ch across: 27 dc.

Row 2 (Right side): Ch 3, turn; dc in next 12 dc, work FPtr around next dc, dc in last 13 dc.

Note: Mark last row as **right** side and bottom edge.

Row 3: Ch 3, turn; dc in next 13 sts, work BPtr around FPtr below last dc made, skip next dc, dc in last 12 dc.

Row 4: Ch 3, turn; dc in next 10 dc, skip next dc, work FPtr around next BPtr, dc in same st, work FPtr around next dc, dc in last 13 dc.

Row 5: Ch 3, turn; dc in next 12 dc, work BPtr around next FPtr, dc in next 2 sts, work BPtr around FPtr **below** last dc made, skip next dc, work Back Popcorn in next dc, dc in last 9 dc.

Row 6: Ch 3, turn; dc in next 8 dc, skip next Popcorn, work FPtr around next BPtr, dc in same st, work Front Popcorn in next dc, dc in next dc, work FPtr around next BPtr, dc in last 13 sts.

Row 7: Ch 3, turn; dc in next 11 dc, skip next dc, work BPtr around next FPtr, dc in same st and in next 4 sts, work BPtr around FPtr **below** last dc made, skip next dc, work Back Popcorn in next dc, dc in last 7 dc.

Row 8: Ch 3, turn; dc in next 6 dc, skip next Popcorn, work FPtr around next BPtr, dc in same st, work Front Popcorn in next dc, dc in next 3 dc, work FPtr around next dc, dc in next BPtr, work FPtr around BPtr **below** dc just made, skip next dc, dc in last 11 dc.

Row 9: Ch 3, turn; dc in next 8 dc, work Back Popcorn in next dc, skip next dc, work BPtr around next FPtr, dc in same st and in next dc, work BPtr around next FPtr, dc in next 5 sts, work Back Popcorn in next FPtr, dc in last 7 dc.

Row 10: Ch 3, turn; dc in next 12 sts, work FPtr around next BPtr, dc in next dc, work Front Popcorn in next dc, dc in next BPtr, work FPtr around BPtr **below** dc just made, skip next Popcorn, dc in last 9 dc.

Row 11: Ch 3, turn; dc in next 6 dc, work Back Popcorn in next dc, skip next dc, work BPtr around next FPtr, dc in same st and in next 4 sts, work BPtr around FPtr **below** last dc made, skip next dc, dc in last 12 dc.

Row 12: Ch 3, turn; dc in next 10 dc, skip next dc, work FPtr around next BPtr, dc in same st, work FPtr around next dc, dc in next 3 dc, work Front Popcorn in next dc, dc in next BPtr, work FPtr around BPtr **below** dc just made, skip next Popcorn, dc in last 7 dc.

Row 13: Ch 3, turn; dc in next 6 dc, work Back Popcorn in next FPtr, dc in next 5 sts, work BPtr around next FPtr, dc in next 2 sts, work BPtr around FPtr **below** last dc made, skip next dc, work Back Popcorn in next dc, dc in last 9 dc.

Rows 14-107: Repeat Rows 6-13, 11 times; then repeat Rows 6-11 once **more**.

Row 108: Ch 3, turn; dc in next 10 dc, skip next dc, work FPtr around next BPtr, dc in same st and in next 4 dc, work Front Popcorn in next dc, dc in next BPtr, work FPtr around BPtr **below** dc just made, skip next Popcorn, dc in last 7 dc.

Row 109: Ch 3, turn; dc in next 6 dc, work Back Popcorn in next FPtr, dc in next 8 sts, work BPtr around FPtr **below** last dc made, skip next dc, work Back Popcorn in next dc, dc in last 9 dc.

Row 110: Ch 3, turn; dc in next 8 dc, skip next Popcorn, work FPtr around next BPtr, dc in same st, work Front Popcorn in next dc, dc in last 15 sts.

Row 111: Ch 3, turn; dc in next 17 sts, work BPtr around FPtr **below** last dc made, skip next dc, work Back Popcorn in next dc, dc in last 7 dc.

Row 112: Ch 3, turn; dc in next 6 dc, skip next Popcorn, work FPtr around next BPtr, dc in same st, work Front Popcorn in next dc, dc in last 17 dc.

Row 113: Ch 3, turn; dc in next 18 sts, work Back Popcorn in next FPtr, dc in last 7 dc.

Rows 114-117: Ch 3, turn; dc in next dc and in each st across.
Finish off.

FLOWER PANEL (Make 1)

With Pink, ch 45 **loosely**.

Row 1: Dc in fourth ch from hook and in each ch across: 43 dc.

Row 2 (Right side): Ch 3, turn; dc in next 18 dc, work FPtr around next dc, dc in last 23 dc.

Note: Mark last row as **right** side and bottom edge.

Row 3: Ch 3, turn; dc in next 22 dc, work BPtr around next FPtr, dc in last 19 dc.

Row 4: Ch 3, turn; dc in next 14 dc, work Right Small Leaf, skip next dc, dc in next 2 dc, skip next dc, working **above** legs of Leaf, work FPtr around next BPtr, dc in same st and in last 23 dc.

Row 5: Ch 3, turn; dc in next 22 dc, work BPtr around next dc, dc in next FPtr, work BPtr around FPtr **below** dc just made, skip next dc, dc in last 17 sts.

Row 6: Ch 3, turn; dc in next 15 dc, skip next dc, work FPtr around next BPtr, dc in same st and in next 2 sts, work FPtr around BPtr **below** last dc made, skip next dc, dc in next 2 dc, work Left Small Leaf, skip next dc, dc in last 19 dc.

Row 7: Ch 3, turn; dc in next 20 sts, skip next dc, work BPtr around next FPtr, dc in same st and in next 4 sts, work BPtr around FPtr **below** last dc made, skip next dc, dc in last 15 dc.

Row 8: Ch 3, turn; dc in next 9 dc, work Right Small Leaf, skip next dc, dc in next 3 dc, skip next dc, working **above** legs of Leaf, work FPtr around next BPtr, dc in same st and in next 2 dc, work Right Small Leaf, skip next dc, dc in next 3 sts, working **above** legs of Leaf, work FPtr around BPtr **below** last dc made, skip next dc, dc in last 20 dc.

Row 9: Ch 3, turn; dc in next 18 sts, skip next dc, work BPtr around next FPtr, dc in same st and in next 7 sts, work BPtr around next FPtr, dc in last 14 sts.

Row 10: Ch 3, turn; dc in next 10 dc, place marker around last dc made for Petal placement, dc in next 3 dc, work FPtr around next BPtr, dc in next 4 dc, place marker around last dc made for Petal placement, dc in next 5 sts, work FPtr around BPtr **below** last dc made, skip next dc, dc in next 2 dc, work Left Small Leaf, skip next dc, dc in last 15 dc.

Row 11: Ch 3, turn; dc in next 16 sts, skip next dc, work BPtr around next FPtr, dc in same st, work BPtr around next dc, dc in next 7 dc, work Lower Petals, skip next dc, work BPtr around next FPtr, dc in last 14 dc.

Row 12: Ch 3, turn; dc in next 13 dc, ch 1, skip next BPtr, dc in next 7 sts, skip next dc, work FPtr around next BPtr, dc in same st and in next 2 sts, work FPtr around BPtr **below** last dc made, skip next dc, dc in last 16 dc.

Row 13: Ch 3, turn; dc in next 14 dc, skip next dc, work BPtr around next FPtr, dc in same st and in next 4 sts, work BPtr around FPtr **below** last dc made, skip next dc, dc in next dc, work Left Petal, skip next dc, dc in next 4 dc, dc in next ch-1 sp and in next 4 dc, work Right Petal, skip next dc, dc in last 9 dc.

Row 14: Ch 3, turn; dc in next 13 sts, work Top Petal, skip next dc, dc in next 5 sts, skip next dc, work FPtr around next BPtr, dc in same st and in next 2 dc, work Left Small Leaf, skip next dc, dc in next 3 sts, work FPtr around BPtr **below** last dc made, skip next dc, dc in next 2 dc, work Left Small Leaf, skip next dc, dc in last 11 dc.

Row 15: Ch 3, turn; dc in next 13 sts, work BPtr around next FPtr, dc in next 8 sts, work BPtr around FPtr **below** last dc made, skip next dc, dc in last 19 sts.

Row 16: Ch 3, turn; dc in next 13 dc, work Right Small Leaf, skip next dc, dc in next 3 dc, skip next dc, working **above** legs of Leaf, work FPtr around next BPtr, dc in same st and in next 5 dc, place marker around last dc made for Petal placement, dc in next 3 dc, work FPtr around next BPtr, dc in next 4 dc, place marker around last dc made for Petal placement, dc in last 10 dc.

Row 17: Ch 3, turn; dc in next 12 dc, work Lower Petals, skip next dc, work BPtr around next FPtr, dc in next 8 dc, skip next dc, work BPtr around next FPtr, dc in same st, working **below** st already around post, work BPtr around FPtr **below** dc just made, skip next dc, dc in last 17 sts.

Row 18: Ch 3, turn; dc in next 15 dc, skip next dc, work FPtr around next BPtr, dc in same st and in next 2 sts, work FPtr around BPtr **below** last dc made, skip next dc, dc in next 7 dc, ch 1, skip next BPtr, dc in last 14 sts.

Row 19: Ch 3, turn; dc in next 8 dc, work Left Petal, skip next dc, dc in next 4 dc, dc in next ch-1 sp and in next 4 dc, work Right Petal, skip next dc, dc in next dc, skip next dc, work BPtr around next FPtr, dc in same st and in next 4 sts, work BPtr around FPtr **below** last dc made, skip next dc, dc in last 15 dc.

Row 20: Ch 3, turn; dc in next 9 dc, work Right Small Leaf, skip next dc, dc in next 3 dc, skip next dc, working **above** legs of Leaf, work FPtr around next BPtr, dc in same st and in next 2 dc, work Right Small Leaf, skip next dc, dc in next 3 sts, working **above** legs of Leaf, work FPtr around BPtr **below** last dc made, skip next dc, dc in next 5 sts, work Top Petal, skip next dc, dc in last 14 sts.

Rows 21-106: Repeat Rows 9-20, 7 times; then repeat Rows 9 and 10 once **more**.

Continued on page 122.

Row 107: Ch 3, turn; dc in next 16 sts, skip next dc, work BPtr around next FPtr, dc in same st and in next 8 dc, work Lower Petals, skip next dc, work BPtr around next FPtr, dc in last 14 dc.

Row 108: Ch 3, turn; dc in next 13 dc, ch 1, skip next BPtr, dc in next 7 sts, work Right Small Leaf, skip next dc, dc in next 3 sts, working **above** legs of Leaf, work FPtr around BPtr **below** last dc made, skip next dc, dc in last 16 dc.

Row 109: Ch 3, turn; dc in next 14 dc, skip next dc, work BPtr around next FPtr, dc in same st and in next 6 sts, work Left Petal, skip next dc, dc in next 4 dc, dc in next ch-1 sp and in next 4 dc, work Right Petal, skip next dc, dc in last 9 dc.

Row 110: Ch 3, turn; dc in next 13 sts, work Top Petal, skip next dc, dc in next 13 sts, work FPtr around BPtr **below** last dc made, skip next dc, dc in next 2 dc, work Left Small Leaf, skip next dc, dc in last 11 dc.

Row 111: Ch 3, turn; dc in next 13 sts, work BPtr around next FPtr, dc in last 28 sts.

Row 112: Ch 3, turn; dc in next 24 dc, place marker around last dc made for Petal placement, dc in next 3 dc, work FPtr around next BPtr, dc in next 4 dc, place marker around last dc made for Petal placement, dc in last 10 dc.

Row 113: Ch 3, turn; dc in next 12 dc, work Lower Petals, skip next dc, work BPtr around next FPtr, dc in last 28 dc.

Row 114: Ch 3, turn; dc in next 27 dc, ch 1, skip next BPtr, dc in last 14 sts.

Row 115: Ch 3, turn; dc in next 8 dc, work Left Petal, skip next dc, dc in next 4 dc, dc in next ch-1 sp and in next 4 dc, work Right Petal, skip next dc, dc in last 23 dc.

Row 116: Ch 3, turn; dc in next 27 sts, work Top Petal, skip next dc, dc in last 14 sts.

Row 117: Ch 3, turn; dc in next dc and in each st across; finish off.

JOINING

Place Flower Panel and one Leaf Panel with **wrong** sides together and bottom edges to your right. Beginning at left edge and working through **both** pieces around posts of dc at end of rows, join Pink with slip st in first row; ch 1, working from **left** to **right**, work 2 reverse sc in same row and in each row across *(Figs. 11a-d, page 126)*, slip st in same row as last reverse sc made; finish off.

Repeat to join Leaf Panel to opposite side of Flower Panel.

Join one Berry Panel to each side of previously joined Panels in same manner.

Join one Leaf Panel to each side of previously joined Panels in same manner.

SIDE TRIM

With **right** side of one long edge facing and working around posts of dc at end of rows, join White with slip st in first row at left edge; ch 1, working from **left** to **right**, work 2 reverse sc in same row and in each row across, slip st in same row as last reverse sc made finish off.

Repeat for opposite edge of Afghan.

Holding five 18" strands of corresponding color yarn together for each fringe, add fringe across short edges of Afghan *(Figs. 20a & b, page 127)*.

Shamrock Wrap

St. Paddy himself would be delighted with our lucky shamrock afghan! The petals in each square are framed by a double crochet border. All of the squares are then whipstitched together and surrounded by a picot edging for a soft springtime effect.

Finished Size: 46" x 66"

MATERIALS
Red Heart Worsted Weight Yarn
[3½ ounces (198 yards) per skein]:
White - 12 skeins
Green - 5 skeins
Crochet hook, size I (5.50 mm) **or** size needed for gauge
Yarn needle

GAUGE: Each Square = 4"

STITCH GUIDE

> **BEGINNING CLUSTER**
> Ch 3, ★ YO twice, insert hook in ring, YO and pull up a loop, (YO and draw through 2 loops on hook) twice; repeat from ★ once **more**, YO and draw through all 3 loops on hook.
>
> **CLUSTER**
> ★ YO twice, insert hook in ring, YO and pull up a loop, (YO and draw through 2 loops on hook) twice; repeat from ★ 2 times **more**, YO and draw through all 4 loops on hook.
>
> **PICOT**
> Ch 3, slip st in third ch from hook.

SQUARE (Make 176)
SHAMROCK

With Green, ch 10; slip st in sixth ch from hook to form a ring, leave remaining 4 chs unworked for stem.

Rnd 1 (Right side): Work beginning Cluster, ch 1, work Cluster, ch 6, place marker around ch-6 just made for Border placement, work (Cluster, ch 1, Cluster, ch 6) twice, slip st in end of stem, ch 6; join with slip st to top of beginning Cluster, finish off: 6 Clusters and 4 loops.
Note: Mark last round as **right** side.

BORDER

Rnd 1: With **right** side facing, join White with sc in marked loop (*see Joining With Sc, page 126*); (3 sc, ch 2, 4 sc) in same loop, hdc in next ch-1 sp, (4 sc, ch 2, 4 sc) in next loop, hdc in next ch-1 sp, (4 sc, ch 2, 4 sc) in next loop, sc in slip st at end of stem, (4 sc, ch 2, 4 sc) in next loop, hdc in last ch-1 sp; join with slip st to first sc: 36 sts and 4 ch-2 sps.

Rnd 2: Ch 3 (**counts as first dc**), ★ dc in next sc and in each st across to next ch-2 sp, (2 dc, ch 2, 2 dc) in ch-2 sp; repeat from ★ 3 times **more**, dc in each st across; join with slip st to first dc, finish off: 52 dc and 4 ch-2 sps.

ASSEMBLY

With White, using photo as a guide for placement, and working through **both** loops of each stitch on **both** pieces, whipstitch Squares together forming 11 vertical strips of 16 Squares each (**Fig. 19b, page 127**), beginning in second ch of first corner ch-2 and ending in first ch of next corner ch-2; then whipstitch strips together in same manner.

EDGING

Rnd 1: With **right** side facing, join White with sc in top right corner ch-2 sp; 2 sc in same sp, † 2 sc in next dc, sc in each dc and in each sp across to within one dc of next corner ch-2 sp, 2 sc in next dc, 4 sc in corner ch-2 sp, 2 sc in next dc, sc in each dc and in each sp across to within one dc of next corner ch-2 sp, 2 sc in next dc †, 3 sc in corner ch-2 sp, repeat from † to † once; join with slip st to first sc, finish off: 824 sc.

Rnd 2: With **right** side facing, join Green with sc in center sc of top right corner 3-sc group; work Picot, (sc in next 4 sc, work Picot) around to last 3 sc, sc in last 3 sc; join with slip st to first sc, finish off.

123

General Instructions

BASIC INFORMATION

ABBREVIATIONS

BPdc	Back Post double crochet(s)
BPhdc	Back Post half double crochet(s)
BPsc	Back Post single crochet(s)
BPtr	Back Post treble crochet(s)
ch(s)	chain(s)
dc	double crochet(s)
dtr	double treble crochet(s)
FP	Front Post
FPdc	Front Post double crochet(s)
FPdtr	Front Post double treble crochet(s)
FPsc	Front Post single crochet(s)
FPtr	Front Post treble crochet(s)
hdc	half double crochet(s)
LDC	Long double crochet(s)
LFPtr	Long Front Post treble crochet(s)
mm	millimeters
Rnd(s)	Round(s)
sc	single crochet(s)
sp(s)	space(s)
st(s)	stitch(es)
tr	treble crochet(s)
tr tr	triple treble crochet(s)
YO	yarn over

SYMBOLS

★ — work instructions following ★ as many **more** times as indicated in addition to the first time.

† to † or ♥ to ♥ — work all instructions from first † to second † or from first ♥ to second ♥ **as many** times as specified.

( ) or [ ] — work enclosed instructions **as many** times as specified by the number immediately following **or** work all enclosed instructions in the stitch or space indicated **or** contains explanatory remarks.

colon (:) — the number(s) given after a colon at the end of a row or round denote(s) the number of stitches or spaces you should have on that row or round.

GAUGE

Gauge is the number of stitches and rows or rounds per inch and is used to determine the finished size of a project. All crochet patterns will specify the gauge that you must match to ensure proper size and to ensure that you have enough yarn to complete the project.

Hook size given in instructions is merely a guide. Because everyone crochets differently — loosely, tightly, or somewhere in between — the finished size can vary, even when crocheters use the very same pattern, yarn, and hook.

Before beginning any crocheted item, it is absolutely necessary for you to crochet a gauge swatch in the pattern stitch indicated and using the weight of yarn and hook size suggested. Your swatch must be large enough to measure your gauge. Lay your swatch on a hard, smooth, flat surface. Then measure it, counting your stitches and rows or rounds carefully. If your swatch is larger or smaller than specified, **make another, changing the hook size to get the correct gauge**. Keep trying until you find the size that will give you the specified gauge. DO NOT HESITATE TO CHANGE HOOK SIZE TO OBTAIN CORRECT GAUGE. Once proper gauge is obtained, measure width of piece approximately every 3" to be sure gauge remains consistent.

BASIC STITCH GUIDE

CHAIN (abbreviated ch)

To work a chain stitch, begin with a slip knot on the hook. Bring the yarn **over** hook from **back** to **front**, catching the yarn with the hook and turning the hook slightly toward you to keep the yarn from slipping off. Draw the yarn through the slip knot (**Fig. 1**).

Fig. 1

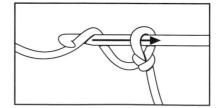

WORKING INTO THE CHAIN

When beginning a row of crochet **Fig. 2a**
in a chain, always skip the first
chain from the hook and work
into the second chain from hook
(for single crochet), third chain
from hook (for half double
crochet), or fourth chain from
hook (for double crochet), etc.
(Fig. 2a).

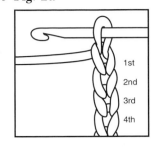

Method 1: Insert hook into back ridge of each chain
indicated **(Fig. 2b)**.
Method 2: Insert hook under top loop **and** the back ridge
of each chain indicated **(Fig. 2c)**.

Fig. 2b

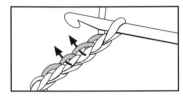

Fig. 2c

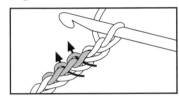

SLIP STITCH *(abbreviated slip st)*

This stitch is used to attach   **Fig. 3**
new yarn, to join work, or to
move the yarn across a group
of stitches without adding
height. Insert hook in stitch
or space indicated, YO and
draw through stitch **and** loop
on hook **(Fig. 3)**.

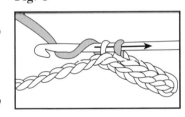

SINGLE CROCHET *(abbreviated sc)*

Insert hook in stitch or space   **Fig. 4**
indicated, YO and pull up a
loop (2 loops on hook), YO
and draw through both loops
on hook **(Fig. 4)**.

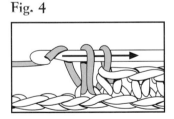

HALF DOUBLE CROCHET

(abbreviated hdc)   **Fig. 5**

YO, insert hook in stitch or
space indicated, YO and pull
up a loop (3 loops on hook),
YO and draw through all
3 loops on hook **(Fig. 5)**.

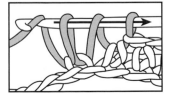

DOUBLE CROCHET

(abbreviated dc)

YO, insert hook in stitch or space indicated, YO and pull
up a loop (3 loops on hook), YO and draw through 2 loops
on hook **(Fig. 6a)**, YO and draw through remaining
2 loops on hook **(Fig. 6b)**.

Fig. 6a

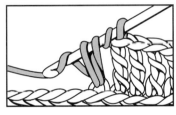

Fig. 6b

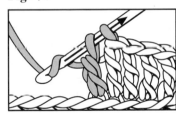

TREBLE CROCHET

(abbreviated tr)

YO twice, insert hook in stitch or space indicated, YO and
pull up a loop (4 loops on hook) **(Fig. 7a)**, (YO and draw
through 2 loops on hook) 3 times **(Fig. 7b)**.

Fig. 7a

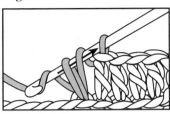

Fig. 7b

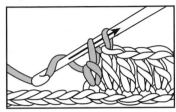

DOUBLE TREBLE CROCHET

(abbreviated dtr)

YO 3 times, insert hook in stitch or space indicated, YO
and pull up a loop (5 loops on hook) **(Fig. 8a)**, (YO and
draw through 2 loops on hook) 4 times **(Fig. 8b)**.

Fig. 8a

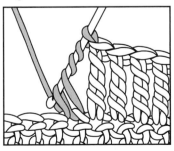

Fig. 8b

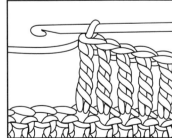

TRIPLE TREBLE CROCHET

(abbreviated tr tr)
YO 4 times, insert hook in stitch or space indicated, YO and pull up a loop (6 loops on hook) **(Fig. 9a)**, (YO and draw through 2 loops on hook) 5 times **(Fig. 9b)**.

Fig. 9a

Fig. 9b

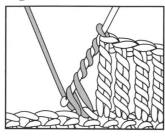

PATTERN STITCHES

LONG DOUBLE CROCHET

(abbreviated LDC)
YO, insert hook in stitch or space indicated, YO and pull up a loop even with loop on hook (3 loops on hook) **(Fig. 10)**, (YO and draw through 2 loops on hook) twice.

Fig. 10

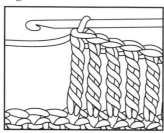

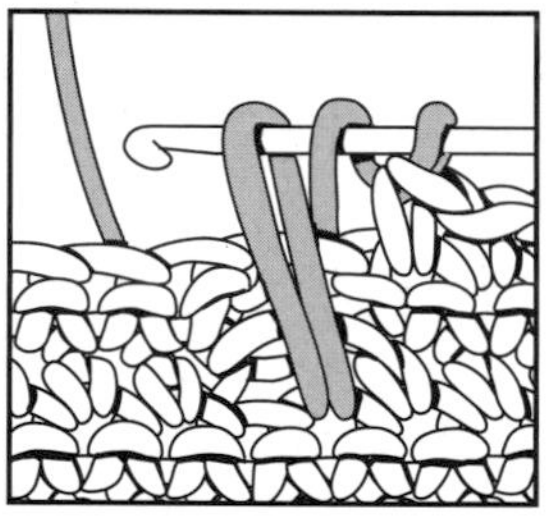

REVERSE SINGLE CROCHET

(abbreviated reverse sc)
Working from **left** to **right**, insert hook in stitch indicated to right of hook **(Fig. 11a)**, YO and draw through, under, and to left of loops on hook (2 loops on hook) **(Fig. 11b)**, YO and draw through both loops on hook **(Fig. 11c)** (reverse sc made, **Fig. 11d**).

Fig. 11a

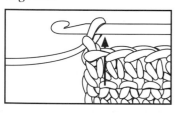

Fig. 11b

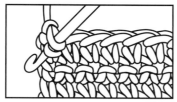

Fig. 11c

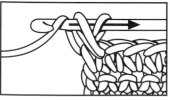

Fig. 11d

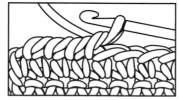

REVERSE HALF DOUBLE CROCHET *(abbreviated reverse hdc)*

Working from **left** to **right**, YO, insert hook in stitch indicated to right of hook **(Fig. 12a)**, YO and draw through, under, and to left of loops on hook (3 loops on hook) **(Fig. 12b)**, YO and draw through all 3 loops on hook **(Fig. 12c)** (reverse hdc made, **Fig. 12d**).

Fig. 12a

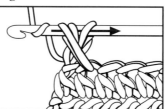

Fig. 12b

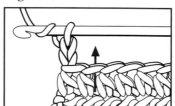

Fig. 12c

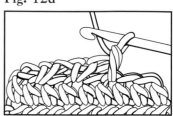

Fig. 12d

POST STITCH

Work around post of stitch indicated, inserting hook in direction of arrow **(Fig. 13)**.

Fig. 13

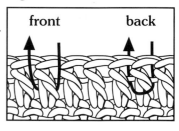

STITCHING TIPS

JOINING WITH SC

When instructed to join with sc, begin with a slip knot on hook. Insert hook in stitch or space indicated, YO and pull up a loop, YO and draw through both loops on hook.

BACK OR FRONT LOOP ONLY

Work only in loop(s) indicated by arrow **(Fig. 14)**.

Fig. 14

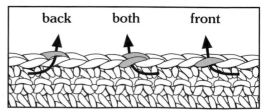

FREE LOOPS

After working in Back or Front Loops Only on a row or round, there will be a ridge of unused loops. These are called the free loops. Later, when instructed to work in the free loops of the same row or round, work in these loops (**Fig. 15a**).

When instructed to work in a free loop of a beginning chain, work in loop indicated by arrow (**Fig. 15b**).

Fig. 15a

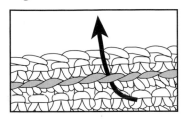

Fig. 15b

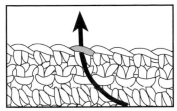

CHANGING COLORS

Work the last stitch to within one step of completion, hook new yarn (**Fig. 16**) and draw through loops on hook. Cut old yarn and work over both ends unless otherwise specified.

Fig. 16

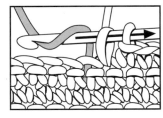

NO-SEW JOINING

The method used to connect Squares or Strips is a no-sew joining also known as "join-as-you-go". After the first Square or Strip is made, each remaining Square or Strip is worked to the last round, then crocheted together as the last round is worked. Hold Squares, Motifs, or Strips with **wrong** sides together. Slip st or sc into sp as indicated (**Fig. 17**).

Fig. 17

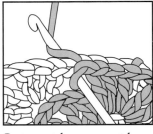

WORKING IN FRONT OF, AROUND, OR BEHIND A STITCH

Work in stitch or space indicated, inserting hook in direction of arrow (**Fig. 18**).

Fig. 18

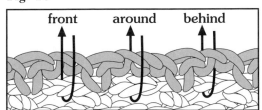

FINISHING

WHIPSTITCH

With **wrong** sides together and beginning in stitch indicated, sew through both pieces once to secure the beginning of the seam, leaving an ample yarn end to weave in later. Insert the needle from **front** to **back** through **inside** loops of each piece (**Fig. 19a**) or through **both** loops (**Fig. 19b**). Bring the needle around and insert it from **front** to **back** through the next loops of **both** pieces. Continue in this manner across to stitch indicated, keeping the sewing yarn fairly loose and being careful to match stitches.

Fig. 19a

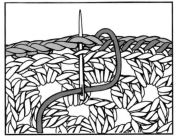

Fig. 19b

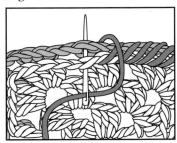

FRINGE

Cut a piece of cardboard 8" wide and 1/2" longer than desired fringe. Wind the yarn **loosely** and **evenly** around the length of the cardboard until the card is filled, then cut across one end; repeat as needed.

Align the number of strands desired and fold in half. With **wrong** side facing and using a crochet hook, draw the folded end up through a stitch, row, or loop, and pull the loose ends through the folded end (**Fig. 20a**); draw the knot up **tightly** (**Fig. 20b**). Repeat, spacing as desired. Lay flat on a hard surface and trim the ends.

Fig. 20a

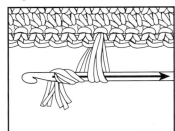

Fig. 20b

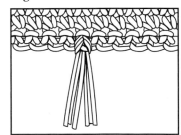

CREDITS

To **Magna IV** Color Imaging of Little Rock, Arkansas, we say *thank you* for the superb color reproduction and excellent pre-press preparation.

For their excellent work, we thank photographers **Ken West**, **Larry Pennington**, **Mark Mathews**, and **Karen Shirey** of Peerless Photography, Little Rock, Arkansas, and **Jerry R. Davis** of Jerry Davis Photography, Little Rock, Arkansas.

We offer a special word of appreciation to the talented designers who created the lovely projects in this book:

Janet L. Akins: *Light & Airy*, page 20
Eleanor Albano-Miles: *Call of the Wild*, page 7; and *Serenity*, page 54
Carol Alexander & Brenda Stratton: *Captivating Crescents*, page 66; and *Flower Patch Silhouette*, page 100
Mary Lamb Becker: *Pretty Petals*, page 52
Norma Cunningham: *Victorian Fans*, page 16
Dot Drake: *Harvest Wrap*, page 30
Betty Edwards: *Reindeer Forest*, page 40
Nancy Fuller: *Kingly Cover-up*, page 26
Sue Galucki: *Big on Ripples*, page 38
Kathleen Garen: *Tribal Spirit*, page 78
Shobha Govindan: *Summer Lace*, page 10
Sarah J. Green: *Double-Cozy Cover-up*, page 50
Nancy Griffin: *Terrific Texture*, page 34; *Patriotic Diamonds*, page 74; and *Christmas Stripes*, page 96
Laurie Halama: *Country Baskets*, page 104
Anne Halliday: *Rich Reflection*, page 36; *It's a Party!*, page 70; *Wrapped in Ruffles*, page 76; and *Bargello Blanket*, page 115
Fran Hetchler: *Blacklight Beauty*, page 28; and *Easter Basket*, page 106
Tammy Hildebrand: *Kaleidoscope*, page 80
Diana B. Husband: *Braided Miles*, page 108
Terry Kimbrough: *Lacy Valentine*, page 12; *Hearts Aplenty*, page 56; *Absolutely Gorgeous*, page 58; *Sweetheart Wrap*, page 62; and *Pansy Perfection*, page 112
Tammy Kreimeyer: *Spring Fantasy*, page 102
Melissa Leapman: *Lap of Luxury*, page 15
Roberta Maier: *Soft Hearts for Baby*, page 8
Leigh K. Nestor: *Noah's Ark*, page 88
Jane Pearson: *Daisy Blanket*, page 116
Carole Prior: *Splendid Stripes*, page 46
Judy Schuler: *Up, Up, & Away!*, page 82
Rhonda Semonis: *Pineapple Dream*, page 64
Barbara Shaffer: *Clam Shell Sensation*, page 32
Mary Ann Sipes: *Stunning Shells*, page 6
Martha Brooks Stein: *American Homecoming*, page 86
Rena Stevens: *Floral Cascade*, page 118
Clare Stringer: *Shamrock Wrap*, page 122
Carole Rutter Tippett: *Appealing Aran*, page 60
Maggie Weldon: *Blue Breeze*, page 18; *Handsome Chevron*, page 24; and *Quick & Toasty*, page 44